Coaching the Mental Game

Acclaim for H. A. Dorfman

Coaching *the* Mental Game

Leadership Philosophies and Strategies for Peak Performance in Sports—and Everyday Life

H. A. Dorfman

Taylor Trade Publishing

Lanham   New York   Boulder   Toronto   Oxford

Published by Taylor Trade Publishing
An Imprint of the Rowman & Littlefield Publishing Group
4501 Forbes Boulevard, Suite 200
Lanham, Maryland 20706

Distributed by National Book Network

The hardback edition of this book was previously cataloged by the
Library of Congress as follows:
Dorfman, H. A. (Harvey A.), 1935–
   Coaching the mental game : leadership philosophies and strategies for peak
performance in sports, and everyday life / H. A. Dorfman.—1st ed.
     p.   cm.
   1. Coaching (Athletics)—Psychological aspects. 2. Leadership. I. Title.
GV711 .D67 2003
796'.07'7019—dc21

                                          2003002022

   ISBN 1-58979-258-0 (pbk : alk. paper)

♾ The paper used in this publication meets the minimum requirements of
American National Standard for Information Sciences—Permanence of
Paper for Printed Library Materials, ANSI/NISO Z39.48–1992.

Manufactured in the United States of America.

Dedicated with love and respect to A. Huntley Parker Jr.

My Personal MVC: Most Valuable Coach.

Born: March 18, 1910
Died: February 10, 2003

I firmly believe that sports are a fundamental part of education. To know of what one is capable, both mentally and physically, is to know the scope of one's freedom.
L. Pearce Williams
From football program:
Cornell vs. Rutgers, 1971

Psychologically, the athlete reaffirms the necessity of play. . . . We knew it from the scriptures and Plato and the Renaissance educators who gave athletes an equal share of the curriculum with the classics and ethics.
Dr. George Sheehan
New York Times, November 10, 1974

I always stress condition with my basketball players. I don't mean physical condition only. You cannot attain and maintain physical condition unless you are morally and mentally conditioned.
John Wooden
UCLA Basketball Coach

My favorite coach was Michael Summey—my eighth-grade AAU coach. He was the first coach who made me believe in myself and love the game of basketball.
Robert Lodge
Millbrook H.S. (NC) Athlete
Class of 2002

Last season in New England . . . [Patriots coach Bill] Belichick started listening to the needs of his players.
Thomas George
New York Times, September 15, 2002

Some of the material in this book previously appeared in:

The Mental Game of Baseball
The Mental ABC's of Pitching
The Mental Keys to Hitting
Pro Magazine
(Published by Street & Smith)

Contents

Introduction

I'd completed this introduction, or so I thought. Then John, a former coaching colleague, made a visit to my North Carolina home. We hadn't seen each other for many years. John and I last worked together in 1968, when he had been my assistant basketball coach at a Long Island secondary school. After I moved to Vermont with my family, he became the head coach, and he also assumed my responsibilities as athletic director. He coached two (or three?) sports and taught there for the rest of his professional career.

We happened to have gone to the same college, though I'd left before John arrived. I went to college after graduating from high school; he went into the service and then attended college. He's a few years older than I am.

We had many "old days" to talk about, of course. I even delighted him by finding some photos of the teams we coached together. And we spoke at length about coaching.

I was surprised when he subsequently brought up the name of a particular coach in college. He played for this man (deceased for many years) on the varsity basketball team. I was a goalie on the fellow's junior varsity soccer team. My visitor, a serious, conscientious, cooperative, loyal, and fair-minded person and coach, revisited an experience he had had with his college basketball coach. He told a story I'd never heard about a game against Buffalo. John was a good player, and he played well that night in Buffalo. With his team down by one point, John took a last-ditch shot at the buzzer. He missed the shot, but he was fouled. Standing alone at the line, time having run out, John calmly made both free throws—and won the game. He was in a wonderful frame of mind as he rode home on the bus that night: happy, proud, confident. Lauded by his teammates.

He was benched the next game. "I couldn't understand it," he said. "The guy (coach) never said a word to me—nothing! I was crushed; I lost all my confidence. I was never the same player again." John said more, but my point has been served. (See Chapter 7.)

John asked about my experiences with the same coach. I told him that whenever I spoke to the man I felt less good about everything than I had before I spoke with him. He didn't heighten my sense of human sensibility. I then told John a story about a team vote, taken on the bus going to an away game. The coach said he wanted co-captains (there were two or three games remaining in the season). He said the team would know who the captains should be by now. The team manager gave every player a piece of paper and a pencil. We were to vote for two players.

After he had tallied the votes, the coach stood up at the front of the bus and addressed the team. One player had been named on every ballot. (He deserved that honor.) I had the next highest number of votes, so that would make the two of us co-captains.

Not so quick. The guy I edged out for second place was the coach's favorite (certainly a very skillful player) for reasons not necessary to mention. I was the coach's least favorite. One reason worth mentioning is that I was outspoken. Coach didn't appreciate that trait. He appreciated less a profanity-laced outburst in his face one day at practice. His response at the time was "You're never at a loss for an opinion, Dorfman."

Back to the bus: "The vote for the second co-captain was very close, so we'll have a revote," he announced. He said that I had "barely beaten out" the other fellow.

My vote count doubled on the second ballot. I won in a landslide. The coach was disappointed and confused. Both typical modes for him.

John's sensitivity when dealing with and understanding this coach was, apparently, not the same as mine. My perversity inspired me, in spite of the coach, rather than because of him. He was not a bad man; he was a bad coach.

The following year I played for the man to whom this book is dedicated, the man who coached us to the National Soccer Co-Championship (with Penn State). A fine coach and a finer gentleman. We saw each other whenever an opportunity presented itself and communicated regularly. He died in February 2003. Many will miss him, I among them.

Anyhow, when I finished telling John the story about the vote on the bus, he was just shaking his head. I'm not sure he'd been listening that attentively. "I've never forgotten how I felt," he said softly, tears welling up in his eyes. John will be seventy-one years old on his next birthday. And very obviously he still feels it.

John's hurt notwithstanding, many other athletes have suffered worse experiences with poor coaches.

■　　■　　■

Whether good or bad, everything a coach says or does becomes a message that the athletes receive, interpret, and respond to mentally. They too may never forget.

Does the message make sense? Is it fair? Is it honest? Is it rational or emotional? Is it helpful or threatening? Is it consistent with what's been said before? Is the meaning clear? What's its purpose?

These are just a few questions that pass through the consciousness of athletes, professionals and amateurs alike. The answers become evident in time. They then become fixed in the athlete's psyche. And through interpretation and experience these messages are delivered to the muscles, ultimately affecting (predetermining?) individual and team performance.

It's agreed upon "within the ranks": coaches do influence players' performance, for better or for worse. The nature of the influence is determined by the substance and style of the coach's delivery: what a coach says; how and when he or she says it. Who he or she is—as a coach and as a person.

Having acknowledged this, effective coaches strive to understand how best to know themselves and their athletes. How to communicate with their players. How to instruct, direct, and lead. How to "connect" in ways that will enhance the athlete and his or her performance. This connection implies a focus that goes well beyond Xs and Os. Beyond the practical tactics and fundamental mechanics of the sport.

The coach should therefore have an understanding of the athlete's mental makeup and develop appropriate coaching strategies aimed at helping a player's mental approach to performance. Every coach I've ever spoken to recognizes the relationship between the athlete's mental approach and performance. Yet few coaches devote specific time to that aspect of the game. I have asked many of them to tell me why.

The reason/excuse I've heard is a universal one: "I don't have the time." The truth I hear less frequently: "I don't know where to start." Perhaps this book will give impetus and direction for that start.

An important initial step is to recognize that athletes perceive their coaches as a leaders/teachers/mentors. Players respond to the way coaches use the power enacted in these roles. Those responses affect team chemistry, daily practice, and the individual athlete's attitude and behavior during competition.

Position power—the position of authority—helps a coach get an athlete to do what the coach wants done. Personal power helps get the athlete beyond just *doing* what the coach wants—to *wanting* to do it. That requires a coach to have a personal "touch," a skill beyond his (her) authoritarian mantle. I am too old to be naïve. I know some athletes respond to a coach who is an intimidator. But I can speak (and do) of others with great talent who do not—and who might otherwise make a great contribution to the team if he or she were treated differently. Time is devoted to the examination of this important and often misunderstood subject.

The book does *not* advocate team covenants, Zen meditations, role-playing, "blue rooms" for visualization, or raving, threatening "motivational" speeches. Nor does it recommend complex athlete–coach dynamics. Rather, it suggests what I call the "meat and potatoes" approach: the use of *common sense*. Unfortunately, and this is an essential understanding for anyone interested in self-improvement, common sense is not common *practice*. "I know better," is a frequently invoked self-admonition I hear from players and coaches alike. The payoff is in a *doing* that is based on the knowing. The *application* of common sense.

The book's intention is to be instructive—and to help coaches interact with their players in a sensible, thoughtful, effective manner.

Early in my own coaching career I turned for guidance to those I thought had something to offer me. One of my primary sources was UCLA basketball coach—now legend—John Wooden. (Two others were Red Auerbach and Vince Lombardi.) I read and reread Wooden's book on coaching. In November 2000, the ninety-year-old master was honored and interviewed once again. He offered one of his many strong views about coaching, particularly referring to what he believes to be a coach's major responsibility: "He should remember he's there to teach," Wooden said. "He should remember he's there to get a player to learn. . . . If he's recruiting just to have great players, he shouldn't be there. He should be a teacher." Wooden, being reiterative.

When asked if he believed most coaches today act out that role, Wooden smiled benignly and said, "No." Wooden, being realistic.

When asked to talk about former Indiana basketball coach Bob Knight, Wooden simply stated, "He's a good teacher. I didn't like his methods, his vulgarity." A positive for substance; a negative for style. As an addendum, Wooden later recalled the words of Abraham Lincoln: "There's nothing stronger than gentleness." (How to strike a balance is discussed within the context of this book.)

John Wooden did not use the word *win* with his teams—teams that won ten National NCAA Championships in twelve years. But working with professional teams and players, I've had to deal with the term on a daily basis. That's the reality of professional sport—and it's also become the reality at the amateur level, it seems. "The Winning Way" is what I focus on with players and staff members. The *means* to the desired end, which can be controlled.

I, too, am a realist. I'm aware of the pressure frequently put on high school and college coaches by administrators and parents. The pressure to *win*. I recall the words of my father: "Don't ever be afraid to lose your job, kid. Because you won't be very good at it if you are." The imperative to win, at any cost to ethics and values and/or the fear of coaching a losing team, produces distorted and sullied people and institutions.

That's not the goal of an elite teacher. That's not the approach of a good coach.

The precocious young athletes whom coaches love to have on their teams are very often one-dimensional. They are brilliant performers at an early age. But they also tend to be confused and conflicted in their later lives, when they are called upon as human beings to have emotional, social, family, and economic dimensions. Sport has retarded their full personal development instead of enhancing it. I've personally dealt with many players who were "neglected selves." These athletes became painfully aware of their need to attend properly to other dimensions of their being. Their athletic precocity had previously been their only concern—and the seemingly exclusive concern of their coaches.

The role of sports in a young person's education has been well established. Again, the effect can be a positive or a negative. The side on which the experience falls is determined by whether the student-athlete is encouraged to develop into a mature and whole person. Encouraged and assisted, as opposed to discouraged and ignored.

Can successful coaches "get it all right"? I'd say it depends on a couple of considerations. First, the coach's definition of "success." Second, the coach's desire to learn and make changes and adjustments necessary for success.

The rather enthusiastic and positive responses to the format of *The Mental ABC's of Pitching* have encouraged me to treat sections 2 and 3 in a similar fashion. Specific, individual topics are presented and developed. They appear in alphabetical order, allowing coaches convenient access to issues they may wish to refer to at any future time. A handbook of sorts.

The format is as follows:

Section 1—The Coach as Leader, Communicator, Teacher
   THE COACH/LEADER:
Considering Leadership Style and Substance
   THE COACH/COMMUNICATOR:
Considering Strategies and Approaches to Develop and Enhance the
   Coach's Relationship with the Athlete
   THE COACH/TEACHER/LEARNER:
Considering Effective Teaching Philosophies and Approaches and
   Principles of Learning
Section 2—The Mental Game Alphabet: Impact Terms for the Coach
Section 3—The Mental Game, A to Z: Athletes' Impact Terms
Appendices—A, B, C, D, E

This introduction and the nine chapters of the book include a number of references to strategies that are reiterated in sections 2 and 3. I continue to follow Oliver Wendell Holmes's advice that if there is something worth saying, say it over and over, "of course in a little different form each time."

The presentation includes many anecdotal references from more than thirty years of experience: twelve years as a coach at the secondary school level and nineteen years as a mental skills coach/counselor at the professional level. Illustrations are not always sport-specific.

I offer a reminder here: a person's psychic life, essentially, is his or her "real" life—whatever he or she makes it and makes of it. So it's also a hope of mine that the chapters to follow help coaches understand and address their players' lives—in and out of the competitive arenas. The chapters should serve coaches who wish to reaffirm, refine, or develop an informed and thoughtful approach. A "teaching" approach which, again, effectively guides athletes in the direction of their presumed goal: improving as performers and as people.

Based on my own experience, the coaches themselves are the beneficiaries of their own teaching because to teach is to learn. And to give, after all, is to get.

An explanation: I'm certainly sensitive to the viewpoint that no gender bias should exist in interscholastic athletics, whether it relates to the athlete or the coach. (I coached women's basketball for four years.) In writing this introduction, my sensitivity has been all too apparent to me. The use of "he or she" and "his or her" is an attempt to indicate my understanding of the issue. But it is inappropriate to my view of effective writing, distracting the reader and breaking the continuity of thought.

So in the chapters that follow, the word *he* is usually used. It is meant to be inclusive, rather than exclusive. The major intention is to satisfy the writer, assist the reader, and—at the same time—be inoffensive.

As noted above, many coaching philosophies and strategies are relevant to more than one section of this book. These areas are reiterated, reemphasized, and cross-referenced throughout the chapters that follow. An effective coach is a unified whole, rather than a compartmentalized collection of singular viewpoints and skills. It's hoped that the interrelatedness of the material to follow will assist the coach in establishing and/or reinforcing that wholeness.

Ara Parsegian, former head football coach at Notre Dame, expressed the view that good coaches are very special people. That they exert a great influence on young athletes, "more so than teachers, more so than Dad, more so than anybody." It is a sweeping statement, but if it's anywhere close to being accurate the implications are obvious for all who are called "Coach."

H. A. DORFMAN
2003

The Coach as Leader, Communicator, Teacher

- Considering Leadership Style and Substance

- Considering Strategies and Approaches to Develop and Enhance the Coach's Relationship with the Athlete

- Considering Effective Teaching Philosophies & Approaches

One

Leadership and Power(s)

This passion is best stated as a matter of caring and valuing.
It is further characterized by its consistency; it does not erratically
come and go. . . . It is also shaped by tender- as well
as tough-mindedness.
David Loye
The Leadership Passion

The epigraph above provides a good introduction for identifying some of the characteristics of effective leadership. Control of a program doesn't presume effective execution of the responsibilities that go with it. The perennially successful athletic programs are the result, to a great extent, of talented players. Yet to as great an extent (greater?), they can be attributed to enlightened leadership—to an outstanding coach.

Here's a "no-brainer" that a coach must always remember: leaders affect the behavior of the would-be/should-be followers. Let me express it in another way: players follow the coach's lead. If the leadership is misguided, the "followers" will be lost—in a variety of ways. Or they will choose not to follow.

Make no mistake about it, athletes not only need effective leadership, they also desire it. Young people want consistent parameters, direction, order, structure, organization, and discipline (to be defined and discussed in a later chapter). They need it, whether they know it or not. It gives them security, and that, in turn, helps them to be more confident.

One of the coach's first jobs is to provide clarity—so players understand the nature of his leadership credo: what he believes in; where he wants the program to go; what he expects from them. (The parameters, direction, etc.) Having established that, the coach will then be watched carefully by his players. They'll watch to see what he wants from *himself*, and whether he practices what he preaches. The *conduct* of his leadership will be the true mirror of his doctrine. We don't easily fool players, though we may think we do. We more easily fool ourselves.

3

The Power of Authority: Position Power

The ability to handle his authority well implies that the authority figure knows how to manage people. I've had contact with a few major league managers who could manage a baseball game very well, but they couldn't manage people. The leader who knows how to manage people must first know how to manage his power (and himself, of course).

A position of authority does not suggest that the authority figure be a dictator. Authority does imply that "the buck stops" with the person in power. Philosophy, parameters, and final decisions reside with that person, but policy should not be made or applied arbitrarily.

A leader who knows how to manage athletes can direct their mental and behavioral efforts toward a common goal—a goal established by the leader. This becomes the organizational/team credo. "What we stand for" is the way I put it with players. "What we want and how we go about pursuing it."

The credo should be one of his first expressions of position power. I have light-heartedly told teams at initial meetings, "We are a controlled democracy here. You have the freedom to do whatever you want—as long as I approve."

Order is established through position power. "Uni-form," I still explain to professional athletes. "One form. You sacrifice your individuality for the benefit of the whole—the team. To the goal of all the guys wearing the same uniform." (This is treated further in Section 3—The Mental Game, A to Z: Athletes' Impact Terms.)

Credibility

Whenever a coach asserts his position power, he puts his credibility on the line. He's saying, "This is what I know is right; follow it." If players know or discover the coach is wrong or contradicts himself, that power is greatly diminished, eroded, and/or lost.

Recognize your fallibility, and let the players know you recognize the difference between being g-o-o-d and being G-o-d. I've often presented a syllogism, a logical process, to the players.

Major premise: All humans are capable of making mistakes.
Minor premise: I'm a human.
Conclusion: Therefore, I'm capable of making a mistake.

We preach that players should learn from their mistakes. So should coaches, and I've taken great care not to repeat mine. I've put it this way: "This is what I *trust* is right." I trusted that my leadership would elicit their trust in me—and in my views. (See the following sections.)

Think before you speak. Prepare. It's often said that "power corrupts, and absolute power corrupts absolutely." Speak out of intelligence, rather than thinking you can arbitrarily say whatever comes to mind, because you have the power to do so. Very often, the source of the message is your emotional system, and when that's the case, what comes out usually would be better left inside.

At such times, the coach is losing his credibility at the top of his voice. As much as he might wish it, his might will not make it right. My own view is, "*Right* makes might." Followers want their leader to know what he's talking about; know what he is doing. That's what will enhance their mental state—intellectually and psychologically. They learn, and their teacher elicits confidence through his understanding. That's what effective leadership provides. In the follower's mind, the proof is "in the pudding," not in the position power. Effective leaders validate their authority every time they open their mouths. (See the section Personal Power.)

Make it clear how authority will be used. The coach should establish what he expects from the team, as athletes and as people. And he must communicate the fact that there will be consequences when a player does not meet these expectations. Let the punishment fit the crime. A warning? Immediate action? Are there extenuating circumstances? Each coach must decide, but he must be firm, sensible, and consistent.

At a celebration for and of John Wooden, his former coach, Bill Walton recalled Wooden's way of dealing with difficult or resistant players. Walton recalled what the coach would tell that player. "He would say, 'I admire and respect your position. We'll miss you here at UCLA. We've enjoyed your time. Thanks for coming.'" A kinder, gentler "my way or the highway." The authority is expressed and applied with a touch—a velvet fist, you might say. (See chapter 2.) I tell staff members who wield power too severely, "You don't have to drop an atom bomb on an ant."

Nor does a leader have to be a "rule maker." Rather than constructing a complex system of rules and consequences, keep things simple and positive. Clarify your expectations as necessary, accentuating your belief that they facilitate the achievement of team goals, rather than restrict individual freedom. Elaborate rules are often "made to be broken."

An illustration comes immediately to mind. Years ago, when I taught in Vermont, a new secondary wing was added on to our school. Each new room had a water fountain in it. That was a big deal for the students in this small town.

It's fair to say that the teacher across the hall from me had a great need to employ position power with her students. She made a list of rules and taped it to the wall over the fountain in her room. The list (negativisms, at that) included "Don't spit in the sink" and "Don't stick gum on the spout." And a number of other absurd directives and consequences.

The fountain sink in my room was spotless. The sink across the hall, below those posted rules, had gum, spittle, and the power of negative suggestion all over it. What you don't like, don't suggest. What you can't enforce, don't demand, especially using thoughtless, negative language. Trust in authority is gained by the authority showing trust. (See the section Personal Power.)

Consistency

There should be continuity in procedures and responses. Frequent changes in behavior, process, or expectations will cause confusion and concern in players, and will negatively affect their perceptions and performance.

A minor league manager with the Oakland Athletics organization was influenced by one of his coaches. He behaved after a game in a manner that he knew was inappropriate: he "read out his team" in the clubhouse, fulfilling the wishes of the angry coach. This, by itself, was an act that forfeited the manager's leadership.

After the unnecessary butt kicking, the manager felt guilty. A local team booster had brought in a platter of homemade cookies and put them on his desk. The manager took the cookies and served them to the players at their lockers.

It was a mixed message, if ever there was one. When he went back into his office, I asked him, "Which of those two messages do you want them to own?"

The manager had compounded his mistake. We addressed it the next morning. He acknowledged that, though in a position of leadership, he had allowed himself to be led by a subordinate with an ill-conceived, self-serving agenda. The leader had not chosen for himself the behavior he acted out. The players knew it immediately. (The thought-police are always on duty, ever attentive to the ongoing need to confirm or deny the trust given to leadership.)

A less absurd situation arose in a major league spring training camp. The manager delivered a ten-minute "riot-act." The presentation was appropriate in its sternness and intelligence. I read in the players' faces what I interpreted to be attentiveness and positive reactions during that time. The end of the talk, however, undid the positives that had preceded it.

After it was over, the manager asked me what I thought. "Great for the first ten minutes," I said. "You told them what they had to hear. What you said after that was essentially an apology for having said it. What message do you think they left the room with?"

Many failures in leadership come about because of players' muddled mental picture of where the coach is coming from or what he's trying to do. Unless the coach recognizes and remedies this, his inconsistency will become the prevailing pattern. Leadership cannot be asserted under such circumstances. His power becomes a weapon used against him.

Adjustments

Have faith in your philosophy of leadership, but be pragmatic. Only a coach who has faith in himself will have faith in his players. Or get that same faith *from them*. Know how you want to go about directing your team—and do what you know—as long as you see its positive effect.

The ninety-year-old John Wooden again: "My basic philosophy would be the same (now), but you have to change with society to some degree. There has to be a line of demarcation, but you can't be bullheaded."

Pragmatism says, "What works is true." Remaining faithful to an approach that's showing itself to be ineffective—and has been given a fair time of use and evaluation—is an indication of inflexibility. Is it based on stubbornness or are you just a "hoper"?

Adjustments are not frivolous abandonments of philosophy. If the philosophy is based on application, rather than just theory, then the coach will *consistently* be observing how his players respond to him and to his techniques. The ability and willingness to make adjustments are signs of a number of positive attitudes.

First, it shows that the leader/coach is a learner, a seeker. That he is open to new ways and ideas. When you don't learn, you don't know. Henry Adams said, "They know enough who know how to learn."

Second, it shows those who follow that the leader/coach is not arbitrary. Many times the "my-way-or-the-highway" mantra has been invoked by coaches who really mean, "I only know one way." Authority and effective leadership require intelligent command. Intelligence implies knowing what to do, when to do it—and why it should be done in the first place. "Because this is the way I've always done it" doesn't qualify as intelligence. It's constancy, for certain. But it's the type that is directed to repeated failure.

Be flexible. Established procedure and practice are preparatory to competition. Habit creates comfort. Familiar and time-tested coaching approaches provide mental security for players. And for coaches. But I'm sure you would love to compete against a coach who never adapts to game situations. Don't get too comfortable with one approach or routine. If something isn't working, try something else. Change can be uncomfortable, but it can also be necessary.

Many years ago I was a young and inexperienced coach, coaching a high school freshman basketball that was quite talented. Our record reflected that talent, but the first six or seven games were won the hard way. We were always behind at halftime, even against less-talented teams. We talked about this tendency after the first three games; our opponents in those games had been significantly inferior. The pattern continued.

I had been addressing the players' mental approach regularly. I told them that though we had thus far won all the games, those early deficits wouldn't always be made up against more formidable competition. And so on. I even changed the starting lineup, first including more cerebral players, then more "hungry" players. Same result. I decided their lethargy problem was *physical*. Their bodies weren't ready to play. I'm not certain what made me come up with that point of view, but I do know I devoted plenty of time to thinking about the problem.

What to do? I wasn't sure, but made an attempt. We changed our warm-up procedure. Instead of running the traditional layup drill, we played a three-on-three game. The five starters were out there, of course. It looked ridiculous; I *felt* ridiculous. The players were self-conscious and uncertain. They gave me We-hope-you-know-what-you're-doing looks. (I wasn't certain I did.) But whatever they might have felt or believed initially, they *did* get lathered up, which was my purpose—and hope.

The players responded. The tempo immediately after tip-off was much more to my liking. As were the numbers on the scoreboard. Apparently, these young men needed to "prime the pump" before competition. We stayed with the drill, which became, as one player put it, "our new tradition." Whatever it was called, it was believed by the players to be helpful.

Much of life is trial and error. Though we have the power to repeat our mistakes, we have the ability to correct them.

If you are flexible and lead wisely, you'll be followed enthusiastically. The player's belief system will be enhanced. He'll believe in the coach's intellectual ability and transfer that presumed edge to his own mental game. The best professional managers and coaches I've been around are flexible as they lead and connect with players. And they are the "authorities" who gain the reputations of being the smartest in their game.

Socrates was given credit for being the wisest man in Athens. Someone asked him, "Socrates, what is the nature of your wisdom?"

Socrates answered by saying, "Unlike other men, I know how ignorant I am."

It was overstatement, perhaps, if taken literally. But let's take a very literal point from Socrates' words. The ability to formulate a plan of action starts with "knowing"; the ability to make adjustments starts with knowing you don't know everything. (And never will.)

Balance

"Nothing in excess." Solon, another profound Athenian, preached that 2,500 years ago. Balance in life and human behavior was one of the Greeks' great values. Many coaches do not strike a balance—or seek it, apparently.

The coach who is oppressive, overbearing, vulgar, and mean-spirited operates at one end of a continuum. *He abuses his position power.*

The coach who is a self-identified Mr. Nice Guy, every player's every way, operates at the other end. He is permissive, nonconfi tional, and indiscriminately accepting. *He forfeits his position power.*

Balance does not imply the midpoint between those two ex tendencies. Think of a fulcrum. It is a point of balance that is struck according to the weight on each side of the plane that rests on it. If one pound of nails rests on one side of a board and two pounds on the other, the balance point, the fulcrum, will be found by moving the two-pound side of the board (plane) toward the fulcrum. The board has greater length on one side; lesser on the other. Uneven weight must be accommodated to strike the balance.

This from *The Way of Life According to Lao Tzu*:

Not to have edges that catch
But to remain untangled,
Unblinded,
Unconfused,
Is to find balance,
And he who holds balance beyond sway of love or hate,
Beyond reach of profit or loss,
Beyond care of praise or blame,
Has attained the highest post in the world.

Higher, even, than coaching.

In coaching, the greater need must be accommodated. This is not the *coach's* emotional need. Rather the situational need, as assessed intelligently and judiciously by the coach, who "strikes the balance" in order to resolve issues and situations as appropriately as possible.

The effective leader moves along the continuum, able to operate at any point between the extremes. He enacts whatever is required by the situation he faces. The test of his approach, once again, rests with his ability to know what it takes. He may not always be right, but he'll always apply sound judgment while maintaining the strong principles he wishes to represent and convey. Abandoned principles reside with poor judgments.

During leadership training sessions, I've always referred to a favorite philosophical credo of mine. It provides the two poles of the continuum—the either-or extreme points—and a philosophical point of balance that should be struck. Simply stated, the effective leader should be "strong, without being insensitive; compassionate without being weak."

This approach isn't based on "moderation" but on appropriateness. "What is called for here?" is a question I always ask myself when facing a decision or choice of action. "What does the *situation demand*?" I ask. Rather than, "What do *I* demand?" The "*I* word," as I've heard professional players say, "gets tired."

First, look at the extremes of the continuum (the board). Then weigh the possibilities (the nails). Next, strike the balance somewhere between the extremes (finding the fulcrum).

This process can help you in using:

- power without insolence,
- discipline without humiliation,
- authority without arbitrariness,
- confrontation without abuse,
- consistency without inflexibility.

Excess means too much. Even too much of good thing becomes a bad thing. Getting it "just right" is easier with porridge than with people. Effective leaders make the task less daunting by working at it. Through this attentiveness to striking the right balance, they go beyond their position power. They develop (if they don't already have) "a touch."

The Power of "a Touch": Personal Power

A coach who has a personal touch, as suggested in the introduction, goes beyond getting players to do what he wants. His great achievement is in getting them to *want* to do what he wants. Beware: many players are "pleasers." They want to do whatever *anyone* wants them to do, but for the wrong reason. Compulsive followers do not test the efficacy of a coach's personal power. Nor do those who believe that whatever an authority figure says must be true. Those who are healthy (even in their occasional skepticism) and self-assured are not won over by position power exclusively. Those who are resistant or perverse—or just plain difficult—require greater effort and attention. (The coach must decide whether such expenditure of time and effort is possible, practical, and desirable.)

Paying Attention

The coach with personal power is perceptive. He understands his players as individuals. He recognizes their needs and their personal strengths and weaknesses, their makeup. The coach "gets it." Through this understanding he's able to explain some of the behaviors they enact during practice and competition. And in their social and academic lives. Just a moment's insight can lead to a long-term relationship.

Voltaire said that understanding someone makes it impossible to hate him. We can hate the way a player behaves without hating the individual. But sometimes an understanding doesn't lie close to the surface. Players' agendas aren't always obvious, even to the most perceptive coach. Those who make the effort to look deeper into the causal factors and the motives behind the behavior will be better equipped to establish personal power.

Establish an Agenda of Concern

"Connect" with your team members as people, as well as athletes. Caring about players' needs and concerns is a major part of employing personal power. Walter Haas, who was the grand old owner of the Oakland Athletics, said to me, "It's the morally right thing to do—and it's good business." It serves a coach by saving talented players who might otherwise fall through the cracks.

One of my first experiences, immediately after being hired by the Oakland Athletics in 1984, was to attend their Instructional League program. The manager of the team that year was Fred ("Chicken") Stanley, the former major league shortstop. We became good friends, but the relationship didn't start out very amicably. Fred was a hard-driving, my-way-or-else manager. But his way was based on how he'd been treated as player by Billy Martin, the manager during his years with the New York Yankees. Fred applied leadership techniques to these Instructional League kids as they had been applied to him.

I was critical. "It worked for me," he answered defensively. I asked him if there was a player on the team that it hadn't worked for. Could he remember one?

"Sure," he answered immediately. "My roommate. A kid named Jim Mason, an infielder too. He could've been a player. Billy made it tough though. He didn't last."

Our young players were sitting in the dugout before a game as Fred and I talked near the foul lines. "Turn around," I said to him. "Look in the dugout." I pointed to the player seated at the far left end of the bench. "So," I began, "you'll make him and break him, and make him and break him," I said as I continued to point at each individual down the line.

I stopped speaking and again pointed to the first player on the left end of the bench. "Your job is to make him and make *him* and make *him*—and so on," I said as I pointed. Fred wasn't predisposed to like the message, but he knew exactly what I was talking about.

Personal power focuses on the individual player. Each player can make a contribution to the team and enhance himself at the same time. It was not so much Fred Stanley's "job" to accept this point of view as it was his implied *responsibility*—as a staff member in an organization that valued compassionate leadership and effective *teaching*.

By understanding their individual issues and purposes, the coach puts himself in a better position to influence and help his players in a number of ways. A coach or manager's concern for them as people will establish or reinforce a player's understanding that what serves him in the athletic arena will serve him away from it, as well. And vice versa. It *is* the right thing to do.

The organizational focus of the outstanding organizations I've worked for has been on how the staff members could help players become more effective. One of the goals of Walter Haas was that any player who left the organization—whether as a free agent, or traded, retired, or released—"would leave as a better person than he was when he arrived." As for "good business," Oakland played in the postseason five out of six years, with three straight World Series appearances (one championship). A humanistic approach and winning are not mutually exclusive. On the contrary . . .

Such organizations require the people in authority to be more than just "figures." The focus is on what *we* might do to help players get the job done, rather than blaming the players for not being able to get their job done. Winning was a result of a focus on leading, teaching, and developing. Not on blaming and labeling.

A label is an easy out for identifying without really knowing. For not taking the responsibility to really know and not exerting the effort it takes to create a relationship that might give the player (and coach) a chance to develop.

The Coach Is Not the Athlete's "Buddy"

Getting close is not the same as getting too close. I've encountered a number of inexperienced coaches and managers who had mentors from "the old school." I'm from an old school; I qualify as a senior citizen. But all the ideas and theories I was taught there don't have eminent domain in the present. Only the ones that are still valid. Mistaken ideas I cast out, whatever school or era they come from.

One particular view that has been refuted by evidence to the contrary is "You can't get close to the players." Again, it is a matter of balance or extremism. Rationality or emotionality. The coach must define and be sensitive to the words "close" and "too close." And to the nature of the difference. The more effective the coach is, the better able he is to relate and apply his definition to each individual, instead of using a sweeping brush stroke to paint the prospects of every relationship.

The major concern of "old-schoolers," myself included, is with the distinction between an authority figure and a friend. A coach who is "close" to a follower has established a relationship, as Loye says in the chapter epigraph, "of caring and valuing." A leader who gets "too close" is no longer a leader. His presumed concern for the athlete actually serves himself and whatever need he's expressing. He is being led—by that need, or by a manipulative player.

If a coach feels he has to explain the distinction to the athletes, so be it. But explanations are not usually required when the coach's actions are consistently apparent. My own experience has indicated that players get the message easily. They can appreciate the coach's use of personal power without interpreting it as partiality to an individual or leadership weakness. He understands the coach will employ position power when it's appropriate, without selective treatment for those with a "close" relationship.

My two children, now adults, were my students for four years in a special high school course I taught. They knew very well, as did the other students, that I was their father at home and their teacher at school. (Also, as the coach, I had to cut my daughter at tryouts for the women's basketball team. Her understanding of the game was superior, her talent considerably less than that. She understood.)

I never discussed the requirements of our dual relationship with my classes or with my own children. Nevertheless, those coaches who feel that an explanation is needed should provide it. Remember, however, words are meaningless without supporting deeds.

Bill Walton said of Coach Wooden, "He never tried to be your friend. He was your teacher, your coach. He handled us with patience. I was his slowest learner."

What Walton learned slowly is what all coaches should establish quickly: the line between the player and himself. The coach is responsible for drawing that line—as close or as distant as the individual relationship requires.

To Persuade Is to Convince, to Win Over—to Prevail Upon

The power of persuasion is real. Its most convenient utilization is through position power. Its most effective is through personal power. But that doesn't mean pleading or begging your case to a player. It means understanding where a player stands and what makes him move.

As a coach, I first establish with a player that whatever I want from him, he should want also, because it will be good for the team and for him. Any initial resistance is met with a stronger persuasive approach. Prolonged resistance is met with position power.

"Touch" requires some sense of determining who the player is as a person. What motivates him, what inhibits him. What pleases him, what threatens him. He's not always the person he appears to be; he's not always where he seems to be. He should be identified and located, so to speak. And then, perhaps, he's more apt to be led to the place you think he belongs. Use whatever level of persuasion is needed to move him along—your position power being a last resort.

The extent to which the coach's persuasion is subtle or emphatic will be influenced by the individual athlete's responses. By starting with an assumption that the personable and personal approach is appropriate, the coach will be able to change directions as he deems necessary. If he sees that the light touch isn't working, he modifies his approach. He doesn't cater or defer to the player. He leads. But a coach's exclusive use of an authoritarian approach makes it difficult to know where the athlete stands. It will only indicate what makes him jump.

On the other hand, if an oncoming car is speeding toward people standing near me, I don't try to be *reasonable* about getting them out of harm's way. Again, the situation should dictate which power the leader employs—and the degree to which he applies it.

The more personal skills a leader has, the longer the line of his followers. The best coaches can be found at the front of the line, leading. The others are at the back, pushing—and chasing strays.

Keep in Mind

- People in power tend to lose a part of their identity.
- There is a constant tension between yourself and the position you hold.
- It's important (1) to recognize that tension and (2) to respond to situations and people according to what is right, rather than to the tension created by the decision-making responsibility of your position.

Two

Leadership Style

> *Leadership is a word and a concept that has been more*
> *argued. . . . I am not one of the desk-pounding type that likes*
> *to stick out his jaw and look like he is bossing the show.*
> *I would far rather get behind and recognize the frailties and*
> *the requirement of human nature; I would rather try to persuade*
> *a man to go along, because once I have persuaded him, he will stick.*
> *If I scare him, he will stay just as long as he is*
> *scared, and then he is gone.*
> **Dwight D. Eisenhower**

A concept of leadership that is beyond argument is that one who would lead must have the ability to influence people. A leader's position power will influence others through coercion; his personal power will influence through persuasion.

Those who influence exclusively through the power of their authority establish a rather evident, singular style. Those who combine their authority with a personal touch establish a style that can vary according to circumstance. Different coaches will have different styles; they can all be effective.

Eisenhower espoused "the light touch." But when facing pressing situations as a military leader and president of the United States, he was not initially mindful of individual needs, if he was mindful of them at all. The war and the country took precedence. He was not apt to persuade Hitler with his personal power. So a leadership style should first allow for the pragmatic approach discussed in the previous chapter.

Must Our "Style" Be Chained to Our Genes?

Each of us has a predisposition for a particular style. Our genes influence our personalities. They provide us with a *natural instinct* for approaching interpersonal relationships, for example. Are we inclined to be socially aggressive or shy when interacting with others? Talkative or reticent?

Is this the same question asked twice? Not necessarily. There are aggressive people who don't say much. Former Brooklyn Dodger manager Walt Alston didn't say much, until something needed to be said. But he was not a shy leader. Minnesota Viking coach Bud Grant is another such example. Many people are naturally gregarious, while many others talk nonstop in order to cover up their shyness or feelings of inadequacy. (Their style is meant to *compensate* for their genetic predisposition.)

Whatever our natural style may be, we're capable of changing it. We can choose to be victims or beneficiaries of our genes. The trick is to keep the naturally instinctive behaviors that *help* us and change the ones that *hurt* us. Those that inhibit an effective approach to our task or purpose. Any change in behavior will at once reduce the influence of unwanted "natural" habits.

Seeking and *acquiring new instincts*—those not natural to our personality—allow us to "come out of ourselves," or "draw back" from ourselves. We thereby learn to act out behaviors based on a *consciousness based on situational need*, rather than on a self-conscious personal need.

For example, say you were to play the lead role in stage performances of two different plays on consecutive weeks. One week the theater group would put on *Bozo the Clown*; the other week the play would be *Hamlet*. Being a light-hearted fellow with a sense of humor and a flair for the comic, you'd *naturally* tend to enjoy and do a better job of playing Bozo. You might not be sympathetic to Hamlet's continuous agonizing and indecisiveness. But if you *had* to play the part, you would.

And if you continued to work at playing an acceptable Hamlet—playing the part over and over again—you'd become more effective, more convincing—more comfortably *instinctive* in the role. The comfort would develop through the cultivation of a new habit. After all, you knew you couldn't be effective playing Hamlet the way you played Bozo. You adjusted to what the situation called for. You invented a new self, *according to need*.

Great leaders are great actors. They play to the needs of their audience. If you can be a great coach by always being your *natural* self, then so much the better. But the proof is in the effective pudding. Circumstance will allow you that naturalness, or beg for a different style—a different approach.

During my early years of teaching at the secondary school level, I coached both football and basketball. My wife saw "two different people" come home for dinner after practices. She was not happy with my high level of intensity and aggressive manner (style) at home during the football season. During the basketball season, she claimed, I was more "sensitive and approachable."

I pleaded guilty with an explanation. I told her of the differences in the conditions of coaching those two sports. If my reasoning (excuses?) were made into a list, it would appear somewhat as follows:

FOOTBALL—
- One assistant coach, so control of large number of players not ideal.
- Out of doors, so physical setting not optimal for organization and supervision.
- Spread over a wide practice area, often requiring the need to shout to be heard.
- Constant demand for aggressive mental behavior from players.
- Constant demand for aggressive physical behavior from players.
- Physical demonstrations by coaches, requiring aggressive actions.
- High emotional arousal level of players required, as well as mental discipline—a relentless *battle* for balance.

BASKETBALL—
- Indoors.
- Four walls.
- Six baskets.
- Two players at a basket for drills.
- *One* resounding whistle noise required once.
- Talk like a civilized person to players.
- Complete control.

Two different people came home, depending on the season, because two different people were coaching. That was my experience, for what it's worth. I made an adjustment at home, I think. (There was no excuse for not doing so.)

I was more *natural* as a basketball coach, but worked at *acquiring* instincts required for the sport I was coaching—the style I thought necessary—in each sport. I would often remind myself that I wasn't coaching "a sport," but coaching young people who were playing a sport. Individual people with individual mental makeups—playing different sports with specifically unique conditions to be addressed in each activity. And I grew more comfortable with a different style when coaching football, because I focused on what I needed to *do*, rather than how I wanted to *feel*.

■ ■ ■

A young manager was running the Instructional League team during one of Oakland's fall Instructional League programs. On a particular day, the manager wanted to express his extreme displeasure to the team of young minor league players. His unhappiness was based on the way they went about playing the game on the previous day. Their mental approach bothered him particularly, as it had bothered me.

The manager felt I would be better suited to deliver a very strong message, not so much because it was my major area of responsibility, but because he felt his manner of delivery would not rise to the need he perceived. A gentleman, he felt he hadn't yet learned how to vary the style of his delivery according to the situational need. He wanted to watch me do it.

The team was seated in the dugout as I faced them and went off on a rather profane rant that addressed their performance and sensibilities. As I did this, the team we were to play that afternoon filed through the field's gate and went to their dugout on the opposite side of the field. That team was a visiting group from Japan.

After my "talk" was completed, the Japanese interpreter came up to me and asked if I was Mr. Dorfman. (*The Mental Game of Baseball* has a Japanese translation.) I said I was that person. He then said that Mr. Soto, the manager of the team, had heard me speaking to the Oakland players, and he would like me to address the Japanese team sometime.

"Did he even know what I was saying?" I asked.

"No," said the interpreter, "but he liked your aggressive style."

■ ■ ■

Comfort is a word I'm not particularly fond of. When talking with athletes and staff members about changing their approach or style, I have them fold their hands. I then say, "When I say the word 'go,' unfold your hands and then clasp your hands again, this time putting the other thumb on top." Some struggle even to get their fingers properly meshed. But when the task is completed, I ask, "How does it feel?"

The answers have been: "Weird," "Strange," "Funny," "Different." All acknowledged it felt "uncomfortable." Change *is* uncomfortable. It has to be. Our habits give us comfort, whether they're behaviors based on physical or psychological conditioning. All this points to the difficulty in developing a leadership/coaching/teaching style that, as illustrated earlier in the Fred Stanley/Billy Martin anecdote, serves the players' needs, rather than the style grounded in your naturally instinctive behavior.

Growth requires some initial discomfort. We're not naturally Bozo *and* Hamlet. Playing one role will be comfortable. Trying to adapt to the other will be uncomfortable. If we know what style is called for, we focus on getting it right, not getting it comfortable.

Understand There Is a Difference between Style and Substance

Dwight Eisenhower was not George Patton. Vince Lombardi was not Tom Landry. John McGraw was not Connie Mack. Dean Smith is not Bob Knight. Bill Walsh is not Bill Parcells. Invoking the names of these successful leaders is not meant to contrast different styles, so much as it is to illustrate that certain fundamental similarities can be found in all leadership styles.

My ideal, as previously expressed, would be that a coach would be able to elicit effective responses from players with varying mental make-ups and sensitivities. But the reality is that a number of those coaches mentioned above could not. One type of individual responded to them; another often could not.

The misconception is that some players want to be led by "nice guys" and some by "tough guys." But those terms are not mutually exclusive. A tough guy can become an irritant to a tough-minded kid if his style is based exclusively on whatever *he* defines as "toughness." Conversely, a nice guy who aspires to nothing but being accommodating and tolerating unacceptable behavior can wear out whatever welcome he had. Players who want to play the game the right way and—yes, win—come to see such tough guys and nice guys as irritating, rather than inspiring leaders.

Example: Dale Murphy was a fine baseball player. He still is a fine a man. A "nice" man. Murphy played on losing teams in Atlanta. Over the course of that time, the team had a manager who was also a very nice guy. Easygoing, understanding. Tolerant. The dispenser of positive platitudes. The players, Murphy included, liked him. But they were tired of losing and grew tired of the "we'll get 'em tomorrow" cliche.

Eventually, upper management grew tired of his leadership style and fired him. At the time, we talked about the manager's dismissal. Dale expressed his feeling of sorrow for the man. I then asked him, "How do you feel for yourself?"

"Relieved," he said. He wanted a more aggressive leadership style, one that demanded more and forgave less.

■ ■ ■

Item: The *New York Times* (June 23, 2002) ran a notice about a Texas Rangers pitching coach. In part, it said, "Oscar Acosta wore out his welcome faster in Texas than he did in Chicago with the Cubs. The Rangers fired Acosta . . . less than halfway through the season, manager Jerry Narron said, because of 'philosophical differences' and 'communication problems.'

"Acosta, 45, sets out to intimidate his pitchers and coaches (colleagues!) with an intensive, strong-willed, confrontational style. He isolates the pitchers from the rest of the team and at times loudly blames fielders for the pitchers' problems."

Said Acosta's former boss with the Cubs, "He just doesn't get it."

■ ■ ■

"Getting" style is one thing; substance another. The coach who can convey a fundamentally sound philosophy through an appropriate style wins the day. And the players. And, it's hoped, many games.

An outstanding coach is easy to serve and hard to please. Meaning that his style gets players to want to play for him and his consistently high standard (substance) gets them to understand he will be satisfied with nothing less.

Your style is the way you act out your role. The substance is the script. The *substantive* concerns for coaching the mental game, irrespective of a coach's individually unique style, are discussed in chapter 4.

An Effective Style Can Serve the Needs of Any Day's Kids

Jack Horenberger died in December 2000. He had coached college baseball for thirty-seven seasons and basketball for twenty-one seasons at Illinois Wesleyan. Dave Kindred wrote a wonderful tribute to the man a week after his death (*The Sporting News*, December 11, 2000).

To illustrate Horenberger's "touch," Kindred told a story about the coach's handling of a player whose father had died and whose concerns for his mother, his remoteness from home, and related sadness made him despondent and dysfunctional. The player is quoted: "He was into you as a person. . . . Coach told me to get back on track. And he wasn't soft about it either. I'd call it a nice scolding. He said, 'I know you've got it in you. Keep pushing. Everything'll be looking up pretty soon. . . . That day had such an effect on me.'"

Kindred wrote, "The fully amazing part [of the story] is that Horenberger, on that day, was 86 years old, a man born before World War I pumping up a teenager on the eve of the 21st century."

Former Arizona State coach and big-league manager Bobby Winkles played for Horenberger. He told Kindred, "Coach taught me a baseball team is not a democracy. He was a benevolent dictator. I loved the man."

His former players felt the same about old-school Vince Lombardi, another "dictator" of renown. He dictated policy and practice; he cared about the players as people. He got close to them and their families. No generation gap was wide enough to impede Lombardi's formula for success.

I spoke at the St. Louis Cardinals organizational meeting in the fall before the 2000 season. A question was raised about "today's kids." The players of the new millennium. I pointed out that coaches and managers can mute their television sets when Generation X advertisements are run. They don't have to relate to the sound—or to the extreme games of Generation X. "But," I reminded the audience, "you do have to coach and teach a pitcher with a nipple ring and a 'dude' mentality. That's a contractual obligation. The player's 'styling' is not his substance. You've got to know more about him than how he looks and speaks."

I reminded them of the date on the contract they signed. "That date indicates that you're all leaders in the new millennium. You're not being hired to coach kids of the '60s or '70s or '80s. The effective leader addresses the credo of the organization and the need of each player. No compromise of principle and standard; no intolerance for the individual. Whatever his age—or yours."

The Test of a Style Is the Response It Provokes: Two Cases in Point Making

Case One

While working with the Oakland Athletics, I spent a considerable amount of time with a particularly troubled and troubling young player—in person and on the telephone. He was an infielder from the Dominican Republic, brought up by a mother, rejected by a father (perhaps mentally abused), resentful, lonely, despondent.

His moods were brought onto the playing field, and most of his minor league managers and coaches accused him of not hustling. The accusations were correct. They also cited his behavior as an indication that he didn't care—about the game or about becoming a better player. That claim was incorrect.

His talent allowed him to progress from rookie ball to Double-A. He was often disciplined, but coming from a matriarchal home environment, he did not respond well to lecturing and discipline administered by stern male authority figures. He was benched at appropriate times but didn't seem to get that message either. The prevailing description for him was "a kid with a bad attitude."

He had heard from other Latin players that I was the guy who tried to make players "*fuerte en la cabeza*" (strong in the head). The phrase "any port in a storm" probably applies to his allowing me access to his ears initially. He understood English but didn't speak it all that well. (I soon discovered that he spoke it better than he let on to others.)

He understood my agenda; he seemed to trust my concern for him and his self-improvement. I delivered the messages I thought he needed using a gentle style, a light touch. Emphatic, but low-key, a hand often on his shoulder for control and connection at the same time. His behavior improved, albeit slowly. But his skills seemed to have peaked. After a couple of years at the Double-A level, he was released, and he was out of baseball. Other Latin players kept me current as to his whereabouts.

Perhaps three years later, during a series the As were playing in Yankee Stadium, our shortstop, Mike Bordick, came into the dugout just before we were preparing to take batting practice. "Harv," he said, "there's someone who wants to see you." Bordick pointed to the area in the stands behind home plate. I came out of the dugout and the two of us walked to that area.

There, behind the screen, was this former player, a wide grin on his face and two fingers slipped through the screen in an adjusted handshake gesture. Our fingers clasped and then, after years of not having seen or communicated with each other, he spoke his first words of greeting: "Harvey, I've changed."

Case Two

A young minor league outfielder in the organization had been a constant irritant to all staff members and many teammates. He was an aggressive player. He played hard and "got his uniform dirty." But he had a very apparent streak of selfishness. His focus was on his own performance, rather than the team's success. His habitual excuse making kept him from being a good learner and frustrated the coaches. He could be spiteful to teammates and was frequently guilty of verbal cruelty.

This player had been indulged by parents (particularly the mother) and probably by high school and college coaches. He did not respond to being held accountable and took all constructive criticism personally. His responses to my talks with him were respectful (to my face). However, no improvement in his behavior was apparent.

I modified my style and approach over the course of two seasons. Still, no discernible effect.

During a spring training game, in his third year with the organization, he acted out in blatantly obnoxious behavior. I called him out of the dugout and took him behind the chain-link screen—near the water cooler away from the field. My calculated presentation might tastefully be described as in his face. At the top of my voice, my finger in his chest, I recalled a litany of his behaviors over the past two years. And I told him, using strong, descriptive language, of the way I regarded those behaviors. And the way *others* regarded his behavior (and him).

To verify this last point, I first called over his rookie ball manager. With me still shouting, as if the *manager* had been guilty of some terrible deed, I called upon him to corroborate my view of the player's ongoing "bad act." I provided the details and descriptions; the manager had only to say, "Yes," when asked if he agreed.

I followed the same procedure with a minor league trainer—and then with the field coordinator, calling each one over without letting the previous one leave. A gang-up. The player was reduced, to say the least. Finally, to tears.

We kept communicating as if that scene had never been enacted. Over time, his behavior improved, albeit slowly.

Perhaps years five later, I was working for the Tampa Bay Devil Rays during their inaugural season. A number of player/invitees were at that first major league spring training camp. After an introductory talk, the prospective team members were to gather in areas designated by position. The outfielders were to remain where we had all convened.

I was soon approached by the former Oakland player. Before he got close enough for a handshake, he spoke. "Harvey, "I've changed."

Two players, one happily married and the father of two children. He held a civil service job as a postal worker in New York City. He sounded gregarious and upbeat. He certainly seemed to have changed.

The other became an important contributor to his new organization's Triple-A team. He was cooperative and held in high regard by staff and teammates—for his attitude and his approach to the game.

On a couple of occasions I felt like kicking the former in the butt. On one occasion, indelible in my memory, I would have liked to give the latter a sympathetic hug. In neither case did I act out my feeling, simply because it would not have helped the player at that time. It would only have helped me. To the best of my understanding, I adopted a style suitable to the need of each player. The rest was up to him. His choice.

It's Tough to Define What a Good Leader Is, But It's Tougher to Be One

What should be understood about the "argument" alluded to in the epigraph of this chapter is that leadership is not defined easily as it's applied to those who lead. The position of authority identifies the leadership *role*. The degree to which one appropriately influences others identifies the *leader*.

Many effective coaches with many styles are out there leading their athletes. As diverse as those styles may be, they should all be attached to the individual players the coach hopes will follow. Not an easy task. The coach can seemingly "do everything possible" and still not see results with certain players.

It might be wise to consider that, to a great extent, our leadership style is not what we think it is—but what the players think it is. And often, change will not take place within the period of time we are given with the athlete.

Occasionally, change might not take place at all, irrespective of time. In my own experience as a high school coach, I had to remove players from the team because of extreme resistance and insubordination—the proverbial "conduct detrimental to the team." To me, it was more a case of getting the clear signal that the player didn't want to change, didn't want to be led or coached. Or sacrifice *anything* for the goals of the team.

No, it's not always (ever?) easy. But assuming we are making our most thoughtful, sincere, and relentless attempts to lead in the appropriate manner—and in the right direction—it is, again, the player who must finally choose. His choice will be evident to you; all you have to do is turn around and see who's following.

But remember, it's essential to check the mirror regularly—to see who's leading. Two essential questions: Who *is* that person in the mirror? Who do I *want* it to be? Chapter 3 considers them.

Keep in Mind

Leaders:
- Accept personal responsibility.
- Develop athletes and people.
- Work at influencing their athletes' thinking.
- Help each athlete according to his individual needs.
- Focus on objectives, goals, and solutions—not problems.
- Are bosses, not buddies on the job.
- Understand that effective discipline requires attention, fairness, confrontation, and consistency—and an understanding on the athletes' part of your expectations.
- Teach, rather than just expect performance.
- Do not accept incompetence, and explore every avenue to try to help athletes and get them to make necessary adjustments.
- Give recognition to all who deserve it, not just the top performers.
- Are motivators, supervisors, helpers—not manipulators.
- Start by employing personal power but are able to appropriately apply their position power when it is required.

Three

You, the Leader—the Coach

Few men are of one plain, decided color; most are mixed, shaded, and blended; and vary as much, from different situations, as changeable silks do from different lights.
Lord Chesterton
Letters to His Son [1752]

Leadership begins with self-knowledge.
Vince Lombardi,
NFL Coach

Personality

Our personalities are the collections of attributes, dispositions, and tendencies that identify each of us as a single individual. Jean Giraudoux spoke of personality as "an invisible garment woven around us from our earliest years . . . made of the way we eat, the way we walk, the way we greet people." It's also reflected by the way we teach and coach.

The understanding of who we are and what our identity is to others should be clear to us if we aspire to be effective leaders and coaches.

What *is* very clear is the fact that human beings are diverse. Some are friendly; others are antisocial, hostile perhaps. Some are quiet and some are boisterous. Some are sensitive, others insensitive. Some are learners, some are close-minded; some tolerant, others intolerant. Varying degrees exist between the extremes. We're all genetically predisposed to have certain tendencies. Our "garments" may have been woven during childhood, but we don't have to wear them for the rest of our lives.

Who's in Control—of You?

As noted, we don't have to be slaves to our genes. We can change; we can choose our "color" and "shade." Frequently we do so (see first epigraph) because of circumstance. When we adjust to the color of our environment, as chameleons do, we use change as a defense mechanism. We protect ourselves in a social sense. But when we effectively adjust as a leader/coach, we employ a behavior based on what is thought to be the best way to get a particular response from the athlete. In the first case, we're being controlled by the external; in the latter we're in control of ourselves.

I hear coaches imploring their athletes to "just worry about the things you can control." Personality is one of those "things." The athlete's—and the coach's. Coaches can and should learn to master their personalities. Self-mastery leads to self-control. Self-control frees us.

Self-understanding is the initial effort made to gain that freedom.

Two Questions: Who Am I? Who Am I Required to Be?

By being master of ourselves we can, to the extent possible, break the bondage to our genes. We're then able to ask ourselves the question "Who do I choose to be?" rather than ask "Why must I be this way?" Though the task is not necessarily an easy one, we can devote ourselves to adopting any style we may deem appropriate. Our behavior can go beyond our personality if we are determined enough.

■　■　■

During my earliest association with the Oakland Athletics, I met an intelligent, sensitive man. He was the major league manager. His job was in jeopardy and we were speaking about the circumstance. I suggested that he was too mild-mannered—a "gentle-man." Because of this, he was reluctant to assert himself. The team was undisciplined in every sense of the word. Their sloppy play was apparent to everyone, including the manager. His response to my suggestions was "That's the way I am."

And that's the way he remained. Needless to say, he was fired a few weeks later, a self-proclaimed victim of his genes. Let this be clear: he is gainfully employed as I write these words. He is apparently happy not to be responsible for managing players any longer. At the time, *he did want to keep that job.* But he had the wrong answer to the question "Who am I required to be?" He chose to be stuck in his own nature. It didn't work, because he didn't change his approach. Because he didn't get beyond who he was in his mind, he did not reach the demands of his circumstance. He lost his job.

Two other fine people in the Oakland organization's minor league system were *advised* to give up managing for the same reason. They seemed unable to adjust to what was required in order for them to be consistently effective with their players. Fifteen years later, both are still valued members of the Oakland organization. Neither is a manager.

. . .

Yes, we have naturally instinctive tendencies in dealing with other people. But we can acquire and develop new instincts and, with consistent use, they will become "second nature." Certainly there are many ways of doing things—but the things we do ought to be the right things, including the appropriate and effective approaches to leadership. Rather than having a situation determine how he acts because it influences his instinctive behavior (self-defense, perhaps), an effective leader acts upon the circumstance so as to influence it.

Self-Definition

The coach who is the most effective leader knows it. He knows how to define the term—and, more importantly, he knows how to define himself. Knowing oneself is first and foremost for any person who wishes to be a self-actualized adult. In emphasizing the importance of this ancient truth, Vince Lombardi said, "You can't improve on something you don't understand." Gaining that understanding can be an arduous task.

Players I work with call it "Harvey's (expletive deleted) ordeal." It's the ordeal of constantly checking ourselves so as to be more, rather than less, as a person, a coach, and an athlete. Each behavior we enact indicates the direction in which we're moving. Each act can be defined. The good acts make us more; the bad ones make us less. Inappropriate behaviors erode a part of the self we'd like to be.

By avoiding the ordeal of self-evaluation entirely, we deny ourselves the opportunity to expand and enhance our personal and professional selves.

Each day I've asked myself, "Who was I today (or in such-and-such situation)?" And each day I ask, "Was that who I wanted to be?" It's a reality check that, at first, is daunting. It's an ordeal, for sure, but it forces my ego to answer to my brain. And our best answers come from there.

Authority Often Preempts Awareness

It's been said about the human condition that "power corrupts." It can; it has. Many coaches don't examine their style or their points of view, because they believe they are granted immunity from personal identity by their position and authority. But personal power begins with power to assess and control *oneself*.

There's also a more common attitude to recognize here. A milder form of corruption. The many coaches who do not wield their power like Attila the Hun still are apt to focus on their responsibility to exert authority, at the expense of any focus on the person who expresses it.

Themselves. They mean well, but they don't necessarily do well.

Self-awareness is usually not the first thing that comes to a coach's mind when he gets his first job. It certainly wasn't what came to *my* mind. What came to my mind was the excitement of competition, of teaching perhaps, of achievement—and glory. Of keeping my job, at least. (Self-preservation always comes before self-actualization.)

■ ■ ■

My authority as a coach, albeit a young and inexperienced coach, indicated to me that my players' responsibility was to listen to me, learn from me, and do exactly what was dictated to them. To jump through my hoop. (See chapters 5, 6, and 7.) The responses were too often unsatisfactory.

I was young, but my focus and approach remained constant for quite a few years before some awareness kicked in. I remember reading words that struck me, though I don't recall the source: "I am an experiment. When I die the experiment is over. Let others judge the outcome of the whole; I've judged myself on a daily basis."

I had been making judgments about everything *except* myself. I never asked myself, "Why did I do that? (Motive, purpose.) How does it affect my players? (Outcome, consequence.)" I was in charge. If I said it or did it, it must be right. After all, I believed my intentions to be honorable. So, I could rationalize my behaviors; I could disown my faults, blame circumstance or others. I was enacting the philosophy of "might makes right."

It was inappropriate, and I finally smartened up. I took the time to examine my style, my behavior, my motives. Myself. Apparently I'd thought (if I thought about it at all) that my position of authority exempted me from that process. From that *responsibility*. I also thought that others saw me as I wished to be seen. Of course, that's what many, if not most, people think.

■ ■ ■

To expand this point, I refer to an interesting article that appeared in the April 2002 issue of *The New Yorker*. It's about a fellow, Marshall Goldsmith, who has been coaching corporate executives successfully for years. One company "leader" ranked lowest in treating his people with respect. The guy was considered a "hopeless case." Goldsmith described the executive as being "hardworking and brilliant; he didn't lie, cheat, or steal. He was just a complete jerk."

The first agenda was to elicit the view the guy had of himself and the perception he believed others to have of him. "You know how I helped the guy to change?" Goldsmith said. "I asked him, 'How do you treat people at home?' He said, 'Oh, I'm totally different at home.' I said, 'Let's call your wife and kids.' What did his wife say? 'You're a jerk.' Called the kids. 'Jerk.' 'Jerk.'"

After the disclosures, Goldsmith summed up his remarks by asking the executive if he wanted to have a funeral that no one attended. "Because that's where this train is headed."

What I've invoked in my work are appeals to individual coaches and managers who, unaware, lay tracks that lead their coaching "train" to a dead end or a terminus crash, dragging some innocent passengers along for the ride. (The passengers are almost always aware of the direction they're being led.)

■ ■ ■

Honest insight can be painful. Let's say a coach, in honest self-knowledge, says to himself, "I was outcoached tonight. That other guy was much more on top of the game than I was." Any emotional insecurity changes the expressions of that self-awareness to "My kids let me down. They didn't come through when we needed it. And the other team got all the breaks." Whether the latter evaluation is expressed to others or internalized, it can become a rationalization so strong that the person expressing it comes to believe it. Needs to believe it.

The coach who does a poor job of teaching needs to believe "These kids can't retain anything." It's a tough job to be realistic about ourselves, but it's essential. When we aren't aware of our all-too-human tendencies of rationalizing a mistake or weakness, we continue to make the same mistakes and never gain the strength required to help those we're responsible to guide.

Are You Still There?

Are you rolling your eyes? Are you expressing a defiant self-neglect? If so, then Vince Lombardi is up there rolling *his* eyes at *you*. He sees you as a fugitive running from self-understanding.

As for me, having eventually become capable of understanding Lombardi, I recognized that my motivation to be successful, that is, "a winner," should be driven not by personal glory, "but rather for the personal satisfaction that comes from great accomplishment." And that my first great accomplishment would be to understand what was most important to me as a coach and leader and then, in turn, most important to those I coached. If these views were not compatible, whatever personal and professional goals I established wouldn't be reached.

Self-understanding has wrongly been classified by some to be what a friend's wife calls "woo-woo." Something that's "far out there." Mysticism or self-absorption. "Feel-good" folderol. You don't have to penetrate what A. S. Byatt calls "the last wrinkle of your soul." But you should get below the surface of actions, to a level where you can be conscious of your motives and needs.

After deciding to be more conscious of myself and my style, I came to understand that guys are tougher who deal honestly with who they are than those who avoid that process or deny its value.

In my current work, athletes learn to understand their own toughness every time they confront whatever demons they may have. The mentally tough ones learn themselves—and confront whatever self is not working well for them.

Carl Rogers wrote, "No one can explain our behavior more expertly than we ourselves can." Funny how many of us choose to forfeit that expertise—and roll our eyes.

Remember When You Were the Athlete and Not the Coach?

Over the years, I coached against or with many different coaches (and managers). For a significant number, self-awareness wasn't in evidence. Some of these coaches were on a crusade for self-aggrandizement. Others had other agendas. Whatever they were, it was fairly clear that the athlete was an instrument not the subject. These coaches all had been players before becoming coaches. Their current needs obscured their recollections of their past needs.

They were now authorities. On what? On the sport they coached, of course. I've been around staff members who knew how to manage a game, but they couldn't manage people. Themselves included.

■   ■   ■

When asked to run miniseminars for coaches and managers, I take the opportunity to conduct a particular exercise with those I'm speaking to for the first time. I ask the staff gathered in the room to take out the 3x5 cards they've been given and to write down the concerns and needs they remember having had when they were young professional players. This they do. I then have them put the cards down, and I move to another topic.

Hours later, after a break, I have them take the cards out again. I ask each one to turn the card to the blank side and write down the focus of contact and communication he had when communicating with the players he was responsible for.

After this exercise is completed, I ask the staff, "How many of you have written the same thing on each side of the card?" Usually one or two hands—in a full room—are raised. "So this is what seems to be the case," I say. "The issues and needs you had as a player are no longer the issues and concerns you have as a staff member."

Well, that's a no-brainer, immediately clear to everyone. But what also becomes clear is the fact that players focus on their own growth as performers, and that coaches are responsible, theoretically, at least, for this growth, as well. The mental, not just the physical. They are inextricably connected. So in order to be effective, the coach's concerns must reflect an understanding that *players'* mental issues are a major part of the coach's agendas. It is agreed upon in those rooms that a big gap exists between theory and practice.

In order to examine your relative efficacy as a coach, you must first examine your style of coaching—of teaching. Of leading. In other words, you must first examine *yourself*, your own needs and the way you express them to your athletes. (See sections 2, 3.) You must see the see the difference between *your* constant concerns and your athletes'. And then work at bridging the gap.

■ ■ ■

Years ago I was brought in to consult for a university baseball program. I was to spend three days, mostly with the players. My first evening there, I was taken to dinner by the coach and his assistants. During the course of our conversation, I asked the head coach what he felt to be the players' greatest need, in terms of their mental approach to performance.

"We quit," he said. "When we fall behind, we give in."

Before I could respond, the hitting coach turned to him and said, "Tell Harvey what you do when the other team scores early on us." A sheepish look crossed the head coach's face. The hitting coach, who obviously was not intimidated by his "boss," provided the information himself. "Last week, [the opponent] scored five runs in the top of the first. Bill [name changed to protect the guilty party] stormed to the end of the dugout, folded his arms across his chest and didn't say a word to anybody for, I don't know, three or four innings, when we put a few runs on the[score]board."

The coach had made evident his frustration and anger, had disassociated himself from the team, had taken no responsibility for helping anyone, and had cut off lines of communication with his team, other coaches included.

I pointed this out quickly to "Bill" and added, "In other words, *you* quit. You modeled the behavior you hate in the players."

Coach, heal thyself. You're no good for others if you're no good for yourself. First, you'd better recognize your behaviors.

That visit, I spent as much time with the coach as I did with the players.

Examination Time

Abraham Maslow wrote extensively about "self-actualization." The term essentially means self-realization and the realization of one's potential as a healthy and effective adult. He found that self-actualized people he studied shared a few essential characteristics. No one argues about the findings, but how many people (coaches) work hard at developing these characteristics? The outstanding ones.

Examine the list. Assess yourself in terms of the traits as they are evident in your style as a coach and adult. Be honest. Bill Parcells has said, "The one guy I answer to is the guy in the mirror." But that guy had better give you the straight answers. Remember the wicked witch in *Snow White*, who asked the image in the mirror, "Who's the fairest of them all?" The woman heard the answer she wanted, not the one she needed. Dishonesty about ourselves is a mistake too easy to make but too important to allow.

After scanning the list below, determine what you consider to be areas of need. Then be relentless in *doing something* about them.

Self-actualized coaches are:

- *Accepting of themselves.* They don't arbitrarily accept every view they have, but neither do they beat themselves up for their perceived failings. They understand that their personal shortcomings are part of the human condition. They don't accept these shortcomings as inevitable, however, and work diligently at the ordeal of self-improvement.
- *Realistic in their perceptions of themselves and others.* They know themselves to be fallible and therefore don't expect perfection in others. They are honest and understanding in their evaluation of people and circumstances, while maintaining a high standard for themselves and for those they coach and lead.
- *Independent.* They think for themselves, rather than having a "herd mentality." They're sociable with other coaches but not deferential in terms of approach to coaching. They learn by listening to everyone and making independent judgments, based on the merit of the message, rather than the status of the messenger. They "stretch their feet to the length of their own blanket," rather than limiting their reach to the length of others'.
- *Able to be decision makers.* They know where the "buck stops." They are thoughtful, objective, pragmatic in making their decisions, and have the courage of their convictions. They act upon them.
- *Spontaneous.* Nehru spoke of a leader as someone who "can take advantage of conditions themselves when they arise." Leaders aren't bound to the "cookbook" for coaches. They trust their

intuitive "gut feelings," knowing that these messages have sneaked into consciousness from a dark information storage vault within. They aren't afraid to listen to these promptings, and their confidence is not shaken should they occasionally prove to be wrong.

- *Willing to delegate authority to others.* They are not control freaks. They understand the strengths and abilities of subordinates or team members. They are not indiscriminate in delegating responsibility to others. They give it to those who are responsible.
- *Able to communicate a sense of humor.* They intuitively know the importance of and place for humor. Humor is the policeman to the free mind. When we are light-hearted, we are confessing. We're confessing our humanity. More importantly, we're expressing it. Lightening up gives the coach's left brain the break it often needs and too infrequently gets. Note: Sarcasm directed at athletes is not necessarily a "lightening up." In fact, it's particularly "heavy"—often damaging—when directed at those who interpret subtle wit as malice.
- *Creative.* Creative minds, it's been said, have been known to survive bad training. Enough said.
- *Concerned for the well-being of others.* To give is to get. The best teachers and coaches know that.
- *Capable of having close and satisfying relationships with their athletes.* The old chestnut "You can't love your players" has rotted in the fields of time. Yes, there is a line between player and coach. There is also a line between parent and child. What effective coaches understand is the difference between a line and a barrier.

■ ■ ■

Maslow believed that the possibility for self-actualization is embedded in human nature. But "embedded" means fixed firmly in a surrounding mass. Few people exert the energy it takes to strip away that mass. It's a daunting task.

Included in that mass are "deficiency needs," the individual's concerns about the physical and the material. About status and social survival. In contrast, "growth needs" of self-actualization motivate us to develop our potential as human beings.

Self-examination for the purpose of personal and professional growth is a first step. It helps us to be aware of who we've been. Our self-determination indicates who we want to be.

Final words here from Vince Lombardi: "Leaders earn the right to lead. How? They manifest character and integrity. . . . Character is not inherited, it is something that can be, and needs to be, built and disciplined." If we hope to develop these traits in our athletes, why shouldn't we want the same for ourselves? Actually, we need to "have it" in order to "give it."

My own final words on the subject: a self isn't found; it is *made*.

Keep in Mind

- As an effective leader you must know yourself and how you are perceived.
- Part of that awareness is in knowing your strengths and your weaknesses—knowing what you can and cannot do as a coach and being honest with *yourself*, to start with.
- Change is a choice, and personality is not a destiny.

Four

The Substance of Leadership

*Substance, n. that which is solid and practical in
character, quality or importance.*
The American Heritage Dictionary of the English Language

Poet Richard Eberhart wrote, "Style is the perfection of a point of view."
In the context of this chapter, "point of view" is synonymous with the
term *substance*. "Style" is the manner in which a leader presents himself
and his point of view. "Substance" is the essence of what he values in his
world and the characteristics they represent through his behavior.

Though each leader may lack particular qualities and abilities, he
shares a point of view with other effective leaders. He's able to mold the
individual qualities and abilities he does possess into a generally solid
and practical model.

■ ■ ■

If truth were told, I would just as soon not write extensively about the
substance of leadership, mainly because so much has already been written about it. I'm well aware of most readers' familiarity with the subject.
So, my intention is to have this chapter be less than "extensive." Nevertheless, referential points of view must be established, because a good
number of them will be examined in later chapters.

What we should refer to as leaders are the beliefs and behaviors that
make others *want* to follow. Thomas Fuller wrote, "If you command
wisely, you'll be obeyed cheerfully." We don't fool the athletes. They
know what they want, and they know whether the coach is capable and
inclined to help them get it. Effective leaders help the athletes to meet
their appropriate mental needs and get them to change those needs and
approaches that are not helpful to peak performance.

Leaders hold the athletes accountable for "the right stuff." The goal is to have the athletes learn to take that responsibility as their own. But the first responsibility is the leader's, who achieves that goal because he, himself, has that stuff.

Here's the "stuff"—

- *A credo.* Corporations call it a "mission statement." Whatever name it's given, the value of the organization or team must be made clear to all. These are the values of the leader: the philosophies and behaviors that will drive the team and represent it. The standard set for behavior on and off the fields of competition. Playing hard, playing smart, being prompt, being responsible, being unselfish, are a few popular ones. Woodrow Wilson said, "It is not the whip that makes men, but the lure of things that are worthy to be loved." A credo is your statement of what is worthy.
- *Consistency.* Winning isn't a sometime thing, Lombardi said. Neither is leadership. You're either leading—or you're not. You're not when you abandon the acknowledged values, or when you permit the athletes to stray from the course set by these standards. Without leadership there can be no "followship"—and no fellowship of common purpose. If I'm consistent, I'm definable, whether I'm a pain in the butt or a goody-two-shoes. Athletes often say they are most concerned with knowing where they stand. They must determine where the coach stands before that need can ever be satisfied. The coach, of course, should know where he, himself, stands—and be firmly planted there.
- *Authenticity.* What suffers immediately when coaches "let things slide" is the athletes' trust. They understand that establishing a credo is a superficial exercise. What is most real to them is the coach's behavior, not his pronouncements. To paraphrase Sophocles, those don't command who don't enforce. Authenticity is established through consistent behavior. If I'm consistent, I'm authentic. Authenticity is honesty; authenticity is integrity. Both serve to define our character, whether we have them or not.
- *Flexibility.* The ability to adapt to the needs of the circumstance is an imperative for good leadership. Flexibility is *not* inconsistency. Inflexible people are those who would say, as Twain did ironically, that to stay stuck in a rut is consistent and that to climb out of it is inconsistent. Flexibility is the ability to change strategies and beliefs when it's been amply validated that whatever we've believed is no longer true and whatever we've been doing no longer works. It's the ability to recognize what's required at the moment and to spontaneously seize that moment—without being restrained by the burden of convention or convenience. Comfort in foolishness and failure is a consistency that makes those we're supposed to lead

uncomfortable. Very uncomfortable. Write in pencil, not ink.

- *Discipline.* Discipline is too often considered to be a punitive measure. That is not the meaning here. Discipline is order, as opposed to disorder—or chaos. Discipline implies commitment: commitment to the credo and values established; commitment to the relentless pursuit of team and individual goals. Discipline implies accountability and responsibility. Discipline is preparation. Discipline is required in order for the coach and athlete to focus on the singular tasks of competition. I tell athletes, "What you do when no one is watching defines you." Such self-discipline is not the human norm. Doing what is right requires great determination and power of the will. We should require it, teach it on a regular basis—and model it.

- *Preparation.* Leaders who make a commitment to their profession make a commitment to preparation. They recognize the importance of planning, time management, role definition, practice application, assessment, adjustments, and competition strategy. Effective preparation incorporates a number of mental elements and skills already noted or to be discussed subsequently. They include dedication, responsibility, confidence, teaching, repetition, and communication, to name a few. Preparation does not mean the devotion to and formulation of intricate and complicated strategies to outsmart the competition. Lombardi used a few simple plays but prepared his players to execute them perfectly. And those who prepare to do the simple things perfectly are better prepared to do more difficult things easily. Plan your work; work your plan.

- *Rationality.* Mark Twain was fond of saying that the only difference between humans and "lower forms of animal life" is our brain. "And usually man forfeits the difference," he added. Coaching can be an emotional experience. It had better be a rational one, as well. We are primarily responsible as leaders to utilize our intelligence. And though reason alone doesn't identify us, it can and does restrain the emotional responses that are waiting in the weeds to control us in the heat of battle. "To think is to act," Emerson wrote. To be emotional is to react. Rationality is the expression of intelligence over passion. Both are part of being human. One is an essential trait of leadership.

- *Poise.* "Grace under pressure" is how Hemingway defined it. And so many others have tried to get a grip on just what the term "poise" means. A sampling: Herman Melville wrote in *Moby Dick*, "Thinking is, or ought to be, a coolness and calmness." He thought that humans' "poor hearts throb . . . too much for that." The coolness and calmness, the proverbial "even keel," are elements of poise, he believed. In Kipling's famous poem "If," the first reference to manhood relates to poise: "If you can keep your head when all about you/ Are losing theirs . . ./ you'll be a man, my son!" Poise is self-control; poise is self-discipline. It's the ability to face the guillotine, so to speak, without losing your head. Poise in the leader is the first indicator to "the troops" of how the battle will go. Napoleon claimed "a leader is a dealer in hope." (Recall the coach who "lost it"—poise and hope—when the opposition scored five runs in the first inning of a baseball game.) Writer Paul Theroux used a term that is a favorite of mine: "Un-get-at-able," which means that nothing can knock the effective leader off his mental and behavioral balance beam. He can't be got-at. The Vikings of yesteryear believed that no good purpose could be found for showing fear. Such display they felt would signify to observers that they had lost their independence—freedom. In athletic competition, the loss of poise increases the opponent's confidence as it diminishes the athlete— or coach—who loses it. A coach who has "total" poise has the ability to control his emotions, his thinking, and his behavior. His serenity of mind combats chaos. His good example instructs his followers.

- *Courage.* The courage of one's convictions. The courage also to take risks. The courage to confront difficulty—adversity. The courage to be fair and honest. The courage to hold his followers and, above all, himself accountable. The Latin *cor* means "heart." To have courage is to have "heart"; that term is heard often enough in arena of athletic competition. To many, it implies fearlessness. But that isn't the point of courage. To have courage is to act bravely *in spite* of reluctance or fear. Courage is facing adversity and fear and "spitting in its eye." Trying to avoid threatening situations is not an effective strategy. Nor does it bring safety. Rather, it almost guarantees failure. A feeling of vulnerability is reinforced by the lack of courageous behavior. Hardly the makings of effective leadership. Courage allows the leader to express all his other qualities; the absence of courage suppresses them. Stifles them. Challenging fear elevates behavior, elevates the leader, enhances the organization one leads. All people have fears, whether hidden or exposed. Whether a coach, athlete, or accountant. Since one's emotional system is the source of his fears, the environment and activity is less significant than the personality and perception of the fearful person. Athletic competition may just be "fun and games" to a spectator, but it is quite a bit more to the coach and the participant. Courage is acting in spite of these fears. Without fears, one cannot act heroically. All goes if courage goes. Without it, a leader is a leader in name only.

The reader knows there's more to leadership, and I know it also. As noted, it's my intention to address in subsequent pages many of those topics not yet considered. It's my hope to be as thorough as my experience and understanding allows me to be. This I always keep in mind about the best leaders/coaches: they're easy to play for and tough to please.

Keep in Mind

- A coach's team represents something. It should represent what the coach deems to be a form of excellence.
- Consistency means the adherence to the principles that a credo represents, regardless of the results in the arena of competition.
- A coach's honesty and integrity are threads in the athlete's security blanket.
- Flexibility implies calculated change, based on an evident need for that change.
- Discipline includes the setting of parameters and structure; order and determination.
- Preparation is what allows the coach to be ready to teach, ready to practice, which, in turn, allows his athletes to be ready to compete.
- Only those who think effectively lead those who toil.
- Poise is the quality of self-control that allows for effective thinking and acting when the heat is on.
- Courage provides the strength for doing what we know is right.

Five

The Coach Communicates, One Way or Another

Coach O'Brien's got a discipline and at the same time knows how to relate to the players. Even the guys who aren't playing a lot of minutes he's going to be straight with, going to be honest.
Paul Pierce,
Postseason, Post-Pitino Boston Celtics (2002)

I present myself to you in a form suitable to the relationship I wish to achieve with you.
Luigi Pirandello,
The Pleasure of Honesty (1917)

During an interview for a job he was then seeking as a minor league manager in the Oakland organization, Bob Boone was asked to speak about the reputation he had as a catcher who so effectively "handled" pitchers.

Boone, now having managed in the major league for a number of years, responded at that time, "I didn't *handle* pitchers, I *established relationships* with them." His point was that he intended to do the same as a manager.

Good relationships are established through effective communication. Boone's use of the term made a distinction between manipulation and arbitrariness on the part of the message sender and the mutual respect and understanding between the sender and the receiver of whatever is being communicated.

A coach/teacher essentially indicates the type of communication he makes with his athletes based on the choice he makes to either "deal with" them or establish effective "relationships." As Pirandello's words in the epigraph suggest, the "form" of presentation—style and substance—will also influence the terms set between coach and athlete.

■ ■ ■

Item: This clip is about Hall-of-Famer Frank Robinson, Montreal Expos manager, and his "new attitude . . . toned down managerial style, being less abrasive" from *USA Today* (June 18, 2002):

> It seems uncanny that Robinson, who as a player and manager was a horrible loser, can communicate with these athletes. He admits he has changed his approach. "A little softer hand, a little bit more understanding," he said. "I'm willing to listen to them on what they have to say. . . . Being a little bit more compassionate. I make sure each day I have contact with each one of them, say hello, pat them on the back. Make sure, win or lose, I'm in the clubhouse after the game. I try to always leave them with something positive."

Robinson's wife said she'd never seen him happier. To give is to get.

No Form, No Substance?

There are coaches who, for one reason or another, fail to communicate in any essential way with their athletes. In January 2002, Jerry Richardson, the owner of the NFL's Carolina Panthers, proclaimed to the media, "The most important part of a company, or any organization, is communication." He had just fired head coach George Seifert. The area newspaper ran the headline, "Richardson Wants Better Communication Skills in Next Coach."

So, too, apparently, did the players. Fullback Brad Hoover said that one of the traits he wanted to see in the next leader was "a more personable coach, a guy that [relates] to his players and really cares about them."

Seifert had won two Super Bowls in San Francisco. Panthers' cornerback Jimmy Hitchcock said of Seifert: "He's a secretive guy. That's who he is. That doesn't mean he can't coach. Bill Parcells wasn't necessarily a player's coach either. And he won."

On the other hand, New England Patriots coach Bill Belichick was considered to be, according to *New York Times* columnist Dave Anderson, "an introvert, a glowering genius scientist known as Dr. Doom. In his laboratory [as assistant coach to Parcells] his test tubes were the X's and O's. . . . He failed in five seasons as the Cleveland Browns' head coach. Too mysterious. Too secretive."

The introvert changed—and won the Super Bowl in 2002. As Anderson put it, Belichick "attained a stature that for years was thought to be beyond his personality." He communicated effectively with his players. He was no longer introverted.

His was an act of will, not of personality. An acquired instinct, rather than a natural one.

Just Another Mr. Nice Guy? Not.

It's become rather evident that effective communication is essential for coaches in today's world. From the earliest contacts with young athletes to connections made with those competing at the professional level, the athletes and coaches who must "deal with each other" on a regular basis are dependent on both verbal and nonverbal communication. Technological advances may be astounding, but quantity, speed, and coverage have little to do with a coach's relationship with his athletes. Word choice, timing, tonality, body language, facial gesture—silences—(see chapter 6) have everything to do with establishing lines of communication. Some coaches have open, clear lines; others, unfortunately, have vague and short—or closed—lines.

Does sensitivity to the communication indicate that the coach is a wimp—a Mr. Nice Guy, "touchy-feely" type? Those who use such disclaimers are usually those who refuse to make the effort it takes to be truly effective. Some can hide behind won-lost records. Most have records that can't protect their ineffectiveness. Sensitivity to the communication process simply indicates that the coach recognizes the importance of the process. He knows that by "connecting" with his athletes he'll enhance their mental approaches, thereby serving individual goals (his own included) and team goals.

Philadelphia Eagles coach Andy Reid's popularity in that tough sports town has been called "amazing." He came to the Eagles with two years of head coaching experience, yet he has presented himself as a communicator who has earned the respect of his professional athletes.

Quarterback Donavan McNabb said of Reid, "He's the type of guy where what he wants is what he wants. If he doesn't get it, you might not be here long. Players respect that." Communicator? Reid certainly has made clear his values and expectations.

But McNabb wasn't finished. "If you have a coach you can talk to, not just about football, but about anything, that's all you want."

It's been said of Tampa Bay coach Jeff Gruden that connecting is one of his specialties. Some in the media have called Gruden "one of these professional football coaches in a new generation of coaches," young enough to relate to today's athletes.

Coach Steve Mariucci has said, "If you cannot relate (establish a *relationship*) to today's player, you're through as a coach. I think you can be a gentleman and succeed and treat players fairly and like men," he said. "This is not old Rome with Gladiators."

Brian Billick is an "easygoing" coach. It's said that he has his intense moments, but Billick considers himself a teacher, not a screamer. He—and Mariucci and Reid—raise their voices and have their blowouts—and are effective.

"Nice" is not the operative word to describe them as coaches, though each is considered to be a good person. As is Herman Edwards of the

New York Jets, whose goal in his first minicamp with the team was to form a strong bond with and among the players that would aid them in competition.

Mike Freeman of the *New York Times* described this group of NFL coaches as individuals who combine "fairness and communication and intellect to get the job done instead of relying solely on a hammer and vocal cords."

Solely. Occasionally, they do wield a metaphorical hammer that, properly administered, can drive home a point. (Edwards called his own defensive co-coordinator "stern, but it's a good stern.")

And vocal cords are capable of a wide range of volume. The best communicators adjust them according to perceived need.

Baseball columnist Lawrence Rocca suggested in the *Newark Star-Ledger* (May 5, 2002) that two Houston Astros star players were largely responsible for getting two previous managers fired. Rocca also wrote that the two players, Craig Biggio and Jeff Bagwell, "have told friends on other teams they are extremely happy with new no-nonsense manager Jimy Williams because of his communications skills." Williams approaches his players directly and honestly.

Most athletes want and appreciate that approach; almost all of them need it, whether they are professionals or amateurs.

Perception and Communication

"Perceived need." Coaches need to know, not guess, who needs what. The communication process breaks down when we think one thing but the reality is something quite different.

The possibility is great for two people to misunderstand each other. The demanding conditions of competition increase the possibility. Encoding, sending, receiving, and decoding are steps in the seemingly simple process of communicating with one another. It's not actually that simple. The message is often lost within the process. And a relationship can be lost because of a lack of respect for the process itself.

"The Blind Men and the Elephant," a poetic parable written by John Godfrey Saxe, tells of six learned blind men who went to see an elephant "That each by observation / might satisfy his mind." Each man approached the elephant from a different angle; each felt a different part of the animal; each had a different "observation." The one feeling the trunk claimed the elephant was "very like a snake." The one feeling the tail thought the animal to be like a rope. The one feeling the knee thought it like a tree. And so on.

The poem ends, "And so these men of Indostan / Disputed loud and long, / Each in his own opinion / Exceeding stiff and strong. / Though each was partly in the right, / They all were in the wrong!"

If each blind man had experienced each part of the elephant, they would have a shared experience. Then, perhaps, they could come to an agreement about the makeup of the animal. Perhaps. But at least they would all have some specific experience with the elephant's physical "makeup."

Does a coach experience all there is to know about his athlete's mental makeup? Not likely. But a respect for the communication process gives coach and athlete a chance to understand what each wants and needs and knows and feels. The more accurate the perceptions of coach and athlete, the more enhanced their performances will be.

It Isn't Easy

There's the story of a boy excitedly telling his friend of the new pet he's just gotten. His friend, imagining a parrot, asks what kind of pet it is. The boy tells him it's a dog. The friend, imagining a bulldog, asks him what kind of dog it is. The boy says it's a St. Bernard. The friend, imaging a puppy, asks if it's a cute puppy. The boy tells him it's a full-grown dog. The friend, imaging a black dog, asks what color it is. The boy says it's brown and white. The friend, imagining a full-grown, brown St. Bernard with white spots, says, "Why didn't you tell me that in the first place?" The boy, turning to go home to his full-grown white St. Bernard with brown spots, says to himself, "Why doesn't anyone understand me?"

We don't always reach the top rung on the ladder of abstraction. The more we communicate, the better our chances. It's an arduous task. For coaches, it's an essential one.

In 1961 James Thurber, concerned about the precarious relationship between the two superpowers on either side of the Iron Curtain, wrote, "Precision of communication is important, more important than ever, in our era of hair-trigger balances, when a false, or misunderstood word may create as much disaster as a sudden thoughtless act."

Coaching is not life or death (to most), but "precision of communication" should still be a significant concern for those of us in the profession. It certainly affects the performance of the athletes we coach, especially those who often are not understood and/or not understanding.

Rob Sheehan is the director of executive education at the James MacGregor Burns Academy of Leadership at the University of Maryland. Sheehan emphasizes the fact that coaches "see things very differently than the players. It's important to use that different perspective to educate and encourage." (And "to lead your team by example," Sheehan adds.) It's important to first understand what perspectives exist in the athletes' minds.

Communication as Behavior

People most often behave in certain ways because they have a particular reason, motivation, or agenda. Whatever it may be is communicated through behavior. It *becomes* behavior, not by accident but by *cause*. An internal or external stimulus (visual and auditory are the two I concern myself with as a coach) makes an impact on the individual's nervous system. He evaluates, "sizes up the situation," based on the impact of these stimuli, and behaves according to his interpretation. The behavior can be rational—or emotional.

Many coaches fail to establish an effective interaction with their athletes because these coaches don't recognize whether the athletes understand their purpose or message. Whether the athlete has an internal agenda that leads him to interpret criticism, for example, as a personal attack. We see observable behavior; we do not see the internal factors that trigger it.

As a result, an athlete communicates a responsive behavior that may be based on a lack of understanding, lack of self-confidence, or lack of listening skills, to name a few possibilities. The coach, in turn, may interpret the athlete to be resistant, uncooperative, selfish, or stupid. Without connecting on the same level of understanding, the relationship suffers, as does performance.

Words reflect attitude; attitude dictates behavior. Misunderstanding at any level impedes an understanding of behavior. Barriers that might exist can be broken down by a mutual relationship between coach and athlete, a relationship that serves the needs of each. Communicating these specific needs allows behaviors to be understood and/or modified. Once a trusting relationship is established, it's difficult for either party to behave in a way that is counterproductive to mutual needs and goals. To the trust itself.

Item: Florida basketball coach Billy Donovan has said (*Sports Illustrated*, February 2003), "The most important thing to developing chemistry is the players have to believe the coach is being fair. There has to be constant communication."

Whatever style, substance, or silence a coach employs, he's always communicating *something* to his athletes. And he should always be aware of what that *something* is.

Keep in Mind

- A relationship between coach and athlete implies that the coach has established a setting in which the athlete wants to do what the coach sees as necessary and essential. This is an example of the coach's use of personal power, the top priority of superior leaders and the best tool of effective communicators.
- Coaches communicate messages in many ways, including not speaking with their athletes. What's communicated in such cases, whether it's intended or not, is indifference and lack of concern toward the athletes. Needless to say, this perception is not conducive to the athlete's development of a good mental

approach to competition. If he doesn't know what the coach is thinking, he, being human, will usually develop a negative thought. In fact, he'll usually be right, since the coach's inability can hardly be seen as something positive.

- Perception is not necessarily the same as reality. The more the coach communicates with the athlete, the closer the two can come to understanding what is real to each.
- Silence that is calculated is not noncommunication. When intent is clear to a coach, silence is a strategy, not an immature emotional reaction.

Communication: Considering the Process Itself

What a society does for its members, what they could surely not achieve on their own in a lifetime, is to equip them with ready means for entering a world of enormous potential complexity. It does all this by providing means of simplification—most notably, a language and an ordering point of view to go with language.
Jerome Bruner,
On Knowing: Essays from the Left Hand (1962)

Having emphasized the importance of the communication process between coach and athlete, it's appropriate now to examine some of the essential aspects of that process. Some of the essential approaches to the process.

As Bruner says above, language is the tool that makes thinking and communication possible. Through language, ideas are passed on from over the years—from parents to children—from coach to athletes. The "means of simplification," however, is not always apparent, as I've suggested. But let's start at the beginning.

The three ingredients of communicating are:

1. a sender, who refers to things, thoughts, feelings, and actions through language;
2. language—verbal or nonverbal—which is an indicator, a sign;
3. a receiver, who knows something of the "language" and something about what the sender refers to.

Much of an athlete/receiver's behavior is a reaction to the coach/sender's language. He responds to what he thinks he sees or hears. Sometimes he's right, sometimes not. (Remember the elephant, the St. Bernard.)

Nonverbal Language

The coach's direct nonverbal language is made up of gestures (finger pointing, thumbs up, pat on the back, facial scowls, slumping shoulders, rolling eyes, etc.)—what is commonly called "body language." These gestures indicate blame, satisfaction, understanding/encouragement, unhappiness/anger, disappointment, frustration, and the like.

On the brink of elimination in the finals of the 2002 Stanley Cup Playoffs, Coach Paul Maurice of the underdog, overachieving Carolina Hurricanes said, "You understand that your team watches you and re-acts to all things—your body language and what you say. The guys who lead this team—and that's the coach and the veteran players—have to show that fight in them that they are going to keep doing their job." This they did to the undesired end, a final loss in Game 6 to the heavily fa-vored Detroit Red Wings, winners of the Stanley Cup.

■ ■ ■

Indirect nonverbal language includes Xs and Os, game or practice film, whistles or horns, pictures and posters, team logos on T-shirts. These sounds, signs, and symbols are meant to instruct, control, motivate, and so on. In every case, the coach is communicating some kind of message.

I remember the words but not the source: "A calculated silence trav-els faster than light." Silence is also nonverbal, of course. (The operative word in the quote is "calculated.") It is a great tool when used appropri-ately. The coach employs silence as a strategy in order to communicate a message. Those coaches who "ice" their athletes because they're angry or disappointed or frustrated tend to lead the athletes to their own cal-culation: "Coach can't coach."

Verbal Language

This type of language includes any spoken or written words. They may be heard or read. The coach should begin with an understanding that words have no meaning in themselves. We *give* meaning to words. Athletes and coaches have their own meanings, and these meanings de-pend on what the individual refers to with his words.

What is called a "great play" by one coach is a play "that's gotta be made" to another. Consider, as an example, verbal praise sent by a coach and received by an athlete. The words, called referents, may be sent legitimately and yet received as condescending. They may be sent condescendingly and yet be received as legitimate. The "ordered point of view" Bruner speaks of must accompany language. What referents are intended to mean must be understood by all.

A standard referent in competition is "winning." That's the purpose of competition whenever a score is kept. Is winning "the only thing," as

Vince Lombardi is supposed to have said? Well, because the remark was made and published, many coaches have acted upon the message by interpreting it to mean "Winning is the end-all and be-all." Or "Win at all costs." Those who heard it as such have helped put that interpretation into popular sports culture.

What did Lombardi, a coach who espoused character, moral obligation, and self-sacrifice, mean by "sending" such a message? There are those closer to the message sender—former Green Bay Packers lineman Jerry Kramer, for one—who know the popular interpretation is a misinterpretation. They understand that the Hall-of-Fame coach's referent was about means, not ends. About the goal, the will, and the *way* to win, not "only" about the outcome itself.

Beware of Mixed Verbal Messages

Gary Williams's Maryland team won the 2002 NCAA college basketball championship. Before defeating Duke in the championship game, Williams told the media, "You want to win each game. The situation makes it special. You don't put special emphasis on it with your players because what if you lose? You just get ready to play."

Chris Wilcox, a Maryland star who went into the professional draft after his sophomore season as a national champ, had this to say at the time: "This whole week the coach has been uptight on us about Duke. Duke this, Duke that," said Wilcox, who scored a career high 23 points in the Duke game. "I just feel better for my coach because Coach wanted to win this more than we did."

Meaning exactly what? To whom? Why? Plenty of views, I'm sure, in that world of "enormous potential complexity."

But Maryland won after all was said—and done.

"The Map Is Not the Territory"

That's the standard line of semanticists, people who study language and its meaning. It tells us we shouldn't confuse the symbol for the actual thing it represents. So, does the outcome (score) of a competition always represent the way your team played? It does not. Nevertheless, "winning ugly" is still winning. Playing well and losing is still losing.

How does the coach communicate what is most important in his system—what his "territory" actually is: his values, his approach, his philosophy, the means to the end of winning?

Mapping Out the Real Territory in Real Language

1. Be specific, rather than vague. Define your terms!
2. Understand the difference between language that is based on fact (verifiable) and language that is based on opinion or point of

view (interpretation influenced by an athlete's background, intention, needs, and so on, in which case judgments will vary).

3. Avoid false comparisons. Make certain the comparisons used to make a point are apt. An example of a false comparison is talking about the preparation of a sprinter to a miler.

4. Be a coach, not a lawyer. No "party of the first part does hereby . . ." is appropriate. Be as concise as possible. I've been in clubhouses in which what would have been a manager's effective message became lost in a wordy soliloquy. Some coaches fall in love with the sound of their own voice. Athletes want to perform, not sit around listening to speeches.

5. Beware of loaded "color words." Many of those employed by coaches are colored by emotion. The shade is often very dark. Examples: He's a wimp. She folds in the clutch. He's a cancer.

6. Avoid sweeping generalizations. The easiest way to *approach* a point is to make a blanket, all-inclusive statement. It's not the way to *make* the point. At least, to make the point stick. Opinion isn't fact. If a coach can't verify what he says through corroborative evidence, his reach is greater than his grasp.

7. Make distinctions between fact (the final score), inference ("We lost because you didn't come to play"), and value judgment ("The officials were out to get us").

8. Be attentive to the logic of your remarks. The "truth" is based on ideas referring to what's real (not maps). Therefore, physical, intellectual, and psychological contexts should match up when athletes are being addressed. The matches include *time sequence* (Example: "The steps in this drill are . . ."), *space arrangement* ("This is where the defense must line up and move to as . . ."), and *cause-and-effect sequence* ("Lack of preparation and a nonaggressive mental approach usually lead to a poor performance").

Words—and Silences—Have Consequences

The goal for coaches is, as noted, to get athletes to behave effectively. To perform effectively. To compete effectively. Language helps a person to reach his goal, whether it be power, approval, achievement, and/or change. Recognizing the language we use is a required mean to those ends—the achieving of one's goals.

- If the coach's goal is based on technique or strategy, he wants the athlete *to think*. Xs and Os and facts are employed.
- If the coach's goal is to get the athlete to believe in "the system," he wants the athlete *to feel (to trust)*. Language that provokes a positive response and examples of validation is employed.

- If the coach's goal is to have the athlete *act/behave* appropriately, he uses language that arouses and instructs.
- If the coach's goal is *to prepare* his athletes, he uses language that illustrates a systematic plan.

The best communicators know what they're saying, know why they're saying it, know when and how to say it—and know who to say it to. The best communicators start with a respect for the power of language and for the communication process itself. And they have an initial respect for the people with whom they communicate.

Keep in Mind

- The coach and the athletes are both senders and receivers of messages.
- They communicate with each other through verbal and nonverbal language.
- It's imperative that both sender and receiver agree upon the meaning of the message.
- Mixed messages are expressions that create confusion and communicate dishonesty, at worst, and inconsistency, at best.
- Symbol is not substance. Be clear and be real.
- Silence, when used appropriately, is indeed golden.
- A respect for the communication process makes us all better communicators.

Seven

Communication: The When, Where, How, Why—and Who!

Yelling doesn't communicate. It's a whisper in somebody's ear. It's a pat on the back. It's a push at times. Whatever you need to do to communicate. It's not jamming someone up against the wall. It's learning what you can and cannot say to each individual to get the best out of them.
Mo Vaughn,
Major League First Baseman

All speech is a dead language, until it finds a willing and prepared listener.
Robert Louis Stevenson

Those of us whose business it is to communicate must be certain that those we speak to are ready, willing, and able to listen to us. Aside from having the responsibility of knowing what we're talking about, we have the need to know when, where, why, and how to present our message. And much of this is based on the receiver of our supposed words of wisdom. Who is it? How does this person typically respond to messages such as the one we're going to deliver?

And, as Stevenson suggests in the epigraph, is that person prepared to receive our message? If not, what can we do to prepare him?

Who

We should first consider "the who" because, if we are to be as effective as possible, we must know with whom we are communicating: the predisposition and disposition of the athlete we address. His makeup, his probable or possible responses, and his "hot buttons"/"cold buttons." His seeming "buttonlessness." His goals and values, which help us to identify *his needs*. The more we know about them, the better equipped we are to address his mental approach to performance—and identity on the team. (Section 3 will treat this topic extensively.) So an immediate effort is made to be certain that the athlete is or becomes a more "willing and prepared" listener.

Some people respond to directions given gently, some people to those given forcefully. What is needed at any moment depends greatly on the circumstance, but the individual being communicated with is a very significant factor in that circumstance. The individual is a primary consideration, unless the gymnasium is on fire.

When

We've often heard: "Timing is everything." Perhaps it's not everything, but it's up there pretty high on the requirement chart for effective communication. The most brilliant and convincing point of view presented at the wrong time loses its luster and its meaning. It doesn't lose its audience, because it never had one to begin with.

An audience must be receptive, so the sender should be sensitive to the timing of the message he intends to deliver. I can't count how many times people have tried to be helpful to me: coaches, teachers, assistants, students, players, colleagues, a son, a daughter—and I've held up my hand, palm facing them, and said, "Not now."

My wife never has to ask, "When, then?" She knows. So should coaches know when their athletes are best able to "get the message"? This is not to say a coach must canvas his team to find out when he can talk to them. The absurdity of that condition should be obvious. It *is* to say that when an important one-on-one delivery or exchange is conducted between coach and athlete, the receptivity of the athlete should be considered. If he is angry, for example, he is probably deaf and dumb. Let the anger subside, rather than trying to scream through it. If the anger lasts too long, the coach's intervention is required, of course. But that too begs for proper timing.

There may be no ideal time for the delivery of some messages, but the best of what's available should be considered. The major emphasis of my point is that picking the most appropriate time to communicate a particular message to an athlete insinuates a coach's concerned thoughtfulness. That thoughtfulness will be preemptive to behaving in an emotional, ineffective way. It implies that the coach is under control and using his brain, which are two characteristics of the best communicators—and leaders.

Poor timing can be based on impromptu behaviors that are too strong or too weak. Whichever the case, the behavior is often based on the coach's need at the moment, rather than the team's need in the long run.

Where

Recently I received a call from a major league ballplayer. He was struggling with performance, but one of the issues that troubled him most had to do with being confronted by a coach in the dugout between innings. Teammates witnessed and heard the coach's loud and critical message. The player, feeling he was being shown up, did not respond well. His retaliatory words then caused the manager to get involved. "Shut the #^*~ up!" he shouted at the player. The player, wisely, did just that.

The coach was unhappy about what had just taken place on the field and was coaching at the top of his voice. Perhaps, in a sense, the *timing* was right for the player, but the *setting* was not. The player was, indeed, shown up in front of teammates. He'd performed poorly, but not because of lack of effort.

If someone is put into a corner, there's only one place he can go: straight out. In this case, at the coach. The player's intention was to defend himself, to excuse himself, to combat the communication that was embarrassing him in front of teammates. In private, I'd like to believe, he would have shut himself "the #^*~ up" and taken the criticism constructively. But in the dugout, he shouted back, a defense mechanism employed because, clearly, he had been put on the defensive.

Two wrongs do not make this situation right for the player. And my purpose is not to defend him. My purpose is to illustrate that, given a desired outcome for his communication, the coach would not have chosen what did result. He should have been able to predict it (especially if he knew "the who!"—and I believe he did). So, whatever "instructive" message was meant to be delivered evaporated in the dugout air, thick with the breathing of twenty people. We might say the timing of the message was bad, but in a *better place*—private!—the same aggressive message delivered in the same tone of voice would have worked. I can say this with some confidence, having done so myself with this player in the past.

The immediacy of the need to deliver his words provoked the coach to act upon that need instead of directing the player down into the dugout tunnel. That area, a few paces away, would have provided a setting in which a desirable response to information would have resulted, rather than an undesirable reaction to what was interpreted as a personal affront.

■ ■ ■

I was in my mid-twenties and teaching junior high school students in Vermont. I was sitting alone in my classroom, during a free period, when the science teacher across the hall came into my room. "I've got a phone call at the office," he said. "Could you look after my class for a few minutes?"

I went into his room. The kids were not exactly hanging from the rafters, but given some more time, they would have been. Near chaos. I should call it actual chaos, beyond the norm in that classroom. These were the same kids I taught literature to. We knew each other very well. No problem, I thought. Shouting in order to be heard, I directed them to get into their seats. The response was minimal. I was astounded. "What's going on here?" I said to myself.

I shouted louder. Again, louder still. A very marginal response. Suddenly, an epiphany: "Everyone line up!" I bellowed. They did, slowly. "Walk into my room and get into your seats," I shouted. They did, at a decent pace. I waited for a few minutes, then slowly went to my classroom. The proverbial pin could have been heard, had it been dropping. The students (no longer savages) were seated, waiting for me. Order and silence prevailed.

Conditioned environmentally in the science teacher's room—and in mine—these adolescents responded more acutely to *where* they were than who they were with. They marched their conditioned behaviors out of one room and made the adjustment in another room without supervision. The power of place.

More recently, in June 2002, the Toronto Blue Jays changed managers. The general manager said the team needed leadership and direction, and thus the change was made. Later in the month, high-profile outfielder Raul Mondesi was late for a team meeting. He was taken out of the lineup that night and kept out the next night.

Mondesi complained to the media about the manager, as he had complained about circumstances when he played for the Los Angeles Dodgers. Weeks later, he was traded to the Yankees. At this time, he is no longer playing in the major leagues.

His attitude improved. His new manager talked of Mondesi getting a "clean slate" to work with, while at the same time saying that he agreed with the Blue Jays manager's disciplinary actions. "Ten minutes or ten years," Joe Torre said. "He's still late."

Unacceptable to both managers; more acceptable to the player in a new environment: a winning environment in which teammates police their own and those who don't make whatever adjustments are required are soon gone. That is the environment the Blue Jays manager hoped to establish. He knew it would take due diligence and consistency.

■ ■ ■

The competition is over. Coach wants to give his team hell. He gathers them on the field's sideline. The devil gets his due. Is this the best place?

Consider this: a wide-open area (field, court) encourages wide-open attention. Delivery of the message with spectators as possible witnesses does not keep the message "in the house," a phrase of appeal coaches often make to their athletes. A narrow confine (bus, locker room) is more conducive to a narrow focus (attention to the message, not to the surroundings). It is private—and "in the house." The walls of the gym, the locker room, or the bus create a physically controlled environment. The privacy established provides an environment in which team members can trust that the coach is addressing them, rather than publicly posturing for an audience of parents, media, or opponents. Or serving his own internal needs by trying to embarrass them out of disappointment and built-up frustration.

The coach may want to be spontaneous and immediate when he delivers this particular postcompetition response. But one of the meanings of "spontaneous" is "unconstrained and unstudied in manner or behavior." Waiting to deliver the message in the right place might also serve the communicator by allowing for a "studied manner" and an intelligent, rather than emotional, response to what the athletes have just been through in competition.

Practice sessions usually are "in the house," where communication with the team takes place regularly. But individual athletes who require thoughtful, sensitive, and/or strong confrontation should be communicated with where coach and athlete are secured, undisturbed, and unobserved. An athlete's reactions are then more likely to be honest, rather than postured messages and behaviors provoked by self-consciousness. They are more likely to be based on who he is rather than who he wants observers to think he is.

Why

Why? Is the answer to this question too obvious? The answer, in this context, may be short and simple, but the implication is vast and complex.

People generally are more interested in the content of a message than how the message is delivered. Yet, the manner and conditions of delivery have as much impact as what the words contain. (Sometimes more!) The timing, tonality, and language used affect the receiver significantly. So we should all understand what goes into the content, the style, the delivery, the place, and the receiver. Understanding all this helps the coach to look for and learn better ways of connecting and establishing relationships with his athletes. He becomes a communicator looking for signposts to better roads.

The coach uses his communication skills to establish common goals, to express organizational credos, to teach, to discipline, to encourage, to eliminate false perceptions, to air grievances, to ensure appropriate focus, to review and correct mistakes, to motivate the athletes to "play the game hard and play the game right"—to compete.

The games we play aren't complicated. The people who play them are. As coaches, we get an edge when we know the people we teach as well as we know the sport we teach. It's a more challenging task, to be sure. But our explanations, exhortations, and strategies become exponentially more effective as we communicate more effectively. We should not presume that others understand everything we say. Nor should we presume that they believe everything we say.

And this: No matter what we talk about to our athletes, no matter how we say it, no matter when and where—we are always, in some sense, talking about ourselves. If we aspire to be as excellent as we ask our athletes to be, we should understand that our communication (behavior included) not only is primary tool, it is the means by which we are identified.

That's why!

How

How to get your point across well. *How* to get the athlete to understand where you're coming from and where you want him to go. *How* to understand where the athlete is coming from and where he thinks he should be going. *How* to help him change his behavior so you can both get to the appropriate destination as you enjoy the journey.

Many tricks are required, and we don't always know the right one to use. The right ones, after all, are the ones that get the responses we're after. The ones that enhance the athlete as performer and person.

It's challenging for us to communicate exactly what we wish, and I do understand that theory is not the same as practice. To be pragmatic is to believe that what *works* is true. What is presented here has worked for me. Not with everyone and not always. But generally so. I also know that the use of techniques and approaches that are in direct contrast to those I'll suggest very rarely work. (I'm being careful not to say "never," though I'm tempted.)

Listen

Listening is the most neglected language skill. Those in positions of power are particularly neglectful, because they tend to believe they're responsible to tell, rather than hear. The two responsibilities—skills—are not mutually exclusive.

Carl Rogers, a preeminent psychologist, wrote, "The biggest block to personal communication is man's inability to listen intelligently, understandingly, and skillfully to another person."

He might have added "patiently." I've seen coaches who had been informed of their need to be better listeners allow the athlete to speak, then abruptly shut him off after what seemed to be a limited time allowance. Needless to say, the coach who did that was waiting for the athlete to shut up, rather than truly listening to what he said.

The coach who really listens provides the athlete with a sense of participation in the team's well-being. Certainly, if the athlete is talking about himself, the athlete has the opportunity to clarify and suggest. His own well-being is being enhanced by this opportunity and by the fact that the coach gets valuable insights into how to help the athlete perform more effectively.

Not everything I hear from athletes is true. Some will take the opportunity to be heard as an opportunity to "blow smoke." They are trying to hide more than they're trying to reveal. Still, if I keep someone talking long enough, the smoke often dissipates, revealing what I need to know.

As a coach, I've asked players what they thought benefited them most in practice routines. Sometimes I made adjustments according to what I heard; sometimes I did not. Listening doesn't imply loss of control for a coach. It implies a gain of athletes' confidence in your respect for them. A desire to create more effective relationships.

It's imperative to help the athlete to be a better listener. When talking to the entire team, the coach should never allow any whispering or asides between athletes. Such behavior is unacceptable. First, it is disrespectful. Rude, if you care for the term. Second, valuable information may be missed by those not engaged by the words of the coach.

I recall my first talk with the team when I was introduced as a new Florida Marlins staff member. As I was speaking, one of the team's starting players leaned over and spoke into the ear of the player standing next to him. I stopped talking. So did he. I continued; so did he. "So-and-so," I said, speaking his name. "One person speaks at a time, and I'm that person right now." He shut it down.

After the talk, the player, with a less-than-aggressive attitude, nevertheless indicated to me that I'd "shown him up" in front of the team. "And you were showing me up until I did," I said. "That's not going to happen. You either learn to listen because you want to or pretend to listen because I want you to. That much is your choice." We developed a good relationship. I was able to help him listen because he understood the value of listening—*after* understanding the imperative.

Regular, short talks can be given daily. They should have a purpose and meaning, of course. The coach might have an athlete speak to the team about a particular subject from time to time. Whatever the topic, the purpose of these talks is also to help develop the athletes' listening skills.

Ask Questions

This skill is closely related to the listening skill. If I ask a question, I'd better be certain to listen carefully to the answer. Questions are powerful language tools. They make the athlete speak about something the coach wants to know. Avoidance of a direct answer, a direct answer ("right" or "wrong"), or silence should indicate *something* to the coach. Socrates was considered to be the best teacher in Athens. His major teaching device was to ask questions, forcing the student to think, to speak, to explain—to know.

Socrates' favorite question was "Why?" Many motives are discovered as a result of this question being asked. It's an arrogant and presumptuous coach who thinks he always knows the athletes' motives for doing whatever it is that displeased him.

Many times I've spoken to a player and he has nodded in agreement and understanding as a look passed between us that indicated there was no understanding. Years ago, when talking about theory or strategy to individual players, I began the practice of asking them to repeat what I'd just said. I could then be assured that they had been attentive and understood my message—or that they had not done one or the other.

Asking an athlete "Do you know what I mean?" or "Do you understand?" allows him to continue to not know or misunderstand. All that's required is a nod or "Yes." Such questions should be avoided.

During my years with professional baseball teams, I communicated with many Latino players who did not want to appear as if they didn't understand me. The usual practice, as noted, was to ask them, "What did I just say?" They were never annoyed; they appreciated the security of being certain themselves that they knew what was expected of them. Most athletes feel the same. Better safe than sorry.

Be Objective. Think about What You've Heard

I ask plenty of questions, and I'm not always thrilled by the responses I get. If I have any hope of using the player's response effectively, I must be thoughtful and assess what he's said objectively. Many times, if an athlete is asked to be truthful, he will be just that. Sometimes the truth may bother us; it should also help us. Depersonalizing the message may be a difficult thing to do in some cases. When that *is* the case, the best immediate response is to think first and speak later. Rationality needs time; emotionality just needs opportunity.

Be in Control of Yourself

What a coach communicates when he's not in control of his emotions is that he's not in control of his brain. He forfeits his intelligence and the trust the players have in him as an effective leader. They follow because they're intimidated, not because they are confident—in him or in themselves because of him.

Shaquille O'Neal, speaking of Lakers coach Phil Jackson, said, "If the general's OK, the troops are OK." It stands to reason that the coach who isn't OK is "leading" non-OK troops. (The Lakers' 2002 NBA sweep was Jackson's third championship "3-peat"—one as a player, two as a coach.)

Be Aware of Your Tonality

Whether asking or telling, the coach's tone of voice will indicate something to the athlete. Part of being in control is having appropriate tonality. There's that word *appropriate* again. It means the coach has been thoughtful about what the situation and the athletes need. The tone is based on that need, not the emotional need of the coach. I have an indelible memory of a college baseball coach, in the third base coach's box during a game, screaming to his hitter in the batter's box, "Relax, G., dammit!" Another mixed message, delivered in a tone of voice that would threaten a gorilla. It may be laughable to me and the reader, perhaps. It wasn't to the player, who became more tense after the coach's plea. The hitter had no chance of relaxing; he stood with the bat on his shoulder as a third called strike split home plate. Immobilized, dammit.

If a coach's intent is to encourage, his tone should be compatible with his purpose. If a coach's intent is to arouse, some energy is required. I've heard some coaches' high-powered words lose their power because of no-power tonality. In writing about the introduction of Bart Starr, Green Bay's quarterback, to his new coach, Vince Lombardi, writer David Maraniss wrote of the quarterback's internal response. "You could tell that the coach believed in what he was doing. His tone of voice, his posture, his manner, it all made you believe."

If unhappiness is the coach's prevailing feeling, let the unhappiness be conveyed in a manner that indicates it's based on unacceptable behavior or execution. Let it not be conveyed as empty phrases wrapped in an angry tone.

Sarcasm is powerful. It can hurt. It can confuse. A sarcastic tone of voice is one that indicates, to those smart enough to get it, a message of contradiction. Of criticism without correction. Of disrespect. Those lacking the ability to understand the sarcasm of tone will be spared the hurt of the moment and deprived of the opportunity to know that what they've done is not acceptable to the coach. Sarcasm is a refuge for coaches who don't know how to teach or don't care how the athletes may feel.

A coach with a touch is a coach with a tone that's consistent with his thoughtful intent.

Be Just as Aware of Your Language

Knowing *what to say* is essential to effective communication for the obvious reason that the words that come from our mouths are immediately en route to someone else's ears and brain. Their interpretation may be based on any number of other elements of communication already discussed, but, above all, people are held by their words.

Let me get back to sarcasm for a moment. Just as a tone can be sarcastic, so can words. Being laughed at is the most painful form of ridicule. Coaches who employ sarcasm are clever and cruel. I told a manager this once and he said to me, "But the guy laughs along with the rest of us."

What "the guy" did was try to deflect the hurt by denying it. He had a history of being a class-clown type, and this was his way of being accepted. His self-esteem was lower than whale waste. The manager, to his credit, then called the player in and talked about all this. I met with the player also. The behavior of both manager and player changed dramatically. So did the player's performance. As did his self-respect.

Whether initiating the communication or responding to the words of others, a coach's words are his most powerful tools. They should be weighed, rather than counted. A Japanese proverb says, "The tongue is only three inches long, yet it can kill a man six feet high."

When time and thought are available to prepare what will be said, the opportunity to "hit the target" or "press the right buttons" is greater. When responding to the needs of the moment, I try to give respect to the next words I speak by *pausing*, taking that time to consider and choose those words.

When asking an athlete a question, I often add, "Thinking is allowed." People believe they have to fill up silences with whatever jumps into their mind. I try to assure players that the answer I want is the thoughtful one, the intelligent one, rather than a knee-jerk response. I hold myself to the same standard of language.

■ ■ ■

Be very respectful of the word *is*. *Is* means fact, truth, certainty. *Is* is an absolute. So are these words: definitely, positively, absolutely, all, everyone, no one, never, always. They'd better hold up, or else the speaker is wrong, often at the top of his voice. When not certain, employ qualifiers such as seems, appears, might, in my opinion, perhaps. When I *know*, I don't hold back. Then, and only then.

Coaches should talk in specifics, rather than generalizations. They should use positive language, rather than negative, telling athletes what they want them to do, rather than what they don't want them to do. Coaches should speak in language that addresses solutions, not just problems. Coaches should avoid name calling or labeling; they should speak about the behavior, rather than the person. About task, rather than result. About what can be controlled, rather than what cannot. (See Section 2.)

During John Wooden's last year coaching the UCLA Bruins basketball team, his use of language was monitored for research purposes. The results indicated that almost 75 percent of his time on the court was spent giving specific instructions—teaching. A demand for hustle was 12 percent of his communications. Praise took up 7 percent, verbal butt-kicking 6 percent. As noted earlier in the book, John Wooden believed that the best coaches were the most effective teachers. Obviously, his communication was based on that belief. (See Section 1, chapter 8.)

Remember Why, How, and When to Use Silence

The coach should have a defined objective for employing silence. The objective in saying nothing is to create the right tension level at which the athlete feels the need to begin or continue talking in order to break the silence. When the silence becomes a stare-down, it is time for the coach to speak.

Go to the Source, Usually

When an issue exists between the coach and an athlete or group of athletes, the coach's first thought should be of treating it directly. Telling someone else to confront the issue for him is not usually an effective tactic. Much is lost in the communication of the "He said, She said" process, including the athlete's perception of the coach as leader. Confronting difficulty directly is part of establishing order and respect.

Good: coach and assistant coaches discussing athletes' *behaviors* and possible motives in their offices.

Bad: coach and assistant coaches disparaging their athletes in their offices. The "He can't learn; she can't play" or "He's a screw-off; she's a loser" is an absence of an effective communication process and usually a loss of the athlete. In that sense, both coach and athlete are "losers."

Coaches should find ways to help their athletes, rather than burying them under a barrage of criticism that the athletes themselves will never hear. Knowing what's wrong is essential to the effective coach. So is thinking about how to get it right and communicating those thoughts to the athletes.

At times the indirect method may be used, not because of a reluctance to be direct, but because it will be a more effective method of communicating. I've told a number of individual team captains to deliver a message to another team member when I thought the player would, for any number of reasons, be better able to receive it from a source other than me.

■ ■ ■

When Fred Stanley was a utility infielder on Yankees teams managed by Billy Martin, Martin would often scream at him, even though Stanley wasn't playing. The message would actually be for Reggie Jackson, who, the manager believed, would not handle Martin's belligerent directness.

Bobby Knight, known for his bellicose approach, claimed he would "aim something strong to a guy who can take it in that form, but really mean it for the guy standing next to him, who maybe wouldn't respond as well to such a 'strongly' worded message. So the kid who sort of overhears may think, 'Damn—I don't want that said to me.'"

But eyeball to eyeball is usually the best way to communicate constructive criticism, positive reinforcement, disciplinary demands, personal advice, individual instruction. Usually, both athlete and coach will find it to be the best approach.

Communicate Only Appropriate Information

One of the tendencies of coaches who want to connect with or ple their athletes is to tell them too much, for instance, talk about matt that the athlete shouldn't be privy to. An example is the coach who reveals his inner feelings about an upcoming competition. The coach isn't confident and he conveys that to the athlete. He's easing his mind by venting, at the expense of the athlete's positive frame of mind.

Another example based on my experience is the coach who talks to some players about his feelings related to other team members. The coach has a particular athlete whom he likes—and then uses him as a confidant.

A coach who's constantly talking about administrative foul-ups or frustrations with any part of the program is putting himself on the level of the athlete. Perhaps below, because the mature athletes understand this type of communication for what it is: weakness.

Tell the players what they need to know. They do not need to know about the coach's personal life and issues. Provide information that is manageable, rather than swamping athletes with more than they can assimilate.

Make certain the athletes know what is expected of them. Presume they don't know, rather than presuming they do know. Better to reiterate and review than have them uninformed and unprepared. I've heard coaches say, "If they want to know, they can ask." That attitude can indicate any number of things. The most obvious are laziness, disinterest, and a lack of understanding of how athletes typically behave. The coach's responsibility is to tell, to connect—to communicate—not to wait.

■ ■ ■

Promises should be avoided. When, as a young boy, I would say to my father, "Promise?" he'd answer, "Promises make fools happy." Athletes can be foolish enough to want reassurances. Coaches should not be foolish enough to reassure by making promises.

A professional hockey coach promises his unhappy player he'll be getting more ice time. A trade is made the next day; the new player—who is not as talented or valuable to the team—will get the time promised to the guy already there. "He lied to me," says the player.

Any reassurance along those lines should be made using qualifying language, conditional or situational truths. Example: "As things stand now, you'll get more time." Things stand in a different way tomorrow; the coach didn't lie.

Other qualifying language:

- If nothing changes . . .
- At this time, I'm inclined to say yes, but . . .
- In all probability . . .
- It seems likely . . .
- As of today . . .
- Unless something happens that . . .
- There's a real good chance . . .

Recognize Resistance

I do not speak here about insubordination, an in-your-face refusal to follow the coach's plan, rule, or edict. Relatively speaking, that's easy to respond to. Personal power has very apparently not worked with the athlete. Position power is called for.

I recall a player in Oakland's minor league system years ago who would play the game the way he decided. During one of these games, as a third baseman, he was called to from the dugout by the manager, who waved him away from the player's position too close to the third base line. The player moved two steps. When the manager directed his attention elsewhere, the player moved back to his original position. His next position was on the bench. (The manager had other eyes following the player, who had a history of resisting authority.)

Many years earlier, I had to throw my star player off our school's football team for open and frequent resistance. He came back to play basketball for me that same year, with a greater understanding—and sullen cooperation. (I'll refer to him again in a later section.)

Those are examples of overt resistance. But more often, players resist in subtle, covert ways. They may shake their heads up and down when the coach is speaking to them, but their later actions contradict their earlier signs of acceptance. Their real response is hidden from the coach at the time of communication. It is revealed through the athlete's behavior later.

The athlete's resistance is often based on a lack of belief that what the coach is saying is best for him. Sometimes the topic is related to technique or mechanics; sometimes strategy; sometimes the adherence to team rules or procedures. Whatever the case may be, the tools the coach has used to communicate with this resistant player up to this point have not worked. The athlete has not been convinced. (See CHANGE*, section 2.)

Item: John Wooden remembers that Andy Hill didn't like him. Hill sat on the UCLA bench behind Henry Bibby for three years. Hill recalls, "In my mind, he was like my nemesis. . . . I had an inflated opinion of my ability. My first day of practice as a sophomore in 1969 was the first

Vietnam moratorium. I asked him to call off practice. He said, 'Andy, you don't ever have to come.'"

Many years later, Hill thought he understood, but he wanted to make sure. "I was never one of his acolytes, but I wanted some clarity. . . . I needed to talk to him. I needed to say, 'Thanks.' There's a beauty and symmetry of what this man has done. He never talked about winning—only total effort. On one level, he appeared conservative and controlling, but ultimately we were incredibly free to play the game. It took me more than twenty-five years to figure it out."

■ ■ ■

Coaches should be aware that resistance can be subtle. They should always be on the lookout for indicators.

Be Persuasive

A new approach is a change, and change creates discomfort in people. They tend to defend the "old way" because that is their habit. It may be a bad habit. As Mark Twain has said about bad habits, "It's easier to stay out than get out." The coach sees that the athlete hasn't stayed out, so he must find ways to help him get out.

Look athletes in the eye. Be clear as to what the motive is behind the mandate. Speak at a slower rate so the athlete is able to absorb information without a tense, defensive stance. Be brief and to the point. Talk about what is desired, rather than about the athlete. Be optimistic about the eventual outcome. Be encouraging. Be persuasive.

The coach should recognize and interpret frustration, tension, and anger, all of which may be expressed nonverbally. And the coach must approach the resistant athlete when the athlete is in an optimal mood to be receptive. Sensitivity to timing is another indicator that the coach is at least trying to employ personal power, rather than arbitrarily hammering away at the athlete and driving the resistance deeper into the psyche. The power of persuasion is a power that convinces an athlete that what the coach wants for him is the same as what the athlete should want for himself. That's the substance of it; how it's done is the style. What works is true, as usual. (See CHANGE*, section 2.)

■ ■ ■

Item: Referring to the style of play the Kansas City Royals must employ in order to be successful, a reference was made in a column written by Dick Kaegel (*Sports Illustrated*, June 10, 2002) to the team's need to "manufacture runs," because it had no bonafide home-run threat.

Kaegel wrote:

> Fired manager Tony Muser knew that. But perhaps [Tony] Pena [who replaced Muser] is a better salesman. Pena has a fervent disciple in, of all people, notoriously free-swinging and formerly home run-conscious right fielder Mark Quinn, who rarely took a ball last season. He is now stressing patience and is praising the virtues of small ball, saying that reading pitchers, taking the extra base and hitting behind the runner are more fun than waiting for a three-run bomb. Pena's communication skills are getting the message through.

To a player who previously did not acknowledge the effectiveness of that approach. "More fun"? That's persuasion at its best.

■ ■ ■

Some players are more independent than others. They need to assert their individuality and independence. I wanted to have players like that. I tried to take advantage of that tendency by giving them more responsibility. That should *not* be interpreted as meaning more latitude for cooperation with me. But giving a spirited horse some play in the reins will allow it the freedom to do what's right on his own. What's right. Reining him in when it's not right is the rider's responsibility. The coach's.

Some players are eager to please. They don't resist the coach; they resist learning. Their agenda is to make the coach like them, so they are indiscriminate about anything else related to their game. They can't know themselves as competitors because they only focus on the coach's responses to them. They are almost always other-directed, rather than being self-directed.

This tendency does not bode well for such an athlete during competition. It is a resistance to self-development. It might please the coach, because the athlete is "easy to handle." And that's just what it is: manipulation. Because the athlete doesn't understand what a coach–athlete relationship is. The coach should identify this tendency and instruct accordingly. Point out the behavior to the athlete, and convince him that he doesn't please by being a yes-man but by asserting himself on the field and having an aggressive approach.

Coaches tend to like the "easy" athletes and have an initial aversion to any athlete who might challenge their ideas or their way of doing things. A coach, in his position of authority, may believe that he is being challenged. This is not usually so. What is being challenged is an idea. The best teachers are those who challenge their students and challenge ideas. It works both ways. (See chapter 8.)

More locker room clichés: "This kid won't listen." "This kid is nothing but trouble." Generalizations and labels don't define "the kid." It's easier to identify resistance, even the subtle kind, than it is to work at finding a way to combat resistance—at finding a way to be persuasive, other than dropping the hammer on the athlete immediately, of course.

If a staff member, after many and prolonged attempts, says to me, "I can't get through to this guy," I often suggest that he refer the player to another staff member. I know that often there are "good cop/bad cop" relationships on teams. What one cop can do with a player may be more effective than what another can. My goal is always to get the athlete to do what's right. I don't care who gets him to do it.

Be Persistent

It isn't easy with some people. But, assuming the possible success is worth the effort—make it. And keep making it. As suggested previously, try different approaches, different times, different settings. My own experience has shown me that taking a player to lunch, for instance, can somehow provide a setting that helps this player to change his view of who I am and/or "what I want" from him—the words he expresses over a bowl of soup. Hadn't he heard? Apparently not. Hadn't I been trying to convey that message for months? Yes, and I'd failed in my attempts.

■ ■ ■

Item: The following was reported in *The Cleveland Plain Dealer*, June 2, 2002. It regarded the Indians' young pitching prospect Tim Drew (part of a later trade with the Montreal Expos in July 2002).

"Drew's latest collection of starts (at Class AAA Buffalo) would appear to indicate that yes, he could be destined for good things at the highest level. . . . For Drew to be effective, it is imperative he change speeds and planes.

"The stuff is nothing, however, if Drew fails to keep his ears open. The Indians' brass, particularly Bisons pitching coach Carl Willis, have found the stubborn Drew to be more receptive to instruction," wrote reporter Dennis Manoloff.

Assistant minor league director Russ Atkins was then quoted. "It's not that he didn't have a good attitude before, but the working relationship with the staff is better. He's learning how to learn the game."

■ ■ ■

If it becomes evident that an athlete has been completely unreceptive—resistant in an ongoing and unwavering way—the time has come for the coach to decide he's wasting his time by continuing his efforts. When this has happened to me, I have recognized that the communication process did not succeed. Nothing I, or any others around me, had done helped the player to modify his behavior. I knew I had employed every tactic I was aware of; that I had given the athlete a fair allotment of time to make the adjustment; that I had indicated to him that his behaviors were unacceptable and that the continuance of resistance would result in his removal from the team (the next-to-final position power communication). The reexamination and final assessment were my responsibility.

My next responsibility was to meet with the player and review the chain of events that brought us to this point in our nonrelationship—and then remove him from the team.

A Balanced Approach to the Communication Process Is the Best

The seesaw balance between coach and athlete is reached by having the proper weight distribution of personal communication skills. Each athlete who sits on the other end has his own weight.

A June 2002 newspaper article about former Los Angeles Lakers coach Phil Jackson had this subheading: "Lakers coach meshes philosophy, personalities." It noted that while others call Jackson a Zen master, a philosopher, a psychologist, Lakers star Kobe Bryant simply calls him "a button pusher."

Jackson says he keeps himself and his players in balance, addressing perspective, responsibilities, and behaviors that help each of them to maintain that balance.

A balanced approach to the communication process itself is a requirement. Coach and athlete—sender and/or receiver—are responsible for striking the balance. "With the Lakers, Jackson has succeeded in managing and balancing all the issues [read 'needs'] of superstars Bryant, Shaquille O'Neal," the article's writer, David DuPree, claims (*USA Today*, June 5, 2002).

Whatever metaphor we choose—balancing or button pushing—a coach's effectiveness begins with his sensitivity to the individual athlete's needs. A coach's well-thought-out approach will help him get the best responses from his athletes.

Keep in Mind

The coach who effectively addresses the mental game will consider the many factors that influence the communication process. They include:

- Knowledge of the person with whom we are communicating
- Timing
- Tonality
- Language
- Environment
- Purpose/Motive/Goal

- Questions
- Listening Skill
- Objectivity
- Self-control
- Direct and/or Indirect Approach
- Silence
- Athlete Resistance
- Appropriate/Inappropriate Information
- Persuasion (Personal Power)
- Persistence
- Balanced Approach
- Final Response to Continued Resistance (Position Power)

Eight

Coaching Is Teaching

Ideal Combination: Coach and Teacher.
Headline of article by
Harvey Araton,
The New York Times, December 9, 2001

[Teaching] is the thread that runs through [Alfonso] Soriano's development. He's been placed in an environment where there is little tolerance for rookie mistakes. But the environment also is full of teachers. He has transcended the former and taken advantage of the latter.
Ken Davidoff,
The Sporting News, June 3, 2002

There has never been a good coach who was not a good teacher. What is a good teacher? One who creates the right climate for players to learn.
George Welsh,
Football Coach, U.S. Naval Academy,
U. of Virginia

The term *student-athlete* has for years fallen trippingly from the tongues of school administrators and coaches. Often from forked tongues. While it's generally acknowledged that the concept of student-athlete is an ideal, many of us have been aware of individuals and school programs that fell far short of the ideal. A significant number of programs didn't even seem to aspire to it.

Neither have numbers of coaches aspired to become superior teachers. But that may be changing. An Associated Press release (August 29, 2001) began, "If college basketball coaches have their way, they will no longer be called college basketball coaches. They will be 'teacher-coaches.'"

After a closed-door meeting of some of the country's most identifiable basketball coaches and top administrators—a meeting that went on for two days—moderator Michael Josephson said, "This isn't simply a public relations issue. It's an issue of trying to identify the field of coaching in a way that's maybe been lost in recent years, to identify the coach as first and foremost a teacher. The real serious coaches have treasured that kind of teaching role."

Some of the "serious coaches" in attendance at that meeting were North Carolina teacher-coach Roy Williams, Tubby Smith of Kentucky, Kelvin Sampson of Oklahoma, and Jim Boeheim of Syracuse.

Also present was Jim Haney, executive director of the National Association of Basketball Coaches. Haney answered those who were doubtful—or cynical (mostly noncoaches present at the meeting)—by saying, "It's not as much a title as it is a frame of reference. It's about the everyday responsibility of teachers . . . teaching ethics, core values, demonstrating the value of hard work."

Bill Walton, initially a skeptical and reluctant learner as a star basketball player at UCLA, said of his mentor, John Wooden, after Wooden had received the *Sports Illustrated* Legacy Award in 2000, "We thought he was nuts. But in all his preachings and teachings, everything he told us turned out to be true. He quotes poetry. He has a thousand maxims. . . . He is a man who truly has principles and ideas. He taught life." (Remember Wooden's "Pyramid of Success"? Industriousness, Caring about Others, etc.)

■　■　■

"He taught life." Quite a curriculum. And yet, the most successful and revered coaches are those who have done exactly that, from the soft-spoken but firm John Wooden to the volatile but principled Vince Lombardi.

"The best coaches have something else. They have the good sense to instruct, then get out of the way. They are pedagogues, not demagogues," says Duke coach Mike Krzyzewski. Kareem Abdul-Jabbar, John Wooden's seven-foot Lew Alcindor at UCLA, said of his former coach, "He did his coaching in practice." He taught and let them play. Interesting how Bob Knight, Wooden with his rolled-up program in his fist, and Coach K. all sat or sit on the bench, rather than ranting and pointing and pacing the sidelines during a game. They coached during practice and then let the players play. They instructed during times-out; they did not distract during the game—with posturings and histrionics.

They prepared their teams by teaching them what to do, how to do it, and why it should be done. The technical and the mental aspects of performance. Vince Lombardi presented the logic behind every play he asked his players to execute. "They call it coaching," he said. "But it is teaching. You do not just tell them it is so, but you show them the reasons why it is so, and you repeat and repeat until they are convinced, until they know."

When Packers quarterback Bart Starr was first introduced to Lombardi's teaching, he became invigorated. No more "crap"—this goes "right to the bone," simple and clear, but "refreshingly exciting," Starr said to himself.

He was excited by the fundamentally sound instruction, the sense of it, the clarity. He took that appreciation into the repetitive drills—the drills that I've heard so many athletes call "boring," because they had no appreciation for the value of repetition with a purpose, or for the accountability attached to the regimen. (I've told professional players who complained about "boring drills," "There's no such thing as a boring drill, just a bored person." That could have included the person who ran it without forethought, energy, or discipline.)

Bob Knight has stated, "I have come to believe that the key to successful teaching is *repetition*."

In 1996, as the Florida Marlins team I worked for bussed from the Grand Hyatt Hotel to Shea Stadium to play the Mets, Kevin Brown came over and sat down next to me. He had been frustrated by his previous pitching performance. "How many times are you going to have to tell me the same damn thing before it kicks in?" he asked rhetorically.

The damn thing kept being repeated. It kicked in.

■　■　■

Bob Knight has the philosophy of a teacher. Despite what Shakespeare would call his "antic disposition," Knight's pedagogy is sound. (His style of presentation, not the concern here, has shown itself to be controversial, to put it simply.) His reputation for teaching the technical aspects of the game is well known. And that is part of a team's mental preparation: the security of knowing what to do and how to do it. The essence of execution, the clarity of purpose, the habituation through repetition and self-discipline. And a high standard—doing it until it is done right.

But Knight has provided more than the technical to his players. He has also held them to high standards of behavior—academic, social, and athletic. He has always been clear in what he expected from them (though at times they may not have been sure what to expect from him).

The reader may have heard the old chestnut, "A student performs to the level of his teacher's expectation." Knight has held his players extremely accountable during competition. He has been consistent in his focus, not accepting poor execution, regardless of the score of the game. (See CONSISTENCY*, section 2.)

"What I do is very simple," Knight told *Scholastic Magazine* in 1982. "I teach people how to play a game. And in teaching them how to play, I think that because we are demanding, exacting, simple, and direct, we teach a lot of other values. . . . We are after success, and I certainly think that because of what we teach and the way we teach it, a kid will end up learning a hell of a lot of what it takes to achieve success in anything he does."

It's common knowledge that the vast majority of Lombardi's Green Bay players—actually with almost no exceptions—became successful men in the world beyond football, after their careers on the field had ended. Their most influential teacher got to them even during later stages of their lives—as professionals, as adults. They still had plenty to learn, and Lombardi was emphatically instructive. His students applied the lessons in Super Bowl competition, in their communities, in their family life.

The Student

It's probably useful to focus here on the *object* of the coach's teaching: the athlete. Though each learner brings his own *individual* aptitude and inclination to the "classroom" (see chapter 9, the section Learning), a few *generalizations* about young people—adolescents particularly—might be appropriate.

Junior high schoolers, high schoolers, and college entrants are at critical periods in their development, in terms of biological, psychological, and social integration. They have gone through stages from early childhood, and the teacher should attempt to determine what stage the individual athlete is at. Much of the success of the teacher depends on the athlete's development—healthy or unhealthy—prior to arriving on the scene. The relationship established between teacher-coach and athlete will be enhanced or inhibited by the athlete's past experiences.

So much will have depended on his successful accomplishment of developmental "tasks" in infancy and childhood. So, it serves the teacher to know as much about these young athletes as possible. Not opinions! Information.

Adolescence is a particularly tough time—stormy, prolonged, and sometimes poorly resolved (or unresolved) if there are severe defects. I've dealt with professional athletes who were abused during their early years. Their talent masked their troubled selves, until they reached a level of competition at which what's above the shoulders has to assist what's below them. There was no help coming from their mental state. On the contrary.

The term *prolonged* in the preceding paragraph implies that tough times can be resolved. With patience and effective intervention, a coach can help the athlete work through the process of personal growth. Understanding, support, discipline, responsibility, and self-sacrifice should be part of the social and athletic framework to help the development of adolescent into adult. A teaching framework. (See the section The Curriculum.)

What is called suprapersonal (beyond self) psychological traits are valued behaviors in the athletic arena. I tell players, "'Uniform'—uniform, means one form. When we put it on, we sacrifice a part of the self that's in the uniform for what the uniform represents: an agenda shared by all of us. A common goal, not an individual selfish one." And so on. Young people can more easily get beyond themselves when in a uniform, it seems. (Some more easily than others, I know—from my own experience as a coach.)

Sexual identity and peer pressure—from peers who are not athletes, perhaps—also influence young people. Consider all the psychological responses to a young person's physiological patterns: facial hair, acne, showering in public, body shape, and so on. Any deviation and consequent ridicule can be devastating psychologically, though they may seem insignificant physiologically. Insignificant to *others*.

As I write this I think of a young rookie baseball player in the Northwest League years ago—in Medford, Oregon. He was made sport of—ridiculed—for what the other players called "the 3-B's." Boils, breathing, and balloons. The boils, stress related, were all over his back. And he was asthmatic. The balloon reference, sex related, I'll leave to the reader's imagination.

This guy had plenty to deal with. With others and with himself. Yet over time, with adult understanding, intervention, and support, he grew into manhood—a good husband and father and a very respectable major league pitcher. Still active and effective.

The psychological basis for a sense of individual worth as an adult rests upon the acquisition of competence in a work role as an adolescent. The work of the athlete is to compete effectively. A sense of competence is acquired through reassurance. It comes from the actual experience of succeeding in the important athletic tasks. The challenge to the coach, as a teacher, is to instruct the athlete, to support the athlete, to hold him accountable. To understand him and to help the athlete understand himself.

That's one of the tough tasks that faces every teacher who cares about his students.

One thing further: Coaches of tee ball kids, Pee Wee Leaguers, Kiddy Corps Athletes, and the like are usually *whole-child centered*. As the youngsters get older and more skillful, coaches become *learner-centered*. After a couple of more years, the coaches are *sport-centered*, teaching strategies as well as more sophisticated techniques. At an advanced level (and that can be any time from high school and beyond—especially at the professional level), many coaches become *self-centered*, meaning they want results from competition that puts them in a position to advance their professional standing, that is, recognition and a better job.

The self-centered coach has less personal contact with the athlete (student), and effective teaching diminishes or disappears as the athlete seems to advance. Aside from self-interest, the coach makes the assumption that people normally progress in knowledge and ability proportionate to their chronological age. This isn't true. Typically, people grow and improve in proportion to external motivators, mentors, and teachers. This, plus the fact that the less the coach communicates with the athlete, the less open the athlete becomes. Feeling he's expected to know, the student-athlete often pretends to know. He's afraid to admit he doesn't know.

The more results-oriented coach will tend to focus on winning, rather than on teaching. (See WINNING*, section 2.) It follows, then, that the individual who wishes to be an excellent coach should remind himself to focus on ways to be an effective teacher, one who can treat the athlete's psyche, as well as his brain. The results will more likely satisfy everyone concerned.

The Curriculum

1. Intellectual Factors:
   - Techniques—Skill development, The hows
   - Strategies—The whats, whens, and whys
2. Intellectual/Psychological Factors:
   - Goals
   - Commitment
   - Preparation
   - Concentration
   - Self-esteem
   - Courage
   - Confidence
   - Relaxation
   - Poise
3. Intellectual/Philosophical/Psychological Team Factors:
   - Execution (Approach)
   - Competitiveness
   - Self-sacrifice
   - Adversity
   - Responsibility
   - Attitude
   - Self-discipline
   - Leadership
   - A Winning Way

Those are *some* of the things a coach teaches on a regular basis. Or should. Many of the topics listed (and others) are developed in sections 2 and 3.

Some Considerations Related to Effective Teaching

The most essential tools and approaches for effective teaching, that is, leading and communicating, have been discussed in earlier chapters. Some are worth repeating.

1. **Talk about Positive Ideas and Function.** Education is built on a need to be right. During people's early years, they're taught the "correct facts," the correct deductions to be made from them and the correct way of making these deductions. They learn to be correct by being sensitized to what is incorrect. They learn to apply judgments at every stage and to follow up these judgments with negative labels. They then learn to say (teach), "No, this isn't so." Or "You're wrong on that." Or "That won't work." Or "There's no reason for that." It's an easy approach, but not an instructive one. At least, not an instructive one in terms of achieving what the teacher is actually setting out to accomplish. *First and foremost,* tell athletes what is right, rather than what is wrong. Tell them what to do, rather than what not to do. The mind takes the image presented without consideration for the seemingly incidental words that precede the image word. For example, when a coach tells an athlete, "Don't keep your legs so stiff," the word *don't* doesn't register. The focus is on stiff legs, and that's what the athlete thinks about as he tries to improve his technique. "Bend at the knees" sends a better picture. (Another example: "Don't walk this guy" should be changed to "Throw good low strikes here.") Establishing what to know, believe, and do is more helpful than dwelling on what not to know, not to believe, and not to do.

2. **Assume the Athlete Doesn't Know.** It's better to repeat yourself, because repetition is a primary tool in teaching. Better to repeat something known than omit something unknown. Bob Knight: "One of the important things I have learned is never to make assumptions."

3. **Limit the Information Given During a Particular Teaching Session.** As enthusiastic as the coach may be to provide valuable information, he must recognize that the learner's capacity to absorb and the rate of absorption must be considered. (See chapter 9.) Emphasize a particular procedure or point; keep it simple; make it clear. Overloading the student with information leads to a point of diminishing return, after which the student hardly remembers anything he heard. Kareem-Abdul Jabbar on John Wooden: "He was more a teacher than a coach. He broke basketball down to its basic elements. . . . His ability to make the game simple was part of his genius."

4. **Be Objective, Credible, and Purposeful.** Enthusiastic people tend to exaggerate. Make examples legitimate and believable,

knowing what you're saying and why it is said. Avoid using negative examples by personalizing mistakes members of the team have made. Talk about the situation, not the person. The personal example may be credible to all in the audience—except the person who requires the teaching most. Getting personal (if it's appropriate even then) is saved for a one-on-one setting.

5. **Be Certain That Assistant Coaches Teach the Same Principles, Using the Same Language**. Conflicting or inconsistent language will confuse athletes or mislead them. The same meaning may be intended, but a different presentation results. Teachers should prepare themselves by reviewing how they will present ideas, so as to be "on the same page."

6. **Connect with the Student–Athletes.** In the context of effective teaching, this means:
   - Establishing eye contact with your audience, making sure you look at all, not just one person while you're teaching.
   - Watching for reactions—negative and positive—gaining information as you provide it.
   - When speaking with an individual, use physical contact to "connect" and to control the athlete's attention (e.g., hand on the shoulder or arm, pat on the back).
   - Connecting with all team members, not just the best of them.
   - The athlete who has the most difficulty is the one who requires the most attention. Beware, it's easy to gravitate toward the best student inadvertently (or intentionally!), avoiding those who need more instruction.
   - See #7.

7. **Encourage Feedback.** Ask the students questions—about the presentation, the ideas, the environment that coach and athlete share. Make certain to identify acceptable responses, as opposed to those that are presented for the sole purpose of gaining attention. Establish lines of communication so that negative feedback comes directly to you—allowing you to deal with the individual issue, rather than having the athlete spread it around the locker room. Understand that feedback allows the teacher to be a learner as well. (See chapter 9.)

8. **Create an Atmosphere and Attitudes That Enhance Learning.** Establish, stress, and encourage the goal of having the athlete learn to become a more effective performer. Pay attention daily to the athlete's development, reinforcing any signs of improvement or appropriate effort—participating, so to speak, in his performance enhancement program.

9. **Create an Atmosphere That Teaches and Adheres to a High Standard of Behavior and Execution.** Coaches want athletes to succeed. Athletes want to succeed. The coach's responsibility is in the presentation, in holding the athletes

accountable, in helping them to be accountable. NFL Hall of Fame coach Don Shula said he never let an error go unchallenged. Shula remembered, "Someone once asked me if there wasn't some benefit from overlooking one small flaw. I asked, 'What's a small flaw?'" The best teachers know how to create the group standard, while employing techniques that hit the buttons of each individual athlete. Shula again: "The secret of success is getting inside different personalities and getting the most out of them."

10. **Be an Objective Observer and a Problem Solver**. Here are a couple of contrasting examples that should make the point. In them, the head coach is talking to his assistant coach about a player.
   - "He couldn't catch a pass if there was glue on the ball."
   - "He drops passes that are right in his hands."

   The first statement is a negative projection of what has happened and what will continue to happen. The second statement is an assessment of what has happened to this point. The *responsibility* of a coach who teaches is to assess, get information, create a strategy, and help the athlete implement the strategy. In this scenario, the coach would ask the player questions such as: "Where are your eyes when the ball's coming into your hands?" "What are you thinking when the pass is on the way?" "What do you think is happening on these plays?" Effective coaches expend effort in searching for and teaching solutions. Ineffective coaches see only problems and make absolute, easy judgments.

11. **Use Mistakes as a Vehicle for Teaching, Rather Than Lamenting or Blaming.** An athlete who doesn't make a mistake is an athlete who doesn't achieve—or doesn't exist. It's not only an issue of taking risks, it's an issue of making an effort to do the right thing. It doesn't always happen. What does the teacher do when it doesn't happen? He reiterates how it should be done in order to have it happen. The three questions the coach should teach players who have made a mistake are:
   - What was I trying to do?
   - What went wrong?
   - What do I want to do next time?

   Then move on. (See MISTAKES*, section 3.)

12. **Reinforce Effective Learning, Desirable Approaches, and Appropriate Behaviors.** Some coaches I've met tend to neglect using positive reinforcement. They expect things to be done right, so they take the philosophy that their silence betokens consent. The athletes aren't always that skillful at interpreting silences. Positive reinforcement is a standard teaching technique but not necessarily a standard coaching practice. Offering criticism is a

more common one. Though constructive criticism is a useful tool, acknowledgment of a job well done is a sought-after gesture. Later in the book (POSITIVISM*, section 2), a reference is made to a high school basketball player I coached. She said that I didn't "overflow" my players with "compliments." Well, this player meant that I did not offer personal praise when teaching during practice sessions. What was given was recognition that a player's (or players') execution was correct and acceptable. Exemplary. Outstanding. Terrific. Whatever. The focus was on what happened and why—so it applied to *every* student—*every* player. The remarks were not intended to be compliments, though I certainly was glad when a player's healthy ego needs were satisfied. I was happier, however, when *everyone* understood what was effective and how that efficacy was achieved. (Ego needs were taken care of at other times in other ways.) One further point: a very important aspect of reinforcement is for the teacher to focus on approach, rather than outcome—result.

13. **Be Aware of the Communication Process as You Teach.** Tonality, timing, language, and nonverbal communication all influence the way students receive the teacher's message. (Refer to chapters 5–7.) Be certain all in a group audience are attentive.

14. **Maintain a Consistent Teaching Point of View.** Being influenced by winning or losing, by athletic injuries or athletes' inabilities, by outside expectations—or any other adverse influences— can challenge a coach's perspective. A distorted perspective will create a distorted point of view toward teaching. A coach who loses hope loses motivation. Whatever factors may swirl around a team, they should never gain enough strength to influence the teaching atmosphere. Self-discipline on the teacher's part is required to maintain a healthy environment. Adversity can refine the teacher-coach—or consume him.

15. **Introduce the Factors That Are Involved in the Mental Aspect of Performance, the Obstacles, and the Way to Get Beyond Them.** This, of course, means a formal teaching of the mental game: a regular presentation of the elements for enhancing performance and self. Essentially, sections 2 and 3 serve as curriculum material. Plus whatever else the coach brings to his classroom, experientially and/or referentially.

Keep in Mind

- The best coaches are the best teachers.
- Simplicity and repetition are two elements for effective teaching.

- A student's learning is influenced by his teacher's expectations for him.
- The influence of superior leaders/coaches/teachers will go beyond the arena of competition.
- The best teachers always remember that their students are the ones who must apply all the profound principles offered. The implication: subject matter and learner are both the responsibility of the teacher.
- Effective instruction results from the use of positive language, rather than negative.
- The most comprehensive teaching comes from assuming the student doesn't yet know what should be known.
- The more limited the information presented during one teaching session, the more likely it is to be understood, absorbed, and integrated into behavior.
- Objectivity, credibility, and a sense of purpose reassure the learner and enhance the learning process.
- All those who teach in the program should teach the same thing, using language that is clear and consistent.
- The best teaching outcomes are a result of the teacher connecting with the student, that is, developing a relationship (as discussed earlier in the book).
- It's important to value, encourage, and use feedback.
- Part of teaching is to create and develop learners.
- The best achievement comes from the teacher setting and maintaining high standards.
- Good teachers focus on solutions, rather than problems.
- Mistakes are problems that can lead to solutions if they're considered to be *opportunities* to learn, rather than *failures* to learn.
- Positive reinforcement leads to positive future behaviors.
- Teachers should monitor their own methodology and communication techniques so as always to be as effective as possible.
- Events and people within and surrounding the athletic program often become a challenge to the teacher's philosophy. The thoughtful teacher, one who examines and trusts what he's doing, does it consistently, without regard to those factors.
- The best coaches/teachers learns about the specific aspects of the mental game and utilize this learning in order to teach the individual student, thereby helping him to enhance his performance as an athlete and as a (young) adult.

Nine

Learners: The Coach and the Athlete

[A] man who is so dull / that he can learn only by personal experience / is too dull to learn / anything important by experience.
Don Marquis,
Archy Does His Part

Ted Williams, who knew just about everything there was to know about hitting, was always trying to learn more.
Ernie Harwell,
Hall of Fame Broadcaster

My joy in learning is partly that it enables me to teach.
Seneca,
Letters to Lucilius (first century)

There has always been plenty to learn. There always will be more. For all of us.

The Coach-Learner

Coaches can learn more about themselves, learn more about their sport, learn more about the athletes they coach. They can learn more about the learning process itself. Wise coaches are never above learning, because they know they'll never be beyond learning.

When I was coaching high school basketball in Vermont, I went to a coaching clinic in Boston. Visiting college coaches lectured on pressure defenses, playing offense against zones, rebounding technique, and so on. Most were instructive. Some presentations were impressive.

I was greatly impressed by Dr. Tom Davis, coach at Boston College at the time (later at Iowa, now at Drake), who gave one of the lectures. (His topic was "Using the Bounce Pass to Feed the Low Post.") His presentation was very effective, but that didn't have the most significant impact on me. What impressed me most was the fact that Davis attended other coaches' sessions, notebook in hand, listening, jotting, learning—while other presenters stood in the halls smoking, gabbing, posturing.

Based on many experiences since, I've come to believe that the best coaches are the most eager learners.

Coaches want to know more about catchers' techniques for blocking balls, defending the running game, how to get an edge for a runner by getting him out of the starting blocks quickly, effective drills for heading balls. And so on. But when attending coaching clinics in recent years as a lecturer myself, I've been gratified to hear coaches clearly express their interest in learning about the mental aspects of the game. In their interest to teach it, to incorporate it in their daily program.

■ ■ ■

Major league manager Tony LaRussa is a learner. He's credited with being "a smart manager" and his law degree is often a point of reference. But for me, while working in the Oakland Athletics organization, he illustrated his "smarts" by being so open to learning. He is not without pride, but an incident from the past illustrates that his ego did not get in the way of his brain.

Tony and I were discussing a point of view he had about a player, in particular, and people in general. He asked me what I thought of his viewpoint and I told him I didn't agree with what he had expressed. I also told him why. He was not pleased with my emphatically contrarian belief. That much I could see in the expression on his face. What I couldn't see were the gears operating in his head. He turned moments later and went to another area of the spring training camp.

The next day, a catchers' meeting was held. The pitching coach, the catchers at the camp, and I found a quiet place to conduct the meeting: Tony's office. My eyes happened to move across the front of Tony's (open) locker during a lull in the meeting. There on the top shelf were three books relating to the topic we had briefly discussed the previous day. They were library books. Tony had gone to the Scottsdale (Arizona) public library and checked them out, open to the possibility that he had something to learn beyond and/or in contradiction to what he felt he already knew.

To this day, he continues to express his inquisitiveness about matters of mutual concern/involvement. His questions indicate as much about smarts as his answers. Sometimes more. Tony LaRussa knows this; Socrates knew it 2,500 years ago.

Learning is part of preparation. For athletic competition; for life itself.

■ ■ ■

In speaking about LaRussa, who as I write this is managing the St. Louis

Cardinals, I'm reminded of an icon in that organization: a minor league manager for many years, a major league coach, a mentor to many. His name is George Kissell. After a presentation I made at the Cardinals' organizational meeting two years ago, George came up to me and offered kind words about the talk. Somewhat taken aback, I tried to deflect the praise. "George," I said. "You know this stuff."

"I learn something every day," he said—a statement he made regularly, I was later told. But as proof of his sincerity, he flashed three pages of handwritten notes he'd taken during the presentation. "Here's some real good stuff I didn't know," he said, shaking the papers. George was eighty years old at the time, still with the Cardinal organization after more than sixty years, still in love with learning

■ ■ ■

A willingness to know we don't know it all and that all we do know "ain't necessarily so" are prerequisites for learning and for attaining anything that comes close to true wisdom.

The "too-old-to-learn" line continues to be the excuse of the inflexible or lazy person. An effective learner should have an openness to new ideas or approaches, yet maintain a healthy skepticism about pronounced panaceas, the people with "quick fixes" and "magic wands." And we should all be skeptical about the absolute pronouncements of self-proclaimed wise men. We must be open, but not all-consuming. Not gullible. A healthy balance must be struck.

■ ■ ■

A professor of economics at Yale said, in 1929, "Stocks have reached what looks like a permanently high plateau." The chairman of IBM said, in 1943, "I think there is a world market for maybe five computers." The commissioner at the U.S. Office of Patents said, in 1899, "Everything that can be invented has been invented."

■ ■ ■

New ideas can itch initially. Old habits are much more comfortable. The test of a new approach is in the way it works—or doesn't. The proof is in the nourishment of the pudding, not the texture. It takes time for itches to be relieved. Coaches shouldn't be too hasty in giving up on a new idea.

The best learners are risk takers. Whether we refer to Seward's Ice Box (Alaska), Fulton's Folly (Steamboat), or any visionary whose ideas the masses rejected, we learn that the most impressive learners were the greatest risk takers. Coaches who are risk takers—learners—are not afraid to risk making a mistake. They recognize their mistake as an indication that they've done something that doesn't work, which gets them back to what does.

The best learners always examine what they're doing and expand themselves professionally. They talk with other coaches, read books related to subjects they're unsure of or want to learn more about. But they give themselves reality checks regularly, checking to be certain that what they're doing is the best they know how to do.

Theodore Zeldin wrote, "Again and again, apparently intelligent people ooze contempt to protect themselves from what they cannot understand, as animals defend their territory with foul smells. . . . Or else people become so broad-minded that they do not know where they are going." We should all examine where we want to go—and be as certain as possible to know where we are at the moment. At least we will have learned that.

Not all coaches are open to learning. Everyone doesn't hold the same respect for it as LaRussa, Kissell, Carlos Tosca, and others like them. Nor do all coaches feel the same *responsibility* to learn. To know; to be better prepared.

There is a small number of coaches I've dealt with whose resistant attitudes toward learning were revealed through one or more or all of the following remarks I've noted over the years, after having heard them expressed:

"I'm comfortable."
"It won't work."
"I already know the best way."
"It's not important."
"It doesn't make sense" possibly meaning "I don't understand."
    (Probably meaning "I won't understand.")
"It isn't necessary."
"I don't have the time."

These remarks reflect the attitudes that frustrate the very same coaches when such statements are made by the athletes. Those coaches who were unwilling or unable to improve themselves in this area did not remain employees of the organizations I worked for.

I don't know who wrote it, but I remember reading a long time ago that nothing is more dangerous than an idea, when it's the only one you have.

■　■　■

The most creative coaches are learners. Because their minds are open to new ideas, because they constantly seek out different ways of doing things, of thinking about things—their minds are constantly active. (See GOING AGAINST THE GRAIN and OLD SCHOOL, section 2.)

One of the subjects a coach should interest himself in is the athlete he coaches. And how that athlete learns best. Having gained this knowledge, the coach becomes that much better a teacher. (See sections 2 and 3.)

The Athlete-Learner

The coach should create an environment in which learning is valued. Not just technique or strategy. The coach should acquaint himself with the kinds of thinking patterns that help athletes perform more effectively; he should understand the obstacles that inhibit performance; and he should determine which practice patterns work best—for the individual and for the team. In other words, he should learn about the *mental* and physical aspects of the sport and the athlete—and create an atmosphere in which the athlete is encouraged to learn as well.

■ ■ ■

When I was asked by seven frustrated high school seniors (the varsity basketball team had won just seven games in the past three years) to coach the women's basketball team—they knew I had coached men's basketball on Long Island—I told them, "No, thank you." I'd moved to Vermont with my family and had given up coaching so I could write more regularly. I was also inclined to believe these young women would not take the game seriously enough to suit me (a former chauvinist).

I succumbed reluctantly. But to make my first emphatic point, I told them that the five players who would start the first game of the season would be those who *learned* the most about the game and how it should be played. A written test would be given, I told them.

It was given. Funny how the players with the most physical ability pushed themselves to learn the most, avoiding the embarrassment, I assume, of sitting down, while less skilled players went on the court.

■ ■ ■

Athletes should be encouraged to learn the sport on their own, as well. The mental game is intellectual as well as psychological. Aside from learning about themselves and their performance issues—and having coaches working at addressing these psychological factors—the performers should understand their sport, so as to be better equipped to coach themselves. Before, during, and after their performances.

The best athletes are independent, not dependent. Of course they need coaches, but during the heat of the battle they are best served when they understand what to do and how to do it. At the moment of impact, so to speak. Rather than being brilliant in retrospect. The coach cannot always intervene.

An additional benefit to the athlete who is sport smart is that he's more likely to have a more useful focus during competition—thinking about the competitive situation, rather than how he's feeling at that moment.

■ ■ ■

It's been said that NFL running back Marshall Faulk knows the responsibilities of every player on any play called in the huddle. He himself says that his learning has helped him to be more effective. What seems to observers to be astounding spontaneous reactions are, Faulk explains, actions based on anticipating (knowing) what will happen in front of him.

■ ■ ■

Hall of Fame basketball player Larry Bird said he kept a mental record of the moves made by opposing players. "When you see the same move four or five times, you begin to anticipate what he is going to do," said Bird. "You can also get a lot of steals that way."

Bird constantly utilized his learning skills. His lawyer Bob Woolf said about Bird, "He'll play a golf course once and memorize the location of every tree. When we work out together, he will measure each step on the court to perfect what type of shot he can take and from what distance."

■ ■ ■

Looking forward to the summer before my senior year in college, I thought I'd go up to school, work at the bartending job I'd had the year before, take a literature course, and play baseball in a merchant's league nearby. My plans were changed. A varsity soccer teammate of mine, an All-American fullback on the team that had been National Co-champions the previous year, decided I needed a tutorial before my senior season. The goalie I would compete with for the starting job had far more natural talent than I. Bill (and everyone else, for that matter) knew this. Bill wanted me to have that starting position. (No explanation is necessary here.)

I'd never played soccer before attending college; my knowledge was rudimentary. I'd gotten away with it because of all the All-American and All-State players in front of me. Most had graduated. Not Bill.

"You're going to learn everything there is to learn about playing the

position," he said on the phone, weeks before I was schedul(
for my summer activities.

I did tend bar at night, but there was no literature cou
baseball. Just the two of us out at the field every day. (He
enjoyed the rainy days: "Good conditions to get used t
though I thought I'd already been used to them after three years oi p..._,
ing in a town located right off Lake Ontario.) Conditions aside, I learned
about positioning; I learned about angles; I learned about technique. He
kicked balls from every place on the offense side of the field. Short balls,
long balls, bouncers, penalty kicks, corner kicks. He moved me to and
fro—to appropriate space and place.

I learned what it took to be a better observer during the game. I
learned about things I thought I knew and things I never thought had to
be known. He knew; he taught. He was an extremely verbal person; he
talked and talked. The perfect teacher for me. (See Auditory Learning.)

His "goal" was realized, thanks to his teaching—and his intention to
make me a better learner. (Bill Hughes went on to play and coach professional soccer, and later coached the team at our college. He died a
year or so after his fiftieth birthday.)

■ ■ ■

People learn in a number of ways, but they are often predisposed to
learn best in one particular way. It's helpful to a coach to know which
way an individual athlete is most likely to "get the message" the coach is
sending. I'll use another personal example here.

1. *Visual learning.* The results of the test I took when as a seventeen
   year old I enlisted in the naval reserve indicated that my abilities
   related to spatial relationships were limited, to understate the
   implications of an awful score. My general observation skills
   were and are quite good, but I've never been skillful at learning
   from modeling—from watching someone perform a physical act,
   even a dance step, and imitating the movement or action. I do
   not learn best through *visual* methods.
2. *Auditory learning.* On the verbal section of the Navy's test, I scored
   very high, and I was told by the testing superior to "strike for
   yeoman"—the designation of a sailor whose major duties are
   clerical. In later years, while playing ball in college, I told a coach
   who was being overelaborate in his use of the chalkboard, "Just
   tell me what to do and I'll do it." Being verbal, I learn best
   through *auditory* instruction. Through voice directives and
   commands. I listen; I understand; I perform what I know.
3. *Kinesthetic learning.* My body awareness has always been poor. I
   can sit at my desk for extended periods of time and suddenly
   realize the edge of the chair leg is digging into my ankle. A welt

is apparent; the pain was not. My ability to have repetitious physical actions teach my muscles the habit of doing something right is marginal, at best. A coach who worked with me on my pitching mechanics would constantly implore, "Do you *feel* it?" I never did. And he never figured out how to tell me. I am not a *kinesthetic* learner.

Coaches should make every attempt to discover the particular way an athlete learns, especially the athlete who's having trouble applying mental principles to physical performance. Coaches should be aware of subtle factors that will help him identify this deficit. Bad body language during a practice session or drill that is not going well for the athlete often indicates a learning difficulty. An excuse such as "I didn't hear what you were saying" is one sign I've often been made aware of.

Coaches usually teach in *group* settings. When this is the case, the coach should try to make his presentation/activity inclusive, rather than exclusive. He should deliver the material in ways that consider and accommodate the different types of learning styles, giving all the athletes in the group a better chance to grasp it immediately.

■ ■ ■

People's abilities to learn at a given point in time are not the same or predictable. Understanding that, the coach should continue to reiterate the lesson to the athlete. Repetition, as has already been noted, is an important teaching tool—therefore an essential tool in learning. Over and over. Time and again. Always being as certain as possible that what is being taught is being presented in the way it can best be learned. If not today, then tomorrow.

The more a coach knows about the athlete's inherent tendencies and abilities, the more likely he will be to assist the athlete in his desire for self-improvement on the field of play.

■ ■ ■

A final thought: Plain-spoken Josh Billings proclaimed, "It ain't what a man don't know that makes him a fool, but what he knows that ain't so." Certainly we don't want to be fools, but we should want to learn as much about what we don't know as possible. And help those around us to care as much about learning as we do.

Keep in Mind

- The coach should learn more about himself, his sport, and his individual athletes.

- He should understand that new ideas and new approaches are not immediately comfortable.
- He should give something newly learned or attempted a reasonable amount of time before judging it a bad idea.
- Coaches who are superior learners allow themselves to be wrong in order to be certain of what's right.
- The coach should have an attitude that allows him to learn from anyone at any time.
- Coaches should continuously examine their methodology and expand their horizons.
- The coach should create an environment conducive for athletes' learning.
- The coach should encourage athletes' independent learning of their sport.
- The coach should attempt to discover the particular way each individual athlete learns best.
- The coach should be persistent in his teaching, knowing that the information can register at any unpredictable time.
- The coach should understand and address those issues related to the mental aspects of performance that are most often reference points for *him*. (See section 2.)
- The coach should understand and address those issues related to the mental aspects of performance that are most often reference points for *the athletes* he coaches. (See section 3.)

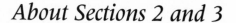

About Sections 2 and 3

The secret of success is getting inside each different personality and getting the most out of each one.
Don Shula, NFL Hall of Fame Coach

The true meaning of a term is to be found by observing what a man does with it, not by what he says about it.
P. W. Bridgman

SECTION 2

The Mental Game Alphabet
Impact Terms for the Coach

SECTION 3

The Mental Game, A to Z
Athletes' Impact Terms

Many athletes—amateurs and professionals—won't tell their coaches what's on their minds because they fear harsh judgments—a response such as "You've gotta be kidding me!" Or "What's your problem?" A pregnant silence can be just as threatening a response.

Knowing or suspecting this kind of guardedness on an athlete's part, a coach can work at helping him develop a more trusting attitude (see APPROACHABILTY and CARING, section 2) and/or understand some of the concerns and needs the athlete might be trying to deal with in his solitary inner self.

Many coaches are aware of the existence of these issues, though many have been reluctant to consider them or address them. Perhaps they've had their own coaching issues to consider. Nevertheless, more and more people *are* talking about the mental aspects of athletic performance. These athletes and coaches want to apply the principles they learn.

■ ■ ■

The two sections that follow present topics, concerns, and trigger words expressed, discussed, debated, and dissected by coaches, managers, sports administrators—and athletes. Quite often they are ill defined and/or misunderstood. Just as often, they are misapplied.

My intention and hope is to provide some clarity about the topics themselves and to bring that clarity to a place where it can help the athlete and his mental game. That place is in the coach's consciousness.

Many of the subjects treated have, in one way or another, already dwelled in the consciousness of the *athlete*. Unfortunately, they too often reside in the neighborhood of neuroses. The coach who is aware of the athlete's concerns, worries, fears, and hidden agendas—his mental state—is the coach who can help "clean up the neighborhood." Who can help the athlete enhance his mental approach to competition and his view of himself.

The coach has two distinct responsibilities in this regard: to deal with the athlete's world and to deal with his own. Section 2 treats "impact terms" that coaches have discussed with me over the years. Many are terms that I myself was concerned with as a coach in my earlier days. Some of these terms seem to have relevance exclusive to the coach. Some are relevant to the coach because they are so critical to his athletes' approaches, attitudes, and performances. Some of the terms also appear in section 3, but are treated from a slightly different perspective—the athlete's perspective.

Section 3 addresses the concerns expressed to me by athletes during my years in coaching and in the field of sport psychology. It also includes topics that, if not of concern to the athlete, *should be*. Many points of view are those that *I've* attempted to provide for them: the anxious athlete, the complacent athlete, the frustrated athlete—the athlete on a quest for peak performance.

Each listing in section 3 includes bullet points at its end. These points attempt to succinctly present the things the coach can say or do to "*address the mental game.*" These points follow the broader discussion of the "athletes' impact terms."

The length of the treatment in each section varies. Some presentations are relatively brief; others are expansive. Cross-referencing and reiteration are very evident, simply because so many of these subjects are interrelated. In a number of cases, cross-references are not mentioned, because they're quite obvious.

Few, if any, of the terms in these sections can be taken out of the context of an athlete's performance. If something impacts on the coach, it has a good chance of affecting his athletes, though the athlete may never know what the catalyst for the coach's behavior was on that given day.

Restraints related to the length of the book dictated the omission of a number of topics originally intended for inclusion. "Keep it under 100 entries," my editor said. Necessity won out over desire: there are "only" ninety-two.

Coaches and readers "out there" may have experienced issues that somehow have not crossed my professional path. Given the years I've been walking, I'd like to believe there are not too many. In any case, my hope is that the sections are comprehensive, though I know they are not all-inclusive.

Before moving beyond section 1, a reminder: leadership inspires; communication connects the coach to the athlete and the team; teaching leads to understanding; and learning allows for a heightened awareness of, among other things, the issues that provoke, inhibit, or enhance performance.

Now, on to those issues.

(Topics that appear in both section 2 and section 3 have an asterisk after the word section to indicate the double entry. The same topic is treated differently in each section.)

Section 2

The Mental Game Alphabet

Impact Terms for the Coach

Section 2 Contents

A

*Adversity**

Anyone can hold the helm when the sea is calm.
Publilius Syrus,
Moral Sayings (first century B.C.)

*Adversity is the trial of principle. Without it a
man hardly knows whether he is honest or not.*
Henry Fielding,
English novelist

Adversity brings the character of people down to the level of their circumstance or up to the level of the challenge it presents.

The trial of adversity will indicate whether we use the experience or it uses us. A coach who knows how to handle adversity well is particularly advantaged. He can understand the impact tough times have and better teach his athletes how to effectively deal with such times and situations. On the other hand, a coach who does not himself cope well with adversity sets himself up as a poor model—and influences his athletes for the worse, rather than for the better.

Adversity is, at the same time, a formidable test and a stern teacher. The confrontation with difficulty, problems, or failure introduces people to themselves. During the course of my daily talks to professional baseball players, before stretching every spring training, I would include a reminder about tough times, reminding them, "If you want to know who you are, pay attention to yourself when things aren't going your way." That's an indicator I always use when observing them during and after competition. And by observing myself—always. Coaching provides challenging tests. The results are not always favorable. (See FRONT-RUNNER, section 2.)

Many coaches can't get past their disappointment. As a result, their approach to their athletes changes. It's all too apparent to the athletes, though not so to the coach himself. I'd always ask my assistant coach to pay attention to the way I presented myself on any given day, but particularly after a tough loss or a terrible practice session. As time went on, I could monitor myself. Awareness, as has been noted in chapter 3, is the starting point for efficacy.

Lucretius wrote, "Look at the man in the midst of doubt and danger. . . . It is then that true utterances are wrung from (his) recesses. . . . The mask is torn off; the reality remains." Many coaches have uttered words they wished to take back. They revealed too much from recesses too deep.

Item: On January 13, 2002, the Associated Press ran a story about the frustration of Temple University basketball coach Don Chaney. Chaney, sixty-nine years old, said, "I could probably quit somewhere this season. There are too many changes that have taken place in young people that I just don't like. There's no sense of urgency (see URGENCY*), no sense of awareness. Now it's not one for the Gipper. They don't want it for anybody." (See ZAPPED, section 2.)

Chaney stayed; the team received a bid to the NCCA Tournament.

I was told at an early age to keep my mouth shut when facing up to adversity. The homily my father more than occasionally provided after complaints regarding my plight was "Suffering's good for you, kid—so long as you survive it." Learn to deal with adversity, he was saying, instead of complaining about it. He followed up with "Instead of cursing the darkness, light a candle." I've used that one often, most effectively with pitcher Kevin Brown, who faced down much adversity in 2002.

There's a wide gap between survive and thrive, and I've always asked the players I coached to use tough times to make them tougher. To help them face up to such times, be *aggressive* in the face of the adversity, and trust that they will persevere. And thrive because of it, at best. In spite of it, at least.

Most of what I know and what I am is directly attributable to what I went through as a bed-ridden youth. As it turned out, it was, as my father said, "good for me." I wouldn't change the circumstances if I could.

Item: The headline of an article in the *New York Times* (January 13, 2002): "The Lions Struggle in Silence All Season Long." The NFL's Detroit team was notorious at this point because of its 0–12 record. But they seemed unique in that there were no stories—"even with off-the-record sources," the article said—about finger pointing, fighting, or inside political turmoil.

"This team never came apart and we had every reason to," said receiver Johnny Morton.

Coach Marty Mornhinweg had this to say: "We went through about four or five seasons of adversity. This team never wavered, didn't make excuses, took the high road and stayed together. These type of things, what we went through in the locker room, are the rewards for doing that. And I'm proud of them for that."

• • •

For continuing to work hard, to be persistent, and to controʷⁱ
could control—their attitude and approach—and take the
sults like the men they showed themselves to be. From the
through all the players roster.

Anger*

[See VENTING and CONTROL, section 2]

*Anger in many ways is a feast. . . . The chief drawback is that what
you are wolfing down is yourself. The skeleton at the feast is you.*
Frederick Buechner,
Wishful Thinking

People who are continually angry devour, at least, much of what is good
about them. An angry coach loses his capacity to think—to rationally assess, understand, and solve whatever needs a solution. Anger brings on
the loss of control and further results in irrational thinking and dysfunctional behavior. During competition, that is tantamount to becoming a
"skeleton."

One of the dangers of being angry is that once a coach starts on it, he
is apt to get much more than he bargained for. And so do the objects of
his anger.

The coach should have a good reason for it—and be in control of it.
Meaning, anger acted out as a tool—to teach or get one's attention—can
be an effective coaching device. It should be purposeful, calculated, and
controlled. I've had my own anger escalate to the point where I went
over the line of acting into feeling it. At that point, it lost its usefulness—
and, in fact, detracted from what I'd already accomplished. The law of
diminishing returns kicked in.

One million brain cells are destroyed every day. Coaches shouldn't
waste what they have left—and need.

We may ride anger for a short while, but it will ride us in the long
run. Anger can cause us to say or do things that cannot be undone, even
if we wish them to be. Irrevocable acts of passion, Thomas Fuller called
them. We can't *always* be in control of our emotions; it's not human.
And, perhaps, it's not desirable.

W. G. Sebald, I recall, wrote about actually feeling sorry for a fellow
who would never permit anything to provoke him enough to lose his
composure. But we can train ourselves to detonate our explosives in an
unpopulated area. A coach shouldn't confront players when his brain is
not functioning. He should ride out the storm in his soul. Wait to deal

h a volatile issue until the next day, after reflection. Sanity rises with he sun.

I remember being a young coach and having my anger change into a pervasive sense of uneasiness. It made me squirm when I was through with it. It also served as a poor example: a loss of control, poise, straight thinking, and focus on function. All the things coaches hate when their athletes "lose it."

In his novel *The Corrections*, Jonathan Franzen referred to anger as "an autonomous neurological event; no stopping it." For some. But not, I hope, for all.

Appearance

Outside show is a poor substitute for inner worth.
Aesop,
"The Fox and the Mask"

While having a debate with myself about whether or not to include this topic, I was swayed by a call I received from a college athletic director. The call was related to a candidate for a head coaching position—head baseball coach—and this particular candidate had used me as a reference. The words the athletic director used provoked me to make the inclusion.

But first it's essential to establish the relevance of "appearance" to the mental game.

I have, over time, observed what I've interpreted to be a self-consciousness on the part of a number of coaches—amateur and professional. Their self-conscious feelings inhibited a self-assertive behavior. It also indicated a lack of self-trust, which, in turn, got in the way of their establishing healthy relationships with the athletes they coached—especially the most self-assured athletes.

We're not much good for others if we think we're not that good ourselves, whatever the basis is for the feeling. ("Physician, heal thyself.")

Beauty may be in the eye of the beholder, but for a coach the definition of beauty should relate to the way he or she leads and teaches. Every mother is beautiful to an infant whose needs she satisfies.

I'm not oblivious to how people are perceived because of physical appearance, but my major concern is how these people perceive themselves. When their self-image is tainted or damaged, their ability to project themselves is weakened considerably. I've been witness to it. And though novelist Peter Carey wrote, "The skin won't predict the inside of a fruit," a coach must feel good inside that skin.

■ ■ ■

Back to the coaching candidate I spoke of earlier. This young man has tried to get a head coach's job for a couple of years now. He's been an assistant baseball coach at a number of fine colleges. Though he is currently a head coach at a two-year school, he's been turned down as a candidate for a number of jobs at four-year schools.

He does not have an imposing stature. He doesn't have a face that attempts to wear what writer Martin Amis called "the standard sneer of enraptured self-sufficiency." He doesn't have a strong voice. One's appearance is what is first perceived, and many who look for coaches to fill vacancies make decisions before a candidate ever speaks a word.

The articulation of the individual whose candidacy I supported gives the hint of his being the educated and cultured person he is. He's an accomplished violinist. (So was Eddie Basinski, an infielder for the Brooklyn Dodgers in 1944 and 1945.)

This candidate is also very knowledgeable about the game of baseball and about coaching techniques. He knows *how* to coach, how to handle young people. And knows there's plenty more he still has to know.

The athletic director said to me in an e-mail message, "He doesn't make a formidable physical presentation, though he interviewed very well." He did not get that job.

■ ■ ■

Item: From a column by Bob Herbert on the *New York Times* op-ed page (January 24, 2001). Column head: "An Unlikely Coach."

"If you went strictly by appearances, you would never guess that Mr. Willingham is the new head football coach at Notre Dame. Stereotypical, he's not. He's excessively polite and does not seem particularly assertive." No mention of his ability to play a musical instrument. (Mr. Willingham is now coaching at University of Washington.)

■ ■ ■

Item: From a *USA Today* article, written by David DuPree (April 25, 2001), this headline: "Don't Sell Van Gundy Short." The subhead: "Unimposing coach gets most out of Knicks."

The first line stands by itself: "Jeff Van Gundy doesn't look the part."

DuPree continues, "He's in a high-profile, glamour job, yet he looks like a short, rumpled, wispy-haired lawyer who somehow wandered onto the Madison Square Garden floor.

"Van Gundy is used to people making fun of him," the article continues. "Opposing players chuckle at him, other coaches such as Phil Jackson of the Lakers, gibe him and fans razz him." Van Gundy was also made sport of by Pat Riley (whose grooming has been called obsessive).

Irrespective of his appearance, Jeff Van Gundy did a fine job while coaching the Knicks. He had the personal strength to rise above the shallowness of others. One of his players, Alan Houston, said, "Some coaches and some people are more worried about how they look or how they are perceived. But all Jeff worries about is winning games and getting us to be the best we can be. You've got to respect him for that."

The respect Van Gundy, "the shortest coach" in the NBA, received came after he was given the opportunity to coach.

■ ■ ■

It took quite a while for Ralph Friedgen to get a position as a head football coach. Friedgen was given a ten-year contract to coach the University of Maryland in December 2001. For years he had been virtually overlooked as a head coach, though highly valued as an assistant. He actually wasn't overlooked; he was looked over—and found to be, according to one observer, "too fat."

One could say Friedgen was a "minority hiring." (The hiring Maryland AD, by the way, was a woman, Kathy Yow.) After his first season at Maryland, Friedgen was named Associated Press Coach of the Year. He said, "I'm very proud for the school, our assistant coaches, our players and our administration. I really think they are all represented by this award." He might have added to the list the "appearance challenged" of the coaching profession.

■ ■ ■

Aesop's fabled words above probably date back to the sixth century B.C. Nothing's changed in that regard. And when people regard the physical appearance of a coach, they get their initial impression. They put that impression with or against the image or ideal they have in their mind's eye. Hence, a Ralph Friedgen, a Jeff Van Gundy, and individuals I've coached against and worked with have been said to "not look like a coach."

One such individual was in danger of being fired from his job as a minor league baseball coach because he had put on quite a bit of weight. He was still doing the good job he always had, but his boss said, "He looks lousy in a uniform." That was approximately fifteen years ago. He's not with the same organization, but he's still working at doing what he does best: coaching.

Approachability

An ancient father says that a dog we know is better company than a
man whose language we do not understand.
Montaigne

Do your athletes always understand you? Do they try? Do you want them to? Do they always understand themselves? If the answer to any or all of these questions is "No," then the next question must be "Are you approachable?" Or "Are you an intimidator?" "An 'Ice King/ Queen'"?

It's fine to intimidate opponents, but people on the same side of the competitive field of play as the coach are supposed to be able to effectively communicate with him. The coach who gives off signals that he isn't interested in connection and clarification short circuits the communication process and creates a gap between himself and the athlete he coaches. (See CARING, section 2.)

■ ■ ■

Former Kansas City Royals manager Tony Muser entered the 2002 season, the final year of his tenure, with a new point of view. A *Sports Illustrated* clipping reported, "Muser is a taskmaster. . . . He admits to letting losses gnaw at him. For his own well-being, he vows to be more upbeat and looser this season, even relaxing his stolid demeanor in the dugout. In fact, he has proposed a new slogan for 2002: 'Come out and see Tony smile.'" It wouldn't be exclusively for his *own* well-being. Apparently, it wasn't enough to save his job.

Muser was also known as a good storyteller, when he was in the mood. But an athlete's interpretation of the coach's mood can be unreliable. It's up to the coach to make clear that being approachable is part of his coaching credo. Anaheim Angels manager Mike Scioscia made that very clear when he managed in the big leagues for the first time. His players still appreciate it.

Such a perception held by athletes helps their mental game immeasurably. First, they're assured the coach is there to help them. Second, they are assured the coach is not, in their mind, there to intimidate them. We all know that what we can be accused of is not necessarily what is our intention. An approachable coach can clear up miscommunications more effectively and more quickly.

An approachable coach allows the athlete to relax to the extent that he can communicate whatever concerns, uncertainties, or misunderstandings he might have.

Almost without exception, athletes express to me their need to know "where (they) stand" in relation to their role on their team—and their evaluation by their coach. Many seem to need to be reassured, even though they have some idea of their standing. (Even [especially?] professional athletes.) It's difficult for them to know when they don't feel they can approach a coach or manager—*especially when the coach himself never approaches the athlete.*

■ ■ ■

Then there was Scotty Bowman, so successful—at the professional level—who surrounded himself with relatively mature, veteran players who *knew how to handle themselves* (the exception, not the rule) and knew how to deal with an unapproachable coach.

"How to get along with him (Bowman) is to show up, work hard—and keep your mouth shut. And play well defensively," said Detroit captain Steve Yzerman, just before the Red Wings won their 2002 Stanley Cup Championship, Bowman's ninth cup as a coach.

Well, yes, that worked for Bowman. But athletes such as those on the Red Wings don't show up at youth leagues, at junior high school, at high school, or even at college tryouts. And most often, not even at the professional level. The Red Wings were the exception, not the rule. Bowman got what he wanted because he had the power to get rid of what he didn't want. Approachability is not the essential ingredient in that kind of mix.

■ ■ ■

Finally, many coaches have proclaimed to their athletes, "My door is always open." But many athletes understand a message other than that conveyed by the "open-door" assurance. They see contradictions evident in a coach's nonverbal communication and unapproachable manner. Sometimes, even verbal inconsistency. Those coaches conduct themselves in such a way as to indicate that the best way for the athlete to assure his well-being is to pass by that open door.

Approachability is the quality that conveys the message that the coach is as open as the door.

Aspirations

*The Romans . . . held Renown to be a god, and sought out her
harsh attentions, even though her blessing might be bought at the
price of death and disgrace.*
Iain Pears,
The Dream of Scipio

*Every man, in moral intent, is animated by his own intent; he has
something in view which he prizes.*
George Santayana
(1905)

It's fine to do the right thing because it's morally right. But let's be honest; it's right for getting us what we want, as well—and nothing's wrong
with that.

Years ago I expressed my admiration to the owner of the Oakland A's,
Mr. Walter Haas, my boss, for a particularly kind and humanitarian act
he had made. He said to me, "Harvey, it was the morally right thing to
do. But it's also good for business." Doing the right thing can serve more
than one intention.

A coach's professional aspirations often distort the method and manner used to achieve them. In aspiring to make a name for himself, chasing the god named Renown, a coach is apt to use his athletes. Because
winning becomes "everything," all else—by language and logic—is
nothing. The exclusive devotion to winning and supposed self-aggrandizement has always been a potential corrupter of coaches. Too many
succumb, and many young athletes have felt the consequences of this
yielding.

The irony is clear: when a coach's agenda is self-serving, the athletes
perform in ways that are counterproductive to that coach's aims. They
play tight; they play with resentment; they feel a rebelliousness that expresses itself in ways ranging from disdain to subversiveness.

All kinds of things suffer: honesty, respect, the sense of team unity.
Whatever moral credo has been named is a philosophy in name only.

The best way to get what we want is to do things right. The right approach, the right attitude, the right connection with the athletes. One
that starts by serving them will more likely help the coach to reach
whatever professional aspirations he has for "advancement."

Essentially, to focus on one's own personal or professional goals on a
daily basis is to think about ends, not means to ends. It doesn't work; it
doesn't serve the athletes he's coaching.

A college coach I know of bad-mouthed his heavily scouted, draft-
eligible star players during their junior years to those watchful scouts on
the scene. His agenda was to ensure that they would fall in the draft, be

dissatisfied with the prospects of the kind of bonus money they were hoping for—and return to the college for their senior year. He is the ultimate user—driven by self-interest, duplicitous, unethical. The behavior of this coach, though unprincipled, is not unprecedented.

■ ■ ■

Item: Kareem Abdul-Jabbar played for John Wooden's UCLA teams (as Lew Alcindor) from 1966 to 1969. Paying tribute to his former coach, Jabbar wrote (in the *New York Times*, December 10, 2000), "All of the accolades he received never changed his approach because self-promotion and credit were not the things he lived for. If you asked Coach Wooden, he would hope that his players most remembered the impact he had on their lives, not simply the success on the floor. His influence on me was profound."

Big Game/Event

[See URGENCY, section 2]

A thing is important if anyone thinks it important.
Wm. James,
The Principles of Psychology

A big game is big because it carries the weight of perceived or real consequences that distinguish it from other games. It often creates more stress for the coach than for the athletes. To begin with, at least.

I recall being told by a member of an ACC team that his coach, before a "must game," told the players, "If we don't win this one we're through. Do you hear? We're through!" It was a doubly misguided presentation in that it was dressed in negative language. They didn't win; their season ended.

The coach who believes that consistent behavior leads to consistent performance attempts to avoid making distinctions between one event and another. Now, we all know that significant differences define athletic competitions. But the task of the coach is to keep the differences out of the mind-set of the athlete preparing to compete in the event.

The athlete's mind should be on doing all the things he always does to prepare and to perform—*without changing any aspect of that mental routine.* He doesn't plan to "try harder," because this game "really matters." He doesn't entertain a win-or-else approach. He stays balanced and focused on task, as always. Consistently and relentlessly. That should be the goal for an athlete, and intrusive points of view—such as the "urgency" and special meaning of an upcoming event—are likely to be counterproductive.

Maintaining that perspective in the face of a highly coveted outcome is not easy. But when the athlete senses the tension in the coach, it is harder still for him to focus on what is appropriate: task, rather than that desired result. And when a coach proclaims about an event, "This is everything time," muscles tend to tighten—all through the body. Performances tend to deteriorate.

Athletes know what's going on. The wise coach helps them to relax as they ready themselves for competition, rather than project his own anxieties onto them. It is poor leadership—and it doesn't win the big one.

C

Caring

To hear you have to listen. To listen you have to respect.
To respect you have to care.
Benjamin Zucker,
Blue

I believe . . . that coaches can play a greater role in ensuring
that players do not fail.
Herman Edwards,
NFL Coach

When the San Diego Padres manager was called "one of the majors' top five managers," he was credited with having "smooth people skills." The writer Tom Krasovic noted, "Bochy is firm enough to maintain order in the clubhouse and has the players' respect."

"Caring" can be said to mean that a coach (manager, in this case) understands the importance of being an effective communicator. He or she cares that it is a two-way connection between coach and athlete, rather than an arbitrary one. The understanding is that someone with "people skills" is aware and sensitive to the issues in a clubhouse and in an athlete's head. And that's a great start at caring.

Then there are the coaches whose caring goes to the extent of the athlete's life away from the competitive arena. Dean Smith, Lombardi, powerful instruments in the lives of their players.

And then there are those who seem to care too much. Who, in my judgment, are too concerned with what the athlete is thinking. After all, there are areas in the athlete's life and being that are none of the coach's business—unless the athlete chooses to make it the coach's business.

Some coaches are just insecure in terms of wanting to please a particular athlete. Motive, once again, is a litmus test. Often, the coach himself is seeking to be perceived as something or someone. The caring is driven by self-interest, rather than a real—and necessary—involvement with the athlete. Such an ulterior motive is almost always transparent to the recipient, and damaging to the giver.

The safest way to illustrate a caring approach—one that serves the athlete as a competitor and as a person—is to consider a description of

Yankees manager Joe Torre, of whom it has been said he makes "every player on his roster feel respected and needed." That is the elemental concern of all athletes and what every coach should express to them. It will elicit the best responses. It's also extremely helpful in trying to get the most out of the athlete. And what legitimately assists the athlete also benefits the coach.

The caring coach to whom this book is dedicated assisted me immeasurably. I'd like to hope the team—and coach, extensionally—got something back from me.

■ ■ ■

Athletes are more effective as performers and as humans when they recognize that their coach has a genuine concern for them. The coach can best express a caring attitude by:

- Being natural, not forced. Self-conscious or excessive concern for an athlete is artificial. We don't fool them. They know who we are, so let's be that person.
- Understanding their needs and respecting them—as we provide direction and assistance. That is, caring enough to win their appreciation and respect. We don't get love from our athletes by begging for it. And as coaches, we shouldn't need it from them.
- Remembering his own coaches, who cared for him when he did need it as a young person, and by passing it on to others now.
- Remembering any of his coaches who didn't care; remembering the feelings that person provoked and, perhaps, imbedded—and by being certain never to be that coach.

*Change**
[See OLD SCHOOL, section 2]

Even in slight things the experience of the new is rarely without some stirring of foreboding.
Eric Hoffer,
The Ordeal of Change

I don't change with each new trend.
Ralph Lauren,
clothing designer

Change is an ordeal for many, a thing to be avoided entirely for some. As inevitable as change may seem to be, coaches—people—tend to prefer the comfort of what they do to the possible discomfort of change.

■ ■ ■

Change, Gore Vidal has written, is "the nature of life, ar
that's not always the way coaches (or athletes) see it. N
necessarily. There should be a good reason for change
be for not changing. Examination of methods, evaluati
adjustment of goals: all should be considered, so tha
formed and responsive to whatever good information he receivᵤ
whatever source. Why do coaches go to so many seminars and workshops? I presume the reason to be, ultimately, to change. To get better.

Someone less profound than Gore Vidal said, "No one likes change
except a wet baby." But when that child becomes an adult (chronologi-
cally speaking), the discomfort is often in the change itself.

People tend to resist change because they don't know what they're
going to get. Many would rather be in a known unpleasant circumstance than in an unknown better one. Research has shown that abused
women choose to stay with the abuse they know, rather than leave it—
for the uncertainty of future circumstance.

Even a slight change, as Hoffer says in the epigraph, precipitates some
"foreboding," a "stirring" of whatever little insecurity is hiding in one of
the dark corners of our mind. So we hold on to what we know, following the universal instinct for comfort or self-protection.

People hide behind what they've always believed or done, building
what they imagine to be a fortification against fear of what they haven't
experienced or understood. Change often requires courage.

■ ■ ■

Change is an indication of learning. Those who can't change don't learn.
Learning is change. The distinction many coaches make about learning
is simple to understand. They essentially say, "I like to learn things I
don't know, but I don't like to learn things that indicate that what I already know is not effective or good enough." Wrong, perhaps.

The person who lifts weights knows that when he feels "the burn,"
his muscles are developing beyond their capacity. "No pain, no gain,"
the lifter says. When applying the same principle to learning, we can
say, "No pain, no brain," meaning, when we don't ever feel the pain of
changing our thinking, we forfeit our intelligence.

Yes, it's uncomfortable to grow, but coaches must ask themselves a
very basic question: "Is what I'm doing *working*?" If it isn't, a change is
required. It should be made quickly. (For some coaches, change takes
place at glacial speed.) Making that change doesn't (necessarily) mean a
coach has been making mistakes in the past. It does mean that what
worked in the past isn't working now.

.at sense, change is based on the pragmatic view: what works is and what doesn't work should be changed. Some coaches won't .nge the "system" even though it's not suitable for the athletes on the .eam. They try to fit that square peg into a round hole.

Clearly, a change made for the sake of change—for appearance—is foolish. No reason—no rhyme. The fitting cliché: If it ain't broke, don't fix it.

■ ■ ■

If we value personal and professional growth, we should tolerate the discomfort that comes with it.

Character

The measure of a man's real character is what he would do if he knew he would never be found out.
Thomas McCauley,
English writer

One of my standard lines to groups of athletes uses McCauley's words as a reference point. What I say is, "You identify yourself by what you do when no one is watching. The supervised athlete may be the hardest worker, the most selfless and responsible competitor. But how he practices when no one sees him, how he interacts with teammates when the coach is not within listening distance—that's when he defines himself. His character."

Theodore Roosevelt extended the definition to self-awareness and independent self-evaluation, saying, "I care not what others think of what I do, but I care very much about what I think of what I do. That is character!"

I would say that character is the whole of some of the parts presented in this book: values, courage, responsibility, suppressed ego, dedication, mental discipline, will, honesty, trust, caring, and consistency. And more.

■ ■ ■

Athletic competition doesn't teach character, though it will surely reveal it. To develop himself as a competitor and a person, an athlete must face difficulty with intelligence and courage. Many in the game consider that a form of "character." I've heard managers, coaches, and scouts say "character is destiny." It might serve us as well to invert the thought. One's destiny is also his character. Adversity will test us all—and reveal us.

But if character is destiny, then one's destiny can, to an extent, be shaped. Because people can change their expression of self—their "makeup," their character. An athlete's character is initially shaped by a number of factors, noted below.

Though many have argued the point, character *can* be taught. Those who protest too much are either not interested in making the attempt or intimidated by what they consider to be a daunting task. They're right about one thing: it is a daunting task. One that is well worth it, if successful with just one individual.

Vince Lombardi: "Character is not inherited; it is something that can be, and needs to be, built and disciplined."

■ ■ ■

The first step in teaching character is to define it for the athlete. The Greek word character means "impression." But the Greek philosopher Aristotle had a more useful definition: "Character is that which reveals moral purpose, exposing the things a man chooses and avoids." Motive and choices. Character, then, is the relationship between what a person does, what he doesn't do—and the reasons behind his choices.

Many influences *impress* themselves on the individual: parents, siblings, peers, teachers, socioeconomic circumstances, television, the Internet, music, local language and custom, recreational habits. Through these sometimes conflicting impressions and the individual's interpretation of them, character is shaped. The coach, of course, should make whatever impressions would help the athlete to reshape those aspects of his character that require it.

The coach is in a position to influence the athlete's character dramatically. The coach's desire and ability to represent the best philosophical and behavioral model—and, as an educator, to stamp them on the athlete's character, go far in the reshaping.

The athlete recognizes the conscious effort of the coach, and that initial awareness is, in itself, a positive influence. He learns, within the coach's system, what is right and appropriate. And why. And then, how to implement it into behavior.

Philosopher Martin Buber has said that "in this realm of education of character, of wholeness, there is only *one* access to the pupil: his *confidence*." His confidence and trust in the coach, in this case. (See TRUST, section 2.)

Buber said that in this "unreliable world, confidence means the liberating insight that there is human truth."

■ ■ ■

I've found that some young people are capable of developing on their own, if the coach, at least, provides the setting for that growth. The coach should see himself as the operator of an elevator, which can take an athlete from the level of his current circumstance to the height the coach seeks for him. Sociologists tell us that, left to their own devices, most people will rise and fall according to circumstance, rather than self-control. The coach must take that control until the athlete can assume it for himself.

■ ■ ■

"Team chemistry" is, for me, an expression alluding to collective character. The team takes on an aspect that adheres to an agenda in which individual needs are sacrificed for the whole. In which individual goals are compatible with the team's. In which behavior is expressed in a way that promotes unity, rather than separatism.

What I've also found is that only a few core athletes of great character are required for the creation of good team chemistry. They lead because of the strength of their integrity. Others clearly understand they "can't beat 'em, so they join 'em."

I've come to believe that teams with good chemistry—character—all seem to be alike. Teams that have unhappy athletes and chaotic environments seem to have their own particular unhappiness and chaos.

Coaches can't always influence chemistry and character to their entire satisfaction, but they can usually bend athletes to the right shape through their insistent and persistent leadership.

Consistency*

There is nothing in this world constant but inconstancy.
Jonathan Swift,
A Critical Essay upon the Faculties of the Mind

About two decades ago, (Bob) Knight had the best description of himself, saying to reporters at an Atlanta regional, "I don't agree with everything I do."
Dave Anderson,
New York Times, March 10, 2002

Jonathan Swift was not optimistic about people's tendencies. And he didn't even know any bad coaches.

The first point to be made about the value of consistent behavior on the part of the coach is that it helps his athletes gain some peace of mind, because they don't have to be on edge wondering what the coach will spring on them individually or collectively. That predictability (event strategy is not what I speak of here) is a security blanket. It allows the athletes to focus on what *they* are doing, instead of what the coach *may* do.

Consistency relates to how the coach handles issues that arise on a regular basis. Discipline issues, coaching techniques, teaching methodology, communication—dealing with losses, and so on.

A consistent coach does not display mood swings, whether they might be caused by personal problems or professional frustration. He uses the tools of effective communication to establish his points, and he does so with a thought-out sense of purpose, rather than an uncontrolled sense of emotionality.

A high school athlete dropped in at my home to see me a while back. He was frustrated and confused by his coach, who, in the athlete's words, "behaves one way when we're winning and another when we're losing." (See FRONT-RUNNER, section 2.) One of the most consistently inconsistent patterns of coaches' behaviors is their poor reactions to a bad loss. (To *any* loss, for some.) They respond by punishing their athletes, instead of instructing them. They apply seemingly tough hate, rather than tough love. Resentment drips from their sometimes-venomous words to the team or individuals.

Many of the same coaches who *punished* after a loss will be fine after a win. They call the punishment "discipline." (See DISCIPLINE, section 2.) They may run the team into the ground, as I've witnessed a few minor league managers do. This teaches athletes to dislike ("hate," I have heard) running, rather than to appreciate it, if not love it. Running is, after all, a means to a desired end: enhanced physical preparedness.

When running becomes a punitive exercise, it takes on a negative aspect and a negative motive, both of which lead to negative responses. Athletes should want to run hard and often, because it is consistent with the ideal of being fit, playing hard, and being a relentless competitor.

The athletes should *always* see running as a tool for achievement of goals, not a hammer wielded by a frustrated or angry coach on occasions when his inconsistency serves his emotional needs.

He should, Bob Knight notwithstanding, believe in everything he does.

■ ■ ■

Item: The Associated Press NFL Coach of the Year award for 2002 went to Dick Jauron of the Chicago Bears, a team that won its division for the first time since 1990. The threat of losing his job had been evident to the coach and to the players for a couple of (losing) years. His players were elated after Jauron won the award. Many words of praise were offered. Those of center Olin Kreutz spoke to the point made above. "Coach Jau-

. Even when we were losing, he didn't change. This ...and his job was on the line and he didn't change. We ...m him. And we play for him."

■ ■ ■

...st, here are two more quotes about their coaches, provided to ...athletes I've worked with:

He (the coach) has very clear standards for us. One set for the stars, another for the bench guys. (Hypocrite)

He's a nice guy, but he says whatever comes to his mind. I don't think he has a real understanding of what to do and when to do it. (Not consistently prepared)

I chose these two remarks simply because they illustrate other ways in which a coach can express inconsistent behavior or attitude.

With regularity, I tell athletes, "Consistent behavior will get consistent performance." I tell coaches, "If you want your athletes to behave consistently, you must show them how; you must do the same."

■ ■ ■

Item: Mark Twain, in his essay "Consistency": "There are those who would misteach us that to stick in a rut is consistency—and a virtue, and that to climb out of the rut is inconsistency—and a vice."

As previously noted, a rut is not the place for an effective coach. Staying in one is a foolish choice—a foolish consistency that's been described as "the hob-goblin of little minds" by Emerson. He and Twain were both referring to the kind of consistency that indicates that a person is either unwilling or unable to make adjustments to approaches and points of view that have proved to be ineffective or inaccurate. "Stubborn mule consistency," I call it, when addressing athletes or staff members suffering from the affliction.

Aldous Huxley was less gentle. He called an individual who was insistently consistent a "fanatical monomaniac."

If it works, stay with it; if not, make a change. Necessary adjustments aren't indications of inconsistency; they are indications of enlightenment.

We need people who influence their peers and
detoured from their convictions by peers who ⟨
courage to have an

Head Football Coach Emeritus, Penn Stat⟨

Paterno's words above speak volumes. So many talk; so many criticize; so many know so much more than everyone else; so many have no responsibility for anything they say.

The coach has to know, surely. But he has to have the courage to act upon *his* convictions. (See KNOWING vs. DOING, section 2.) Paterno had more to say: "Will those friends of yours who are always after you to compromise your convictions be around when you're in trouble? If they have no convictions, will they have a strong character? If they don't have a strong character, will they be loyal?"

No responses are necessary for these rhetorical questions. The real question is "Who's in control of your personal and coaching life?"

■ ■ ■

As a teenager, I read and revered Don Robertson's book *The Greatest Thing since Sliced Bread*. I wrote down something that spoke loudly to me. More than fifty years later, I still have that paper—and the words: "Bravery is the best thing there is . . . and the smartest. It makes you able to live with yourself. . . . Helps you to sleep nights."

By smartest, Robertson meant the understanding that something else is more important than fear. That something else is the doing of whatever is right and required. The avoidance of the doing makes for an uncomfortable bed at night. The performance of the courageous act is a featherbed for the soul.

■ ■ ■

"Courage means not scaring others." Those words were written by Kingsley Amis. They take me along a different line of thought: Coaches who intimidate their athletes—or attempt to—hide their weakness behind their power. Intimidating those with no power or limited power is not courageous behavior, needless to say. Nor does a coach's intimidating posture enhance athletes' mental approach to their performance. And it certainly doesn't incline the athletes to be motivated in any kind of healthy way. The coach's poor mental state either contaminates the athletes or sends them scurrying to a safer distance.

A coach's healthy expression of courage helps give impetus to the trusting of his athletes—and caring about their well-being.

■ ■ ■

ʃart of being courageous is being confrontational. NFL coach Bill Parcells was fond of saying, "I've never feared confrontation." It's a winning attitude, especially when attached to an addendum: "And I've never sought it."

When Carlos Tosca was named manager of the Toronto Blue Jays in the middle of the 2002 season, he told the media, "I have been known to be confrontational." By alluding to that reputation, Tosca did not mean to imply, "I'll get in your face in a heartbeat." This I know, because I know Carlos Tosca. Very well.

The word *confront* for a coach should mean, as it does to Carlos Tosca, dealing with those everyday important issues of athletes, especially the tough ones. It should indicate that the coach will address any indication of disinterest, disenchantment, lack of hustle, dissension, insubordination, finger pointing, playing without passion, tardiness, absence—need I go on? Whatever unacceptable attitude already exists or is detected in its developmental stage should be identified and met confrontationally and immediately. Stopped and changed, rather than ignored—denied.

When Tosca and I spoke shortly after he was appointed manager of the Blue Jays, he mentioned that he had once asked Atlanta manager Bobby Cox what was the most important piece of advice Cox could give him should he ever be given the responsibility of leading a major league team. Cox told Tosca, "Don't ever sweep unpleasant things under the rug. Confront them."

■ ■ ■

What should be confronted:

- Challenging issues/situations with players, parents, media people, administrators, perhaps. (Some coaches view the issues as threatening, rather than challenging. This interpretation will more likely lead to avoidance, instead of confrontation.)
- Responsibility (vs. excuses and buck passing)
- Adversity (bad games, bad seasons, general bad times)
- Disappointment
- Embarrassment
- Personal problems
- Truth/honesty (vs. denial and duplicity)
- Doing what is right (vs. what is expedient)
- Appropriate strategies that delay gratification (vs. inappropriate ones that provide instant gratification)
- "The person in the glass"

The above are but a few issues that require the courage of confrontation. J. M. Barrie said, "Courage is the thing. All goes if courage goes." Though not always the solution, it is always a salvation.

Criticism

They have a right to censure who have a heart to help.
William Penn,
Some Fruits of Solitude

He was soft to take offense and hard to lay it down.
Alison Weir,
regarding the Duke of Essex, *The Life of Elizabeth I*

Getting It

Coaches must live with criticism, so they should learn to harden themselves. Living with thin skin is very uncomfortable—and distracting. After having gone undefeated in conference play in 2002, Kansas basketball coach Roy Williams was still being criticized for never having won "the big one"—the NCAA Championship. "I have a lot of good company," he said, trying to "lay it down." "But, yes, hearing things said about you that are not nice always hurts a bit."

Even those who have won the big one are not above criticism. Onlookers of every stripe are more fickle than fate, it seems. When things were not going as they historically had, a *Sports Illustrated* article took it upon itself to help the Penn State coach of thirty-five years. They headed the article with, "Old-school Paterno Needs New Approach to Offense." Paterno continued to do what he thought would work. It did. The *Sports Illustrated* issue was either stowed away by collectors or put into the cat's litter box.

University of North Carolina icon Dean Smith was hanged in effigy early in his coaching career at Chapel Hill.

Item: Mack Brown, head football coach at Texas, said (*USA Today*, August 2, 2002): "Most of the coaches who are considered the greatest, who are in the Hall of Fame, had labels at one time that they couldn't do something. . . . I've watched and I've listened, and all of those people have been really criticized. . . . Who would I be to think I'd be different?"

■ ■ ■

Self-confidence allows a coach to respond to criticism with a healthy perspective. Intelligently, rather than emotionally. The prevailing wisdom is "Don't listen to the critics; you're the only one who knows the truth." Think about that. Will every "truth" I know remain a "truth" forever? Is there a better truth out there? Is my truth based on evidence or need?

Shakespeare advised, "Take each man's censure, but reserve thy judgment." The most self-confident coach is willing to *listen* to the opinion of others, evaluate the opinion or criticism, then dismiss it or use it, based on its merit. We listen, but we should filter it all through the sieve of objectivity and intelligence. We *can* learn from criticism. In fact, that's one of the things coaches try to convince their athletes.

But media critics, parents, and people with their own agenda are not the critics I speak of. Their motives are most often self-serving. If they're out to beat the dog, they'll surely find a stick. Saul Bellow called such critics "deaf piano tuners."

A good friend and/or subordinate can be a helpful critic. Or an athlete on the team. Someone who cares, to whom it matters. But the best criticism is self-criticism. Not self-flagellation; there's nothing useful about beating up oneself. (Coaches teach that to athletes also, or should.) The coach should be objective, honest, and rational in evaluating his behavior and strategies.

Rigorous self-evaluation is not the same as constant second-guessing (the I woulda, shoulda, coulda syndrome). I've been around young coaches who would work at justifying every mistake or misconception because it seemed to them to be a sign of imperfection. Well, they are imperfect, as are all of us. "Understand it, correct it and move on," I've told them. The response to valid self-criticism should not be, "I've gotta be perfect." It should be, "I now know how to be better." That's self-criticism at its reasonable best.

As noted, a coach can ask someone he trusts to "monitor" him as a helpful critic. This person will not necessarily be an assistant coach, who, (a) may be afraid to be critical or (b) may be too anxious to be just that, in order to serve his own agenda. Of course, the coach who asks someone for criticism but really only wants praise will gain nothing but resentment from whatever is offered.

Criticism will continue to come. It's a kind of tax a coach pays to spectators for his power over their critical opinions. If the coach maintains his perspective, objectivity, and courage, he'll have a mental belligerency based on the trust in his convictions, even in the face of criticism. But learning and change will also be there, if there is validity to what he hears.

As an oft bed-ridden young boy, I was inspired by reading about Theodore Roosevelt, our twenty-sixth president, who was similarly afflicted. In his later years, he had the following to say, an inspiration, I'd think, to those who are often criticized:

It is not the critic who counts, not the man who points out how th
man stumbles or where the doer of deeds could have done them be
credit belongs to the man who is actually in the arena, whose face is
by dust and sweat and blood, who strives valiantly, who errs and com
again and again because there is no effort without error and short
who knows the great devotion, who spends himself in a worthy cause, who
at the best knows in the end the high achievement of triumph and who at
worst, if he fails while daring greatly, knows his place shall never be with
those timid and cold souls who know neither victory nor defeat. *Roosevelt*

Giving It

Because the coach teaches, he will be critical. Understanding that
learning takes place only when the potential learner is in a receptive
mental state, the coach should address the subject at the beginning of
the season. He should help the athletes to understand that criticism is
about their mental and physical preparation, their execution, their technique, their approaches, and responses in competition. They are (or
should be) criticisms addressing better ways to function, to grow as an
athlete, so he can be an effective competitor.

Before teaching all this to the athletes, the coach must himself recognize that if criticism and instruction are offered with personal attacks—
apparent or veiled—in the style and/or language of presentation, the
athlete will only learn to protect himself from that attack.

The most common protection—defense mechanism—is the use of
excuses. (See EXCUSES*, section 3.) By employing an excuse, the athlete is essentially saying, "It wasn't my fault." He wants to avoid taking
responsibility because the coach is, according to the athlete's perception,
implying he is "a loser." The coach should teach that a loser is someone
who doesn't take responsibility for his mistakes. By constantly beating
up the athlete verbally, the coach is encouraging that losing mentality.

Appearances can be deceiving. Some athletes appear to take harshly
offered criticism well. Of those, some actually do know how to use it to
be motivated to learn. Others are just good actors. They take their cue
from the coach and blame themselves for every screw-up. "My bad,"
they say, all too willing to take responsibility. They're not. They actually
protect themselves from the coach by criticizing themselves. Their focus is
on the coach's response, rather than how to correct their mistake. They
don't think about correcting anything when trying to make themselves
feel better.

The litmus test is in the execution. If an athlete continues to make
the same mistakes, the coach's "teaching" style is obviously not working. An attentive coach changes his own approach in such cases.

■ ■ ■

Criticism can just hurt, it can just help, it can hurt and help. The hurt comes from emotional response. The help comes from the rational. When we're at our best, we put our brain in charge.

Despot

Of all the tyrannies of humankind / The worst is that which persecutes the mind.
John Dryden,
The Hind and the Panther

The primary definition of despot is someone who rules with absolute power. A secondary definition, however, takes some of the luster from the label: "a person who wields power oppressively." There is a difference. The first has the ability to be in control. Many who have exerted their control aggressively have been called "benevolent despots." They rule absolutely, but supposedly with consideration and caring for those they rule.

If, however, a coach is oppressive, he is a persecuting presence. *He* may like what he's doing; his athletes will almost always not. His purpose is to serve his own agenda, using those he controls to achieve that purpose. He can say he is concerned about the athletes, but his only concern is that they perform well so as serve his own end. (Review AS-PIRATIONS, section 2.) He feels safe because of the power he wields; he hides whatever humanity he may have inside that fortress.

■ ■ ■

One athlete told me about his high school coach who, when confronted about his despotic behavior, did not deny or redefine it. He justified it. "It's good for them," he said, with a self-satisfied smile.

I was reminded of Aesop's story about the boy who was throwing stones at the frog. When the frog asked the boy to stop, the boy told him, "But it's fun." The frog responded, "What's fun for some is death for others."

One can think of the goose and the gander as well. What was apparently good for the coach was not good for the athletes. It takes a lot for young athletes to stand up to authority, more to stand up to autocrats. I haven't seen any stand up to a despot, though I've seen quite a few whose performances suffered. And a few more who retreated. Quit.

The despot who calls himself a disciplinarian doesn't understand the term and doesn't understand the athlete. (He may or may not understand himself.) John Wooden was a disciplinarian. So was Dean Smith. A despot's statement about discipline is arbitrary. It also sounds as if it could be true. It isn't. In the case cited above, because there are particulars that were brought to my attention, it is blatantly false.

■ ■ ■

Scotty Bowman, the most successful professional hockey coach ever, coached such players as Lemieux, Dominic Hasek, Yzerman, Henri Richard, Breet Hull, Dryden, and Lafleur, and according to an Associated Press report, they "all shared similar feelings" about this despotic coach.

Said the AP report, "None loved him. Some barely tolerated him. Others hated him. All disliked his manipulativeness, his unpredicatbilty, his aloofness, his *imperiousness.*" Yet they wanted to play for him (even though Mario Lemieux, who "so despised him," convinced his team's general manager to have Bowman coach only on game days and not during practices!).

Bowman ran the proverbial "my way or the highway" program. His era began when Lyndon Johnson was the president. His approach was "grandfathered" by contemporary athletes for one simple reason: his teams won. This was, after all, at the professional level.

Today, tolerance for that approach is hard to find at any level. And few can pull it off anyhow. Is the reader one of those who can? Will the school administrators, parents, and athletes give you that power?

If so, does the reader know how to use it? A rhetorical question.

I used to tell students and athletes that I was running "a controlled democracy." I told them they could do whatever they wished—as long as it met with my approval. They understood. But they also understood, I believe, my primary concern for them as students, athletes, and human beings. Leaders will get plenty of latitude when followers trust their motives.

■ ■ ■

A few terms and definitions to consider:

- *Autocrat*—someone with *unlimited* power or authority. (Unlimited, the dangerous word.)
- *Tyrant*—a ruler who exercises power in a harsh, cruel manner.
- *Jerk*—a foolish, rude, or contemptible person.

Those who are still reading this book probably seek to do things in an effective way—a right way, if you will. They are inclined to be learners, seeking new or alternate approaches to coaching. These readers are probably not autocrats or tyrants. Or if they are, they do not want to remain so. And it's most probable that they aren't jerks, though we all are capable of acting like one on occasion. (See LABELS, section 2.)

Finally, it might be useful to consider this irony: the despotic coach is, himself, controlled. By his own ego and its screaming needs. (See EGO, section 2.)

Power without wisdom is tyranny. Wisdom without compassion is pointless.

Difficult Athletes

The squeaky wheel may get the most oil, but it's also the
first to be replaced.
Marilyn Vos Savant,
Of Course I'm for Monogamy

Athletes who are squeaky wheels aren't necessarily the first ones to be replaced, but they surely put the thought in a coach's mind. Athletes who are complainers, or who always have something to say—usually when it is most unappreciated—or who demand and/or require excessive attention for any reason, may do more to detract from the team's social and learning environment than add to it.

I've seen coaches and managers tolerate athletes' unhealthy needs to an extent beyond what I felt to be reasonable. The leaders' justification/rationalization was a no-brainer: the nuisance "could play." Or run. Or swim. I understood, but I didn't accept it. Still don't.

Great effort is made by coaches to effectively communicate with athletes. They do so in the belief that they can eventually exert a positive influence on them. Difficult individuals offer the greatest challenge, because they test the communication and teaching skills of the coach. And, having failed to make the desired connection with the individual, the coach may then be challenged by his own conflicting impulses. He must respond to that lack of success in a rational and controlled manner.

■ ■ ■

Item: NBA player Derrick Coleman had the reputation for years of being a malcontent. The following is part of a clip written about him (*New York Times*, December 17, 2000):

> It is an old story. . . . Derrick Coleman breaking Paul Silas's heart again is worth mentioning, if for no other reason than it shows how some coaches' faith in their players is never rewarded.

Coleman, the No. 1 draft pick 10 years ago, has been Silas's pet project since the Charlotte coach was an assistant with the Nets in the early 1990's and Coleman was a franchise player.

As a rugged rebounder whose career was built on more passion than panache, Silas never had Coleman's talent and skill. Prodding, cajoling, cursing Coleman some days and soothing his ego others, Silas has spent much of the last decade trying to give the forward a piece of his heart.

While Coleman has at time shown the brilliance of his first few years in the league, he is now on the injured list because of a lack of conditioning. He will be stripped of his co-captain title when he returns.

Silas would not give a specific reason why Coleman was losing the title, saying "Do you have to ask why?"

It may be (Coleman's) last chance to show Silas he could have been a Hall of Famer if he hadn't wasted his talent for much of the last decade.

Coleman did not long remain with the Hornets organization.

■ ■ ■

Skin is our largest organ. People who should know have said that it covers a surface of between twelve to twenty-four square feet, depending on how large the individual is. That's a lot of skin to get under. I can recall a number of athletes who have managed to get under every inch of skin I have. Or so it seemed. They were difficult young people; difficult athletes to coach.

The year was 1962. I was coaching freshman football on Long Island. It was the school's first year, its first athletic season. My first coaching job. The first game; the first offensive play we would run.

Before our huddle broke, our quarterback, one of the finest young men I ever coached (attending West Point after graduating from high school), frantically signaled for a time out. He then dashed to the sideline toward me. When he arrived, I said with some animation, "What the hell is going on, Richie?"

I got my answer. "Well, I called the play you gave me and Eddie (our starting halfback) said, 'Screw that play; I've got a better one.'" Eddie was called to the sideline, where he spent the entire game. That squeak became a minor one thereafter. It required minimal, if regular, oiling.

A couple of years later, his younger brother was on the team. He was one of the most exceptionally gifted athletes in the county. He was more difficult than his older brother. I'll spare the reader the details, except to say that he was well lubricated by the coaching staff. But I ran out of oil; I threw him off the team.

His parents came to see me to inform me of my poor judgment and to demand that I change it. I was unyielding. They brought in a hit man—the player's uncle, a priest. He invoked higher themes, to no avail. The family went to the administration to plead a losing case.

The boy played basketball for me during the winter season. He was not the happiest of players, but he cooperated sullenly and was entirely respectful—as well as being a very effective performer. Oil notwithstanding, a hammer seemed to get him to run smoothly. This fine athlete went on to be an All-American lacrosse player in college. I don't know anything about his attitude there.

■ ■ ■

I refer to the two players I mentioned in the introduction, each of whom, meeting me again after a lapse of years, greeted me with "I've changed." Sometimes the process takes a long time—and attitudes and behaviors change beyond the vision of the coach.

Nevertheless, the coach who has applied the right grade and amount of oil must trust that his care was part of the experience that helped the athlete find a better way. That includes the experience of being taken off a team.

■ ■ ■

The beginnings of many good athletes are ransomed to the treatment of them by parents, friends, and early coaches. Permissiveness, catering to, allowing complete freedom without responsibility or discipline: the sum of these indulgences can indeed be exorbitant. Through such treatment, the perspectives of young people—young athletes—are distorted. The behavior driven by that perspective often leads in later years to difficulty for a coach who, rightly, will not accept the behavior.

Bill Walton remembers his basketball coach's approach when the counter-culture Walton was a player for John Wooden at UCLA. Walton recalled how Wooden dealt with those who rebelled on occasion, who stuck to their individual agendas. "(Coach Wooden) would say, 'I admire and respect your position. We'll miss you here at UCLA. We've enjoyed your time. Thanks for coming.'"

The point is reached with some athletes when the final "persuasion" becomes the presentation of choice the athlete must make: to abandon his selfishness or abandon the premises.

■ ■ ■

We tend to like what is most easily understood. Many athletes are tough to understand, and we're often not motivated to want to delve into a nuisance's agenda or background. These players are difficult for the coach and usually for themselves.

Following are a few questions coaches might consider before approaching difficult athletes:

- Do I understand the problem in terms of cause?
- Whose problem is it? Could the coach be the precipitant?
- What is the message the athlete is trying to convey through the behavior?
- Does the athlete recognize it as a problem?
- Can he do what is required if he wants to?
- Does he know what the coach wants him to do?
- Does he know how to do it?
- Do obstacles exist that are beyond his control?
- What does he get as a result of his unacceptable behavior?
- What does he consider his choices to be, if he sees himself as having any?

■ ■ ■

I don't solve problems for athletes these days either; I try to help them solve problems for themselves. I try to provide clarity. Their behavior is their choice, and as a coach I held them responsible for it. As a facilitator, I still do. They must see what they do; they must see the motives behind the actions; they must understand that all behavior has consequences. Trying to help the athlete come to a solution is part of a coach's responsibility. So, too, is being certain to make every attempt to help the athlete change unacceptable behavior. To solve the problem—one way or another.

And this: just as there are difficult athletes, so too are there difficult coaches. By that I do not mean demanding coaches or stern coaches. I don't even mean some autocratic coaches (though they can be bad coaches because of other behaviors). My euphemistic term *difficult coach* really means *harmful* coach, and I've seen an alarming number of them operating at the amateur and the professional level. That is another subject for another time. But the relevance here is clear enough: coaches must be certain they are part of the athlete's solution, not part of their problem.

Disci
(See MENTAL DISCIPLINE*, s

It has always been my thought that the most importan...
ingredient to success in athletics or life is discipline. I have many
times felt that this word is the most ill-defined in all our language.
My definition of the word is as follows: 1. Do what has to be done;
2. When it has to be done; 3. As well as it can be done; and 4. Do it
that way all the time.
Bob Knight,
Basketball Coach, Texas Tech

Dis-ci-pline, n. 1. training expected to produce a specific character or
pattern of behavior, especially training that produces moral or
mental improvement. 2. Controlled behavior resulting from
disciplinary training; self-control. 3a. Control obtained by enforcing
compliance or order. b. A systematic method to obtain obedience. c. A
state of order based on submission to rules and authority. 4.
Punishment meant to correct or train. tr. v. 1. To train by instruction
and practice, especially to teach self-control.
The American Heritage Dictionary of the English Language

"Training!" The burden of discipline rests first on the shoulders of the coach. It's wonderful to have athletes join your team who are already self-disciplined—but coaches shouldn't count on it.

I've often told players about research done many years ago regarding students who had never cheated on exams. I ask the players to name the number one reason. Some respond that the students were ethical, had "high moral values." Some said that smart students are prepared and didn't need to cheat. Some had a few off-the-wall responses, and a few had the right reason, according to answers given by the students themselves. They were afraid they might be caught. Edgar Watson, in *Ventures in Common Sense*, wrote, "Principle is not as powerful in keeping people straight as a policeman." (Review CHARACTER, section 2.)

NFL Hall of Fame quarterback Norm Van Brocklin's remark crossed the border of coaching into parenting. "If you don't discipline them," he said, "they won't know you love them."

The point I wish to make here is not so much about the human condition as it is about the responsibility of the coach to teach discipline. Self-discipline is a valuable asset, but it's extremely rare. Personal desire resides in most people's hearts; personal resolve is most often homeless.

New Year's resolutions point out the problem people have with self-discipline. Research has shown that 25 percent of those who make these resolutions break them within two weeks. Another few weeks go by and another 25 percent are "homeless." Very few resolutions end up establishing permanent residency.

Without the will, desire cannot find its way. (See WILL, section 3.) Vince Lombardi understood that discipline is part of the will. It began with the athlete's adherence to the coach's will. "A disciplined person is one who follows the will of the one who gives the orders. You teach discipline by doing it over and over, by repetition and rote."

So the coach who is a disciplinarian is the coach who *teaches* discipline. Or should. Athletes need it—and want it. My experience has indicated to me that these athletes appreciate greatly those who create parameters—and hold team members accountable for staying within them.

Item: Olympic figure skater Angela Nikodinov, referring to coach Frank Carroll (*New York Times*, January 13, 2002): "I need someone to look after me, not to let myself make decisions, not to give me any options, not to let my emotions get in the way."

Columnist George Vecsey went on to say, "Many coaches exert huge emotional influence on their skaters because the need is there."

And so it is—in almost all the athletes I've come across. Certainly the degree of need varies, but through the "emotional influence" I've exerted, I have always tried to bring the athlete to self-discipline. And as they say, the process can be an ordeal—for the athlete surely, for the coach as well. "Exhausting work," pitcher Rick Rodriguez once said to me. (He's a coach now, exhausting his athletes, I trust.)

Naturally, there will be those athletes who don't appreciate being exhausted. They are either mentally lazy or have been indulged for too long by parents or permissive coaches.

Item: NHL free agent center Bobby Holik was considering his options. He had heard that the New York Rangers were interested in signing him. When told that some of the Rangers players had not wanted a disciplinarian as a new coach, Holik said: "They have to figure out who's going to run the team, the coach or the players. If the players want to coach, they should become coaches. . . . If a coach demands you play hard, that's your job. That's how it should be. If a team wants to be successful, that's what you need for it to be" (*New York Times*, April 30, 2002).

Common sense, but not common practice.

Item: Coaches have been fired because it was felt they exerted too little discipline. Whether his perception was accurate or not, New Jersey Devils General Manager Lou Lamorello (*USA Today*, January 29, 2002) felt his team needed, among other things, "discipline and accountability." He fired Larry Robinson, implying that Robinson provided neither.

Writer Kevin Allen, writing about an event the week before the firing: "The criticism of Robinson was that he wasn't tough enough on players. After a loss last week, captain Scott Stevens called on Robinson to start benching players to send a message."

■ ■ ■

Leadership through fear works—in the short haul. Everyone knew Billy Martin operated that way. And he always outlived his welcome—and efficacy. After a while, athletes either shrivel in the face of their tasks, or become immune and deaf to instruction, or leave.

Item: (*New York Times*, January 21, 2001): "If the Bill Parcells era with the Jets looked like leadership by fear, as receiver Wayne Chrebet described the atmosphere last week, (Herman) Edwards may define leadership by ebullience. The sarcasm and biting words that marked the public remarks of Parcells and Al Groh have been replaced by a delivery made with all the gusto of a football evangelist."

■ ■ ■

What's left to say is simple, I think. Discipline is not meant to be punitive. It can be, but punishment is not Bob Knight's agenda; it wasn't John Wooden's. It's meant to provide structure, order, direction, purpose, focus. The coach responds to the athlete's undisciplined behavior by holding him accountable. ("The bench is a coach's best friend," Wooden taught me.) If the coach doesn't respond, he sends the message that accountability, among other things, is not part of the team's credo. That the wish to win is not supported by the way to win. To win the competition and to win the athlete's respect.

■ ■ ■

The words that pleased me most as a coach came from an opposing coach who had presented the state championship trophy to our high school basketball team. (We had defeated this coach's team in the tournament's semifinal round.) The coach then spoke to the audience as I was handed the championship ball. These words I heard clearly: "This is the best disciplined high school team I have ever seen." I didn't hear what else was said. It probably didn't matter.

E

Ego

As Ambrose Bierce's words made sport of egotists, he reminds us that, to an extent, we are all guilty of behaviors and desires that could so define us. And Agnes Repplier's words remind us that the egotist is a joyful—and appropriate—target for critics.

There are a number of operative words that are often used interchangeably and misused intermittently. Because of this, a great need of definition and clarification is in order, to enable me to properly express my thoughts on this topic.

■　■　■

Ego: (a) The self, particularly as distinguished from the outside world and other selves. (b) An exaggerated sense of self-importance. (c) An appropriate pride in oneself; self-esteem. *The American Heritage Dictionary* provides this sentence as an example: "A leader needs enough self-esteem to take a lot of criticism." (Review CRITICISM, section 2!)

We can see that the *ego* can serve us or enslave us.

A newborn is all *id*, which demands instant gratification. The baby slowly learns to delay gratification, getting more in touch with the realities of time, place, and circumstances that don't allow for needs to be met immediately. These reactions become part of a new subsystem of the personality—the *ego*. As time passes, the conflict between need and reality lessens. The individual develops skills that keep him connected with reality.

Or not. Some individuals don't make a very effective adjustment. I tell athletes and coaches that their "screaming needs" are getting in the way of their brains. When this happens, poor choices are made. The child is telling the adult what to do, based on feelings rather than a sensible assessment of reality.

The person who is grounded has an *ego*, according to definition (c), that allows him to represent himself with "an appropriate pride."

Egotist: Obviously, this term is not complimentary. It considers the inappropriate expression of the *ego*. An egotist is considered to be conceited and boastful; selfish and self-centered.

Pride: (a) A sense of one's own appropriate dignity and value; a respect for one's self. (b) Arrogant or disdainful behavior or treatment of others; haughtiness.

Once again, a word is defined by the way a person represents it. Pride has been called one of the seven deadly sins. It qualifies as such when a person overestimates himself by reason of self-love. When that kind of pride controls decision making, intelligence flies out the gymnasium window.

It is *not* a sin, I'd say, for us to have proper valuations of ourselves, a self-respect based on what is worthy and right—tempered by humility, of course.

Arrogance: An overbearing pride. Possessing or showing an excessive sense of self-worth or importance, based on the assumption of one's being superior to others people.

■ ■ ■

So there we are: either the beauty or the beast. Capable of both. Why all this? Because we are all complex individuals and if we are expected to lead and teach others, we'd better know what we're about and what those we want to follow us are about. The complexity goes beyond us to the very definition of us by others. So we're left with trusting self-definition. It should be accurate and honest.

■ ■ ■

Let me use a popular example of human complexity: Bob Knight. John Feinstein wrote one of a number of books about the man and the coach. Knight claimed he read a few pages of the Feinstein book about him and "put it down, sick and never read another word." (And there was also that ESPN movie, poorly done, in my estimation.) Since then, a book has been written *by* Knight *with* Bob Hammel.

Feinstein was quoted as saying (*USA Today*, March 5, 2002), "There are parts of (Knight) that are very admirable, and he's a great coach. To deny his greatness as a coach and to not see the good in him is ridiculous. To deny his flaws is ridiculous because he's got them all."

A paperback published in 2002 tried to capture the positives and negatives of Knight, and emphasized the contrasts by having front and back covers titled so as to reflect "the good side" and "the dark side."

What is a "dark side"? For my purpose here, it is the application of the worst of the definitions of all the terms listed above.

From his own book *Knight, My Story*, this report from Grandpa Knight and his superior understanding of his two-year-old grandson, whose mother and father attempt to discipline him by employing the "1-2-3" timeout approach:

> Naturally, he doesn't stop what he's doing that brought all this on in the first place, because "timeout" just makes him go sit down in a chair till he feels like getting up.
>
> That's where my new Texas word could come in handy. I can skip all the counting and say, "You little sum-bitch, you sit in that chair till I tell you to get up."

This public reporting of a family matter, this arbitrary evaluation and absurd application of language, was both arrogant and insensitive. (See above definitions.) It is the presentation of a man who, as Gore Vidal put it, "struts sitting down."

In contrast, Feinstein's book offered an anecdote about Knight's reminder to his players that they had all had a Thanksgiving dinner prepared by the team doctor's wife. Knight wanted to know if any of the players had communicated with the woman to offer thanks—or had sent flowers.

Wrote Feinstein, "No hands go up, and he says, 'This is what I'm saying. Because you guys are so absorbed and so selfish, you have no chance to play basketball well.'"

Feinstein continued, "To Knight, coaching isn't just screaming and yelling and cursing, and that little scene shows it so well, and it wasn't in the (ESPN) movie."

Do we deserve praise as adults when we help some people and hurt others? Well, each act is what it is, but the good and dark acts of a person don't indicate a healthy balance because the score turns out to be 50-50. Who keeps score? The persons who are beneficiaries of someone's goodness and those who are adversely affected by an inflated *ego*.

A good coaching credo to consider: First, do no harm. It might help to remind the coach to stay off his dark side.

■ ■ ■

Basketball coaches now posture on the sidelines. Dean Smith didn't, Wooden didn't, Coach K doesn't. (Knight usually doesn't—unless he's angry, which is more than occasionally.) Nor do many others. But many *do*. I witnessed an area high school coach this past season, pacing the sidelines with the ever-present towel over his shoulder (another John Thompson imitator). His facial expressions were affectations: displeasure, frustration, anger. His yelling at his players was a distraction to them. And how could he have been focused on the game when he was apparently so focused on himself? "Look at me," "Hear me," he seemed to be saying to onlookers. He was just another coach pedaling around on what Bellow calls an "egocycle."

■ ■ ■

An *ego* out of control encourages the arrogance of power. It's already been said that power without wisdom is tyranny. In many cases, the coach is being tyrannized by his own ego needs. (Refer to DESPOT, section 2.)

■ ■ ■

Every criticism that invokes the ego is not necessarily a valid one. Petty jealousies have led coaches to call fellow coaches arrogant so-and-so's or egomaniacs. It is not uncommon, based on my experience. I can think of a particular college coach with whom I've worked closely. He has been very successful and very much disliked by most opposing coaches. Every person I've met who knows him (and it's not tough to do if one cares to make the effort), likes him. That's not his goal. He's aggressive and competitive and successful. Threatening, in other words, to those who are insecure or inferior in their own judgment of themselves.

St. Louis Rams coach Mike Martz has been called "arrogant." Another successful, aggressive coach. (Refer to CRITICISM, section 2.)

■ ■ ■

Coaches and managers have pointed out peers on the other side of the competitive arena or field. "That arrogant S.O.B. thinks he's the greatest who ever lived," one fellow remarked. I remember it well, because I knew the guy who was being referred to. My response was "No, he doesn't."

Many people cover their insecurities by affecting an exaggerated sense of self. Especially those with position power, such as a coach. Overcompensation it's called. People who are observers or who are directly affected by such a coach don't have the time or inclination to get beneath the surface and understand. It's clear enough to them that personal power is not one of the coach's assets.

■ ■ ■

Coaches aren't effective leaders when they're following their underdeveloped ego.

Keep checking that "person in the glass" to see if the image has become bigger than the mirror.

Expectations

I have never hurried to meet a public expectation without leaving myself behind.
Frank Moore Colby,
The Colby Essays (1926)

What Observers Expect

Athletes aren't the only ones to be affected by expectations. Heavy is the head that wears the crown, and if coach is king, he knows additional weight put on his head by the expectations of others.

Parents, fans, and the media all have their own ideas about what a program or organization should do. They seem to share the same idea: win.

I'm thinking of a nice man who died not too long ago. He lived in Vermont and attended our high school basketball games regularly. Whenever we lost, he'd find me in the small community—at the post office usually—and ask me, "What's wrong with this team?" On certain occasions, his laser stare seemed to communicate a different message: "What's wrong with *you*?" When we won, he was silent. I looked forward to his silences, but I didn't expect them. Even after we won the state championship, he offered no comments. There are people who are bound tighter to the failures of others than to the successes.

Many fans and parents attending events wish to be gratified, to see their neighbors' sons and daughters be successful. To have their own children show their "stuff."

I expected my teams to play the game the way they were taught. I couldn't be effective by concerning myself with what others expected. It wouldn't be fair to the athletes, because they would then become the victims of my caving in to outside pressure.

What the Coach Expects

People often acknowledge that students or athletes rise to the expectations of their teacher or coach. They should remember that people will also sink to the low level someone else theoretically determines for them. Or stagnate because of a limited expectation. Whatever the case, the athlete will be greatly affected by his coach's expectations.

■ ■ ■

After Muhammad Ali won the gold medal at the 1960 Olympics, he said he went immediately to visit one of his teachers at her classroom. "Remember when you said I would never be nuthin'?" Ali (Clay, at the time) asked. It was a rhetorical question.

Ali's teacher was wrong on two counts: one, accuracy of judgment; two, the very expression of it—because it was not meant to be a motivational tactic.

The "greatest" can rise above the limited expectations of their teachers and coaches. But they are, by far, the exceptions to the rule. And if considering the use of "you ain't gonna be nuthin'" as a provocative motivational challenge, first recall the goose and the gander tale, so as to be reminded that what might make one athlete, might just as easily break another.

■ ■ ■

To be considered:

- All research supports the belief that a coach's expectations will influence his treatment of individual athletes. His behavior toward the individual will often differ according to his evaluation of the athlete's ability.
- The coach's manner of treatment for each athlete will affect the athlete's performance, his ability to learn, and his rate of learning.
- The coach's different manner of communicating with athletes of differing ability will indicate to them his view of their competence. The indication will affect the athlete's self-concept, motivation, and self-trust, which will all impact on performance. The result will be that the athletes who are evaluated to be superior and communicated with accordingly will behave and perform in such a way as to reinforce the coach's positive expectation.
- The same will be true of those who are thought to be inferior performers and for whom the coach has limited or negative expectations.

■ ■ ■

A coach's initial judgment of an athlete may be accurate or inaccurate. It depends upon his instrument of measure: the opinions of others, film from the athlete's past, pressure from parents or community, or whatever personal predispositions and biases the coach may have. Mistakes will be made.

I own up to the dubious distinction of cutting a tall, ungainly young basketball player the first time he tried out for my team. He went on to break the rebounding record at NYU, previously held by NBA player

Happy Hairston. My team captain had implored me to keep the young man. I told him that when he could teach him to chew gum and walk at the same time, I would consider it. Oops.

What the Athlete Expects

The athlete should expect what he's *taught* to expect by good coaches: that he will give his best effort whenever he competes. Mentally and physically. That he will focus on his performance goals, not the expectations of others, focusing on executing the task of the moment, bringing a relaxed intensity and a relentless spirit to the competition. Responding to adverse situations with intelligence. Thinking and acting impeccably.

Item: Philadelphia third baseman Scott Rolen, amid criticism and trade talks, before he eventually went to St. Louis (*USA Today*, July 10, 2002): "If my name is in the lineup, it's my job to go out and play to the best of my ability. If I haven't measured up to expectations, I'm not going to make excuses. I do have emotions and feelings. But when you get knocked down a bit, you have to pick yourself back up."

Songwriter Ira Gershwin would say, "Who could ask for anything more?" There will always be those who could. But they shouldn't matter.

Front-Runner
(Review CONSISTENCY*, section 3)

. . . A corkhead who bobs to the convenient surface.
Saul Bellow,
writer

Right to the point: Many athletes have complained to me about their coaches or managers. The complaints are sometimes valid, sometimes not. The predominant valid issues are (a) the coach or manager doesn't ever communicate; or (b) the coach or manager only communicates to those athletes who are performing well.

A front-running coach, the athletes say, is "all over me when I'm kicking butt, but when I'm scuffling, he avoids me like the plague." And that, of course, is when the athlete most needs to be communicated with. Reassured, helped, straightened out, put at ease—*coached.*

The front-runner drapes himself around those who are succeeding, so as to share the glory. He wishes to be seen in the spotlight of the athlete's achievement, credit to them inferred.

The front-running coach does not want responsibility for the athlete's failures. No arm draping in these circumstances; finger pointing, perhaps, or just avoidance. Disassociation. And some resentment.

It certainly is easier to like someone who's doing everything we ask than those who aren't. But athletes are usually not getting it done, not because they are resistant to what we teach, but because they are unable sometimes—or often—to understand what we want or, if they do understand, to integrate it into action.

Those are the athletes we should be most attentive to. The others seem to be taking care of business. It isn't a question of oiling a "squeaky wheel"; it is a case of fixing a wheel that has fallen off. That's what coaches do: understand, teach, help the athlete to fix himself. Pay attention to the wobbly wheel, in other words.

Years ago, when I was working with the Oakland Athletics, I walked passed pitcher Juaquin Andujar during a spring training practice session, headed for a player who had asked to speak with me. "Hey!" he shouted after me. "You no talk to me?"

"I don't have to talk with you," I replied. "You're doing fine."

"You no even say, 'Hello'?" he responded with a big smile.

"Hello, Juaquin," I shouted, returning the smile (reminded that talking *with* may not be necessary, but talking *to* is what good communicators should always do).

G

Game Face

Prepare a face to meet a face.
T. S. Eliot,
poet

During a postgame television interview, Bob Knight claimed he never could understand what a game face was. Perhaps because he sleeps with it and eats with it—only one face. His facial contortions during the interview—and his verbal responses, as well—were reactions to just another reporter's question that irritated him more than he already had been. If Knight doesn't know what a game face is, every other coach I've talked with about the subject seems to.

Essentially, a facial expression is a form of communication. Body language conveys a message and the athlete's face is part of the body. To begin with, it can convey whether the athlete is prepared and intensely focused on task and has a seriousness of purpose. To end with, it is an opportunity to get an edge if the opponent is faint of heart and susceptible to intimidation. Trust me, many are.

The athlete's posture should be strong, giving off signals of aggressiveness and invulnerability. The face should send the same signals. I tell athletes that "the look" is part of his possible edge. The look also establishes an attitude: a "this face in your face" attitude.

I'm not talking about some foolish affectation here, just a look that shows the athlete means business. He's prepared and ready to go throughout the competition—until his performance is over.

Over! During the final minute or so of a game our women's basketball team was winning, en route to the Vermont State Championship, we had our point guard on the foul line taking a free throw. Two of our players were positioned back on the defensive foul line. Everyone knew there wasn't enough time left for the opponents to have a chance to win the game—and the championship. This included the two defensive players, who were grinning and laughing at and with each other as they stood on the opponents' foul line.

I shouted one of their names and they both turned toward me. I just had to stare at them. They got the message and put their faces back on.

That is the way they were taught to play the game, but the anticipation of victory made them celebrate prematurely. Inappropriately. Such a "letting down" can be dangerous in competition. It wasn't in this context, but if consistency is such a valued aspect of a coach's program for athletes, he should always behave accordingly. A consistent game face should be part of the athlete's competition agenda.

■ ■ ■

On one occasion during an Instructional League baseball game in Scottsdale, Arizona, a pitcher struggled mightily during his performance. He had a particularly arduous and ineffective inning, which bothered him immensely. This I knew. When the inning was over and he walked off the mound, he had a cavalier grin on his face. The message he was sending to anyone watching was, "I don't care. It doesn't bother me."

He cared, and we both knew it. He hurt. He protected his feelings with this weak display of an "I'm-not-a-competitor" face. I was incensed and approached him in the dugout, letting him know in no uncertain terms about what he'd done and why he'd done it.

After the game, we had a less animated discussion of what a facial expression reveals—and should reveal. He understood his weakness; he was contrite. He later became known as "a bulldog," pitching many years in the major leagues. He retired recently, his scowl still intact.

■ ■ ■

I've been on buses after losses. At the amateur and professional levels. One example I observed directly was of a minor league manager who wouldn't allow anyone to talk after a loss. Absurd. The game is over. There shouldn't be a celebration, but some healthy perspective is missing from a coach who doesn't allow quiet communication between players.

The effective managers I've known of have gone through the bus and made contact with players, or sat down next to one who needed some teaching or consoling. There were no Mardi Gras faces evident, but no funereal looks either.

A letter I received from a parent told of a coach who "busted" the entire team on a high school baseball team because "he caught one of them smiling after a loss." (This, of course, is punishment for losing.) I wonder if the coach makes bed checks for game faces. A good thing taken to an extreme becomes a bad thing.

■ ■ ■

When we compete, we should act like competitors. Coaches should teach their players that acting like a warrior can encourage warrior-like behavior. A warrior's face will reflect his heart. An infantry? charge into battle wearing a smile.

When I was coaching, my own game face was very evi wife. Early in our marriage, before attending games, she'd sä will you recognize me?" I always did—after the game was o' didn't recognize anything but the game before and during. N a matter of face as of focus. This I explained to her satisfaction.

■ ■ ■

Item: Lenny Wilkens, former coach of the Toronto Raptors, had this to say about his star player, Vince Carter (*The Sporting News*, January 28, 2002): "the mental toughness is starting to happen. You'll see sometimes he comes out and he's ready to go. He's not smiling at everybody, and that's what I like, when I see that."

Gamers

I've always believed that the desire must come from within, not as a result of being driven by coaches or parents.
Dawn Fraser,
swimmer, winner of three Olympic Gold Medals

Elbow-grease is the best polish.
English Proverb

The "gamers," as I've defined them, are those athletes who are driven by internal motivation to be the best they can be. They are very often not the most talented athletes. Most often, perhaps. Speaking for myself, I know that if I didn't *always* give my best effort I would either embarrass myself or not be able to get playing time. My skill was not great enough to mask a lack of intense effort.

Many precocious talents are able to do just that. They're so much better than those they compete against that it's easy for them to get away with a limited effort. Until the playing field levels. Then they have a difficult time of it, because they have not developed the ability to go all out all the time. This has been very much in evidence to me in my work with professional athletes.

So too is it evident that the "blue-collar guys," the "down-and-dirty guys" are gamers by that necessity to survive. By the instinct and drive to survive. A precocious athlete doesn't think about survival until "it hits the fan"—eventually. A David Eckstein, a Joe McEwing—even à Pete Rose is ducking the fan at an early age. They expend all their energy;

attentiveness is always there. They compete aggressively. They can't ,ord to do otherwise. They're gamers.

When Pete Rose first became the manager of the Cincinnati Reds, he gathered his team and told them a story, the theme of which qualifies him as "being a gamer."

The story was about a major league baseball game. One team was losing 7-0. Two men were out in the ninth inning. No one was on base. The batter hit a comebacker to the pitcher. Easy out. But the batter-runner busted his butt, going hard down the first base line. The pitcher who'd fielded the ball had nonchalantly turned to make an easy throw to first, presuming the runner to be going at a leisurely pace. Surprised by the runner's proximity to the base, the pitcher then hurried his throw. It was a bad throw, past the first baseman. The runner was safe.

The team then went on to score eight runs and win the game, 8-7. True story, said Rose to his players. He ought to know. He was the runner who hit the comebacker. That's a gamer, in the truest sense of the word. All out, all the time.

■ ■ ■

Many athletes call themselves gamers, using it as an excuse for not being effective in practice. This can result from lack of interest, lack of motivation, or blatant laziness. I consider all to be indicative of a lack of self-discipline. I adhere to the principle that an unprepared athlete is prepared to fail. Coaches who accept limited effort in practice from self-proclaimed gamers are supporting a weak assumption and creating a double standard.

The gamer, as Dawn Fraser's words in the epigraph suggest, is one who rises to the occasion because he or she is *self-motivated. And* motivated by competition, which the gamer sees as a challenge, not a threat. This attitude that brings performance up when the challenge is greatest—the stakes are highest.

Not every athlete is an elite Olympian, however. Many must be externally motivated by their coach. Yet I have seen gamers develop from slackers and worriers. That's what education can do, and the coach is an educator.

Being a gamer is not about talent; it's about attitude. Given the differences between a young person with limited talent and one with exceptional talent, survival of the fittest will force the lesser talent, if he or she aspires to compete, to bring an "A Game" to the arena every time. Limited as the talent is, he gives everything he has, done the right way. And, it should be noted, great talent and great attitude are not mutually exclusive.

Any athlete who doesn't know how to how to keep his elbows greased at all times requires instruction from the coach.

Going against the Grain

Genius, in truth, means little more than the faculty of perceiving in an unhabitual way.
William James,
The Principles of Psychology

(Redskins Coach Steve Spurrier) is never afraid to do what he believes will work, even though others tell him it won't. He has strong convictions.
Dan Henning,
offensive coordinator, Carolina Panthers

NFL center Jeff Mitchell, who played for Steve Spurrier at the University of Florida, offered his view before his former coach's first season in the NFL. "Steve being Steve, he's come into the league and hasn't asked anybody how to do it. He's doing it his way."

Coaches who wish to be creative and independent thinkers must regularly be willing to challenge conventional wisdom, the opinions of others. Immanuel Kant was emphatic on the subject. "Enlightenment is humanity's departure from its self-imposed immaturity. This immaturity is self-imposed when its cause is not lack of intelligence but a failure of courage to think without someone else's guidance. Dare to know!"

Coaches should not be governed by the tyranny of custom. They should adopt an attitude of "enlightened perversity." The operative term is *enlightened*. It's easy to just be perverse, that is, contrary, perhaps stubborn, even cranky. The enlightened coach is perverse in that he does not cater to custom, doing things "his way"—and *knowing why* he's doing them that way. (See GUT FEELING, section 2.)

Someone who goes against the grain for the sole purpose of establishing an identity as an "independent individual" with his peers (or anyone else, for that matter) is behaving self-consciously. He's being controlled by what he wants others to see, rather than what he wants to do. He's more interested in the grain, not the going.

Nor does going against the grain mean doing things differently for the sake of the difference. It doesn't mean being a leaf in the wind of coaching's fads and follies. Basketball players now huddle together regularly before free throws. They didn't always. Dean Smith's North Carolina teams began this practice. What was unusual became usual. That's but one small example.

A coach should have the willingness to take risks—to not always play "by the book"—this book included. The world's best chefs have learned what ingredients should be included in their dishes, but they become the best when they outgrow the cookbooks. I say they have "touch." A little of this, a little of that. People who have a touch pay attention. They are open; they are learners; they are creative experimenters. They take risks.

■ ■ ■

Just as there are those who affect an independent posture for the sake of appearances, there are those who will never have the courage required for independent thought for the very same sake. Such coaches "dare not kill themselves for fear of what the neighbors will say" (Cycil Connelly, *The Unjust Grave*). (See NICE PERSON*, section 2.)

Item: Sportswriter Jo Haakenson's assessment of Mike Scioscia after two years as the manager of the California Angels: "He isn't afraid to be unconventional."

■ ■ ■

Item: From *The Sporting News*, June 24, 2002: Detroit Red Wings player, Igor Larionov speaking of retiring coach Scotty Bowman, winner of ten Stanley Cups, said, "He was a genius." Teammate Mathieu Dandenault elaborated. "I'll remember Scotty for what he was, a great thinker and he always tried to stay ahead of the game. . . . *He's got his own ways, and that's why he's the best.*" (Italics are mine.)

Gut Feeling

*(Intuition is) the supra-logic that cuts out all routine processes of
thought and leaps straight from problem to answer.*
Robert Graves,
poet

Gut feelings are real. They are intuitive responses to something a person "knows" but doesn't really know he knows.

Do you know what I'm saying? An intuitive understanding comes from a lower level of consciousness. It's "down there"—an understanding that you haven't touched but have felt. The gut feeling is telling the coach to match this particular wrestler against that particular opponent. To make this particular substitution during a game or that particular lineup change. Or to run this play at this time.

It isn't playing Pin the Tail on the Donkey. There's no blindfold; it's just a little dark down there in the gut. But intuition can be led out of the darkness by a guiding light: self-trust.

Major league manager Tony LaRussa would say to me, "I just have that gut feeling," when a rational explanation was not at the ready to support some strategy he was going to employ or decision he wanted to make. It often went "against the grain."

Because the word *feeling* seems to identify the source, the term is often misunderstood. There is a voice within that says this approach/decision is the right one. It isn't at the front of our brain, but we sense it in our depths.

It's not just a hunch or guess. It may not be the most rational answer to an issue, but it seems, somehow, to be the most reasonable. Robert Graves wrote that "'reasonable' has warm connotations; 'rational' has coldly inhuman ones." Perhaps he disclaimed rationality a bit too much, but the warmth he mentions comes from the blood, sending us a message to do what our heart is telling us to do. Or our gut.

Yes, a gut feeling has some rational basis. It's a soft voice exerting influence over a louder voice. Most often, it can be trusted. If this hasn't been the reader's experience, he should stop listening to it.

Athletes can have gut feelings also. But a performer's *ad lib* during competition may wrench the gut of the coach, who might then wrench the athlete out of the game or event.

A coach can follow his deeper intuition; an athlete should follow his surface instincts.

Honesty

(See TRUST, section 2)

> *You can never be dishonest or lie to a player or try to give him anything less than the squarest deal possible. Try to lie and you lose the team. That means, you say something then turn around and do something else.*
> **Paul Brown,**
> NFL coach, Hall of Famer

Paul Brown was a self-proclaimed "tough ass." No one argued with the description. But he understood very well that part of an athlete's education is to be honest with himself and to be honest with his coach. And, that there must be reciprocity for this to happen.

We tend, as people, to respond in kind. If I perceive someone as being a "straight-shooter," my own aim to be honest is encouraged. Every teacher or coach I ever had was clearly identified by me as being either truthful or untruthful. Not right or wrong, but honest or dishonest in intent. I never have to agree with everything a person says, but I certainly have to trust the speaker believes what he or she is saying to me.

It's not that hard to know whether a person you're around all the time is authentic in this regard. Athletes whom I speak to for the first time hear a standard introduction from me: "If I'm full of it, you'll be the first to know it." We don't fool them, though we may fool ourselves.

Credibility is the coach's most important asset. It is taken from him if he is discovered to be dishonest.

Item: An article that presented itself as a "manager analysis" (*Sports Illustrated*, February 18, 2002) praised the job Mike Scioscia had done in his first two years as the leader of the Anaheim Angels. It referred to his "open-door policy and honest approach." His players appreciated it—and responded to it.

■ ■ ■

An athlete's number one "security blanket" has been represented to me over the years by the same phrase, repeated often: "I just want to know where I stand." For a variety of reasons, many coaches and managers have a difficult time providing that truth for the athletes. If they don't avoid the issue, they seem to make it worse by making statements that are not accurate or making promises they can't keep.

As noted elsewhere, "situational truths" are remarks made that include qualifying language and convey the meaning of possibility or probability, not of certainty. For example, when telling players what their role on the team "is"—the coach uses language such as:

At this time . . .
Right now . . .
It appears as if . . .
If everything remains the same (does it ever?) . . .

■ ■ ■

Novelist Penelope Fitzgerald has written that truth ensures trust, not victory. Well, I may not win a game because of it, but I always win my "self" and, most often, the athletes I'm coaching.

Coaches must give honesty to get it. Athletes need to be trustful and trustworthy—and they learn to (or not to) by what they hear and see. You don't get honesty by demanding it. Here, I ask the reader to forgive my use of personal references, but they surely help to support and emphasize a few specific points that are important to make.

Brian Graham was a player in the Oakland organization in the 1980s, during my tenure with the As. He is currently the director of player personnel for the Pittsburgh Pirates. Speaking to the media on the subject of honesty, Brian referred to me as "probably the most blatantly honest, tough baseball guy I've met in my twenty years in the game." He went on, "And yet everybody respects him. He can tell you some things that really hurt your feelings. But when you look back two days later and put your feelings aside, you realize he's right."

Tim Belcher pitched in the major leagues for fifteen years. He now works for the Cleveland Indians as a special assistant to the general manager. He told a writer, "When you talk to Harv, you get the truth from him, whether you like it or not."

Pitcher Al Leiter, when asked about my approach, has said, "Most pro athletes don't want to hear the truth about themselves. . . ." Los Angeles pitcher Kevin Brown summed up the rest of what Leiter had to say with a succinct statement: "Harvey doesn't let you fool yourself."

The points emphasized by the preceding references are:

- Honesty can seem "blatant" to the person to whom it is being directed. "Blatant: Totally or offensively conspicuous." So says *The American Heritage Dictionary*. As Leiter suggests, many people do not appreciate hearing the truth, especially when it is about themselves or their behavior.

- Feelings can be hurt by what Iris Murdoch called "the hard idea of truth."
- I'm not usually interested in the listener's feelings, because they change after the moment of impact, when he realizes that the speaker's intention is to help rather than hurt.
- These feelings are salved when the "honest" person's aforementioned intent is wrapped in a message that is appropriate and accurate. In other words, a valid truth.
- Self-deception is easily achieved. Self-enlightenment is difficult, but well worth the effort—on the part of instructor and student of that self. The instructor—the coach—must be relentless in its pursuit.

■ ■ ■

Yet I must qualify and clarify a bit: It is important to be discriminating, to know to whom you speak. Brian Graham could handle the style I used when being honest to him. So could Al Leiter, Tim Belcher, and Kevin Brown. Not every athlete can handle particular truths or particular styles used to present them. I recall a major leaguer coming to me disgruntled with our team's new manager—a smokescreen for his unhappiness at the new role the manager had assigned him. The player made five points, all rationalizations and inaccuracies, so far as I was concerned. I refuted them one at a time. He never spoke to me again. Some athletes don't covet honesty. They want unconditional agreement with whatever they believe—or wish to.

Others are just extremely sensitive for their own good, though they know what's good for them. When speaking with them I soften my instruction and criticism, sometimes conveying a message that, using John Banville's words, is "slightly out of true." There is a readiness process some people must go through before they can effectively deal with hard truths about themselves or their actions. A defensive person quickly becomes deaf. He must learn to hear something before he can hear everything.

I would never do to these overly sensitive types what I did with the Grahams and Belchers, because it would break them. The Grahams and Belchers are provoked by truths, as uncomfortable as they may be initially. They get past the discomfort. They appreciate whatever has merit—whatever is honest and true. And they then integrate their understanding into behavior. Into *action* on the field of competition.

Athletes are pragmatic. What works is true. The coach's job is to know what works. When "honesty" is good information, when it is expressed in a tone that allows the athlete to hear it, and when it is appropriately timed—it will work. For both sender and receiver.

Intimidation

If you can't bite, don't show your teeth.
Yiddish Proverb

Athletes have their own proverb: "If you can't walk the walk, don't talk the talk." Even words spoken in the third century B.C. allude to the point: "A dog is not considered good because of his barking."

But as clever as all these words may be, they miss the bull's-eye on my "intimidation target."

■ ■ ■

What *does not* qualify as intimidation as it is to be received:

In-your-face stares
Trash talk (all varieties)
Splendid uniforms
Intricate warm-up drills
Size/Skill
Media predictions
History

What *does* qualify as intimidation as it is to be applied:

Body language that exudes confidence and courage
Enthusiastic language that reinforces teammates
Uniforms that match
Purposeful preparation
Size/Skill
Tradition (of winning way)
Appropriate focus
Aggressiveness
Relentlessness
Intelligence
Poise
Mental toughness

■ ■ ■

If a coach sets out to intimidate by having his athletes act in ways that are meant to influence the opponents, he's focused on the other team, rather than his own. He's focusing on an end that requires responses from people other than his own athletes. He addresses possible ends, rather than required means. The behaviors of his athletes most often will be self-conscious (often ridiculous, as I've witnessed them) and misguided posturing.

The goal for a coach is to have his athletes do all the things that make *them* effective, aggressive, persistent competitors. That *sends* the message of intimidation—if the opposition is susceptible. They *receive* and interpret the message.

Whether the other team finds it meaningless or meaningful, the coach concerns himself only with his athletes' *consistent* delivery of the message—*to all opponents*. So however the receivers may feel about it, the senders' confidence will come from their own actions.

■ ■ ■

Former major league pitcher Jim Abbott said his California Angels teams noticed the way the Oakland As of the late 1980s and early 1990s carried themselves. "We didn't get the feeling we were going to beat them. And we usually didn't."

■ ■ ■

Note: I never allowed my basketball teams to watch the opposing team warm up. I told them I would watch for tendencies and so on. (Left-handed shooters, weak outside shots, etc.) They would take care of their own preparation. I wanted to instill in them the idea that the opponent didn't matter to them. Their own approach is what mattered. If opponents were affected/distracted by that tendency of ours, so much the better.

■ ■ ■

In BODY LANGUAGE, section 3, I mention an incident about my reaction to two of my high school players. They were smiling on the court as the clock ticked down in a state championship basketball game. I wasn't happy. Not just because that might be construed as "showing up" the opponents, but because it was counter to seriousness of purpose we wished to instill in our players. A purpose that doesn't end until outs are made, a whistle blows, or a finish line is crossed.

And, albeit secondarily, we wanted to project that sense to the other team's players—if they cared to notice. As Jim Abbott's comments indicate, many do.

■ ■ ■

But in the final analysis, teams intimidate most by the way they compete. They compete by preparing. A team that prepares to be intimidating can validate itself only by enacting all of the mental and physical *behaviors* that will give it the edge it seeks in competition.

J

Journalists (Media)

Journalism—an ability to meet the challenge of filling the space.
Rebecca West,
New York Herald Tribune

Four hostile newspapers are more to be feared than a thousand bayonets.
Napoleon I,
Maxims

The less said, the better. A double meaning.

I've been a journalist. I have also been a coach. I understand the responsibility of both. My allegiance comes down on the side of the coach. Why? Because I've seen more journalists take advantage of coaches (and athletes) than I've seen coaches take advantage of journalists. That simple.

I recognize the coach's responsibility to deal with the print media—and with the radio and television interviewer. But the responsibility is not one that should compel him to reveal matters that are privy to staff and athletes. He should be cautious in his remarks and not allow his emotions after a game to accommodate the desire of the media folk. That desire is, of course, to hear some provocative remarks come out of the coach's mouth.

Historian Daniel J. Boorstin wrote, "There was a time when the reader of an unexciting newspaper would remark, 'How dull the world is today!' Nowadays he says, 'What a dull newspaper!'" Journalists don't want dull stories. Coaches can make them more interesting for the reader and more damaging for himself and his team. Beware.

I counsel athletes to give standard responses to leading questions. To talk about observable behavior, not internal agendas—their feelings, their distractions, their "worries."

I advise coaches and managers to force the interviewer to ask specific questions, rather than vague, broad questions that will capitalize on the responder's tendency to talk himself into a place he doesn't want to be.

The specific question allows the interviewee to then say, "I don't care to respond to that."

As a coach, I've had a journalist try to put answers in my mouth. This is done frequently by poor interviewers who speak for five minutes then ask, "Is that right." If the coach responds with, "Yes," the journalist's remarks are wrapped in quotation marks and attributed to the coach.

I remember saying to such a journalist, "Are you *asking* me or *telling* me?" after he interpreted a decision I had made during a game in a negative manner, then begged for confirmation. A fellow named Baltasar Gracian wrote, "Evil report carries farther than any applause." That was in 1647! It still applies, unfortunately.

■ ■ ■

Caveat for coaches: Do not use the newspapers as a forum for criticizing one of your athletes. You will have a rapt audience as you speak—and a "ripped" athlete the next day. Coach through direct communication with the athletes, not through the media. Let the athlete hear it first, at least.

■ ■ ■

Finally, I remember our team bus getting into an accident on the way home from a basketball game on Long Island. A speeding car hit us on the driver's side as we moved through an intersection. I was thrown out of my seat, with only minor damage done to my leg. The driver was in shock. The players were stunned. The media was on the scene, seemingly, in no time.

But first there was time enough for me to talk with the players. One of them, a fellow who was known in school as a very difficult young man, was the first to be confronted by the eager young reporter.

"Tell me what happened," he said to the player, notebook and pencil poised. The large young man folded his arms across his chest and replied, "No comment." A proud look washed across his face as he turned to look at me.

■ ■ ■

As I remarked at the top of these pages—and on that bus—the less said, the better.

K

Knowing vs. Doing

A wise man knows that he has only one enemy—himself. This is an enemy difficult to ignore and full of cunning. It assails one with doubts and fear. It always seeks to loosen and lead one away from one's goal It is an enemy never to be forgotten but constantly outwitted.
Ben Hecht,
playwright

(He) combined deeds and insight into a decisive intervention.
Iain Pears,
The Dream of Scipio

The major battle I've had to address with coaches and managers—and athletes—is the battle fought daily between what a person knows he should do and what he actually does. It is a constant internal warring that goes on between people's conflicting impulses.

The battle waged is between certainty and doubt, trust and distrust, confidence and insecurity, energy and slothfulness, understanding and ego need, strength and weakness, compassion and insensitivity.

Any of those battles sound familiar?

Courage is a key. (Review COURAGE*, section 2.) I always tell people, "All I want from you is intelligence and courage. But if you can only give me one of those, what do you think I'd want?"

The answer is courage. We're smart enough to know what's right and what's not. We're not always brave enough to do it. My purpose in asking the question is to establish the value of courage, not to discount the value of intelligence. My focus is on a person's need to have the courage of his conviction: to act out what he knows or believes to be true.

■ ■ ■

The coach must take control. Of what? First and foremost, control of his thoughts. Thinking is inevitable. Right thinking is invaluable. Right thinking is an expression of a coach's intelligence, as opposed to his anxiety or frustration or uncertainty. Intelligence will short-circuit the trouble. Thinking cannot be stopped; it can be changed. Intelligent thought is blood for the brain.

The coach should be aware of what thoughts are being processed when there is difficulty during competition. He can make necessary adjustments by applying intelligent thought. Appropriate thinking will save him; uncontrolled thinking will destroy him. Is what he is thinking relevant to the circumstance? Is it based on false perception? Fear? Time must be taken to determine these answers and get the right information to the muscles. In the contest between a coach's emotionality and his rationality, intelligent reasoning should always be the victor.

■ ■ ■

When a coach is on "cruise control," he is still thinking. But it is a kind of automatic process, during which he focuses intently on the task. This process indicates a task-oriented thought process—so natural that the coach may have no heightened sense of it. Because he is not thinking about thinking. He is thinking about the competition.

But, as noted, a coach usually becomes aware of his thinking when trouble arises. When his thoughts are based on irrelevancies (e.g., consequences), he is not using his intelligence. When his thoughts focus on himself (e.g., "What will I say to the media?"), he is not using his intelligence. They are counterproductive thoughts. Distracting thoughts. The *wrong* thoughts. And they *are the thoughts* that can creep into a coach's mind; I have heard them expressed to me after the battle was won—or lost.

■ ■ ■

All research indicates that people's behavior is influenced by what they are thinking. When thinking is directed internally on the coach's feelings and self-interest, his tension level will increase. Anxiety or fear is often the result. He may think about his discomfort or any number of negative triggers ("This is a bad day" or "We can't get a break"). Behavior will be directed by these thoughts. The problem will be exacerbated, rather than alleviated. The coaching performance will suffer, as will the coach.

By employing his intelligence, the coach can direct his thoughts to his task, thereby giving himself a chance to enact the appropriate behavior during competition. Intelligent thoughts are the medicine—the cure. Emotional thinking is the poison.

The coach who thinks about what the situation requires, rather than what he requires, "coaches smart," rather than "stupid." (Coaching "scared" inevitably becomes coaching "dumb.") Remember Mark Twain said that there is very little difference between man and other animals—and usually man forfeits the difference? He was talking about man's brain. A coach forfeits the difference when he thinks in any way but an intelligent way. Too often, his left brain takes a nap; it must always be on duty.

Every coach is smart enough to know the difference between his best thoughts and his worst. By continually disciplining his mind, he'll be able to help himself out of whatever trouble may arise. The results may not always go his way, but his thoughts will. When they do, the coach provides himself, during the high-wire act of competition, with what novelist Lawrence Durrell called "the safety net of logic and reason."

■ ■ ■

If thoughts are "rays of power," as novelist Iris Murdoch suggested, intelligent thought will provide power for the *coach*; unreasoned thought will provide power for the *circumstance* he is facing. The ultimate power is in the doing. Those whose actions are based on appropriate thinking patterns have the ultimate power.

I call some people "hopers." They say things to me such as "I hope it will work out." My response is "What's 'it'?" "It" won't work things out for you; you are responsible to work them out. These people can't make a decision, so they hope matters will solve themselves. Coaches who sit, watch, and allow circumstance to gain control over them and their predicament are most often doomed to fail.

A college coach once said to me, "Do something, Dorfman, even if it's wrong." It was good advice. The problem is not always in having a weak thought, it's in having a weak constitution.

Darrin Straus said it very well (in *The Real McCoy*): "Indecision is the cage his hope is flying against." We must *act decisively* on what we know is right. As I frequently remind the people I communicate with, "If you want to hear the song, you don't stand around reading the sheet music. You play the tune—now, and up-tempo."

■ ■ ■

Some things the coach should remember, so as to encourage and provoke him to do what he knows:

- Often the thought process is hardly discernible, because focus is both narrow and concentrated, whereas the emotional signals are like fire engines sounding.
- It is important that he catch himself when he agrees with someone or something while really thinking the contrary.
- When difficulty arises, an intelligent response will arrest it, whereas an emotional response will avoid it, exacerbate it, and

prolong it—and lead him to act in direct contrast to what he'd wished to do. It's helpful to use simple keys (phrases) to provoke right action, based on right thinking.

- It's essential to be determined to "stop the bleeding" by gathering and employing thoughts directed to how he wants to go about doing something, rather than giving in to highly improbable or imagined consequences.
- The most essential tool is courage—having the courage of one's convictions; then, acting upon those convictions.

■ ■ ■

It's not about knowing what's right; it *is* about *doing* what's right. Frequently seen Nike ads annoy me because they tell people, "Just do it." The word "just" implies a simple task. It isn't simple; it's necessary though.

L

Labels

To generalize is to be an Idiot. To Particularize is the Alone
Distinction of Merit.
William Blake,
poet

I feel there is more to be learned by finding out what's going on in a
player's mind than by calling him a "bonehead" or "idiot."
Davey Johnson,
major league manager

Those were strong words expressed by Blake. But he understood the danger of applying general remarks to particular circumstances—or people. It's convenient but without merit. General opinions—labels—cannot be and should not be trusted.

A map is not the territory itself; a label is not the person.

An aura of other people's invention surrounds an athlete who is identified with a sweeping generalization. The invention often is the creation of the athlete's coach, who has decided to "put the athlete in a box" with a label on it. "Lazy." "Bad attitude." "Can't produce when it counts."

Perhaps the athlete's *behaviors* in the past have reflected laziness or a poor attitude or tension in tough spots. But a person can learn to change a behavior. Especially if he has a concerned and effective teacher. A label maker has a full-time job making judgments and so has no time left to help the person make the necessary changes.

Coaches are responsible for teaching their athletes and helping them to develop in every possible way—including the development of more acceptable and effective behaviors. The ease with which labels are attached to athletes create the greater ease of putting all the responsibility for change on the athlete. Or, it presumes no change is possible: "He *is* what he is."

The word is not the fact. Identify what a player *does*, rather than what you think he or she *is*. Focus on behaviors, not the person. It's convenient to attach something like "She's a wimp" or "He's gutless." The generalization offers no all-inclusive support or explanation. Does the coach know the athlete? Does he understand the motives behind the behavior? The easiest way to avoid the effort of knowing and understanding is to arbitrarily attach a label.

■　■　■

Here are some contrasting evaluation statements/responses:

1. Personal Label: "This kid's a choker."
   Coach's follow-up response is to treat the athlete accordingly.
2. Sweeping Generalization: "This kid can't take the heat."
   Coach's follow-up response is to treat the athlete accordingly.
3. Assessment of Behavior: "This kid didn't perform effectively when _____." (Fill in the *situation*.)
   Coach's follow-up behavior is to discuss with the athlete the behavior and to help him/her recognize the inhibitors. Then to determine strategies that can be applied to the next performance, working on these approaches during practice sessions.

The head coach and the assistant coaches should always be careful of the all-too-human tendency to attach a broad label to a person's specific action. Discussions of athletes that include that kind of evaluative language rarely serve the best interests of the staff and the team. They never serve the athlete fairly.

■　■　■

When an athlete acts in a particular way once, is he going to act that way forever? Mark Twain knew about the human tendency to take a particular experience and apply it without further thought to all future experiences. In the coach's case, it's the experience of seeing an athlete fail and assuming he will continue to fail. As noted, the label encourages the coach to avoid responsibility for that failure, attaching "blame" or "fault" with the label—and disregarding the possibility that a person may act differently in different circumstances.

Twain believed we sometimes behaved more like animals than people. He noted the human tendency to generalize:

> We should be careful to get out of an experience only the wisdom that is in it—and stop there; lest we be like the cat that sits down on a hot stove lid. She will never sit down on a hot stove lid again, and that is well; but also she will never sit down on a cold one anymore.

■　■　■

Coaches should:

- Recognize that the focus should be on the *behavior*, not on trying to *define the person* with an all-inclusive label.
- Make an attempt to understand the mental factors that dictated whatever behavior the coach would like to see the athlete change.
- Acknowledge that people can change.
- Take the responsibility of helping the athlete to understand what mental inhibitors get in the way of effective performance.
- Help the athlete to make changes, rather than prematurely "giving up" on him.
- Recognize that a person acts in different ways, according to the circumstance in which he finds himself.
- Create roles for an athlete that he is more likely to be successful in, accommodating his situational abilities.

■ ■ ■

People should not trap athletes with labels. They end up in the trap themselves. Coaches can be most effective by addressing specifics, instead of mouthing generalities. As semanticist Wendell Johnson said, "To a mouse, cheese is cheese; that's why mousetraps work."

Luck

Good chance and bad chance occur in every life. No two persons do the same with them. Some suck out every advantage. Some collapse at the first mischance.
Gustav Eckstein,
The Body Has a Mind

Some folk want their luck buttered.
Thomas Hardy,
The Mayor of Casterbridge

The golden opportunity you are seeking is in yourself. It is not in your environment; it is not in luck or chance, or the help of others; it is in yourself alone.
Orison Swett Marden

It always amazes me how people I deal with, when given the opportunity or having it forced on him, will express their understanding of the realities of life. But when they wallow in pools of self-pity, cursing their fate, bitterly ticking off the advantages they perceive others around him to have, they present sad laments and sorry projections of themselves as coaches, competitors, and human beings. (Review ADVER-SITY.)

To countervail the fates, many coaches and athletes resort to obsessive behaviors, justifying them as part of their preparation. (See HABIT, section 3.) Others, instead of working at enhancing whatever weaknesses they may have, accept their shortcomings as an act of fate—bad luck. Rather than light a candle, they curse the darkness. Still others are in constant states of negative anticipation, waiting for the fates to act in opposition to their desires. Eeyore, of *Winnie the Pooh* fame, begins a picnic with his friends by saying, "Don't blame me if it rains." What fun.

That's the way some athletes and coaches approach competition. Their anticipation of failure becomes a self-fulfilling prophecy. They play or coach right into the loss, then say, "I knew that would happen." Bad luck. The fates conspired against them.

■　■　■

It was English writer G. K. Chesterton who said, "I do not believe in a fate that falls on men however they act; but I do believe in a fate that falls on them unless they act."

Profound words, I think. Luck be damned. We must do something. Something right; something we know, something we trust. And in the trust, keep doing it. If we need to make an adjustment because we've trusted it long enough to see it isn't working, we don't change the outfit we wear; we change the approach to what we're doing. The coaching approach or the performance approach.

■　■　■

The engine of superstition is unlimited desire accompanied by limited self-trust. Francis Bacon wrote that all people have a blind side, and that side is their homage to luck—superstition. Unfortunately, too many coaches and athletes develop the habit. The great ones manage to do well *in spite* of their catering to an indifferent fate. Not because of it. They are the exceptions, not the rule.

Let me quote the famous Serenity Prayer here. "God grant me the serenity to accept things I cannot change, courage to change things I can and wisdom to know the difference."

To *know the difference* between what each of us can control—and what we cannot. That understanding comes from the place where the brain resides. We are not in charge of changing our luck. We are in charge of changing our strategies. That requires thought, not rubbing the head of the team manager or crossing our legs in a particular way.

■　■　■

During the 1998 season, when we were both with the Tampa Bay Devil Rays, I asked Wade Boggs about his "lucky" rituals and superstitions. "They make me feel comfortable," he told me. "What about changing your shoes or batting gloves after a bad at-bat?" I asked. "Do you really think that is responsible for a good at-bat if one follows the change?" He was hesitant. To get to the point, this is what we established as we spoke: he had never changed his hitting approach over the course of his career. "I hit just the way I did in high school," he confessed.

Getting 3,000 hits indicates consistency. A consistent approach provided Boggs his bread *and* butter.

■ ■ ■

When all is said about luck, what remains to be done is to take responsibility and have courage in the face of bad fortune; take advantage of good fortune.

Mental Toughness

Mental toughness is many things and rather difficult to explain. Its qualities are sacrifice and self-denial. Also, most importantly, it is combined with a perfectly disciplined will that refuses to give in. It's a state of mind—you could call it character in action.
Vince Lombardi,
NFL coach, Hall of Famer

When speaking with athletes, I prefer to use the term *mental discipline*, rather than *mental toughness*. And in section 3, I do just that. But coaches love the idea of mental toughness, as do I, and because this section leans toward the coach's concerns, mental toughness it is.

Whatever it's called, it's very inclusive. To be tough and/or disciplined in one's mind is to be able to keep all possible distractions at bay while consistently focusing on and executing the task of the moment.

Bob Knight has his own emphatic view on the subject. (What a surprise.) Interestingly, he too prefers the term *discipline*. Though his syntax is shaky, his point is firmly appropriate.

Said Knight, "It has always been my thought that the most important single ingredient to success in athletics or life is discipline. I have many times felt that this word is the most ill-defined in all of our language. [See PATIENCE, section 2.] My definition of the word is as follows: 1. Do what has to be done; 2. When it has to be done; 3. As well as it can be done; and 4. Do it that way all the time."

■ ■ ■

Item: Former UNC basketball coach Matt Doherty, after his team lost to Virginia, matching the school record for home losses in a season (Associated Press, January 13, 2002): "'The challenge now is with the emotional investment we made because we didn't get rewarded,' Doherty said. 'Do we have the intestinal fortitude, the toughness to come back with the same kind of energy and bring it next week?'"

165

His answer came sooner than he would have liked and contrary to what he would have liked.

Item: Doherty again, after his Tar Heels had a bad loss to Connecticut (*Asheville Citizen-Times*, January 23, 2002): "To me toughness is a huge issue. Toughness is something you should bring to the table every game, every day of practice. When we don't it hurts me to say it, but I have to be honest with the public that we were not tough on Saturday (against UConn)."

■ ■ ■

Toughness is a psychological weapon. It can be taught. And I was fortunate to have the opportunity to deliver a powerful lesson.

In 1977, knowing the makeup of the women's basketball team I would have the following year, I initiated a contact that led to a "Goodwill Trip" to Poland—behind the Iron Curtain. We ended up, due to a mistake made on their end, playing against many women who were Olympic aspirants, on university and club teams. Their ages ranged from eighteen to twenty-four. Our ages were fourteen to seventeen.

We played six or seven games in Warsaw and Crakow and in a number of smaller cities. The first game, in Warsaw, before a full house, provided us with a glimpse of what we had in store. Our point guard was 5'3". She was guarded by a woman who was 6'1"—with a wingspan seemingly the width of the court.

They pressed us full court, and we were down by 60 points at the half. The half! I knew it would get worse before it even had a chance of getting better. During a second-half timeout (trailing by 75+), I tried to make a very strong appeal to their perspective, telling them to play the game as hard and as "right" as they were capable. To be unyielding; to ignore the scoreboard; to transcend the humiliation they were feeling. (The crowd, with sympathy that was unintentionally condescending, was rooting for *us* in the second half.)

I asked them why we had come, and answered my own question: to toughen up. That was our agenda, and the circumstance was giving us the best possible chance to address it. "If you can deal with this, no team in Vermont will be able to deal with you," I said, hoping I was even close to being right. I told them that they could either view themselves as being acted upon, and feel like victims, or see themselves as acting out their goals, and feel like mentally tough athletes. "Your choice," I said.

We lost every game in Poland. But each deficit became smaller. The last one we lost by 15 points. I know the players saw what they had done for themselves.

The next year, we lost to a very strong team in the semifinals of the Vermont state championship. The following year we won it.

■ ■ ■

In 1992, I read a book written by Oriana Fallaci entitled *A Man*. A passage struck me at the time. It referred to the protagonist, who was a political prisoner. A major part of the passage follows.

> The true hero never surrenders. . . . He is distinguished from the others not by the great initial exploit or the pride with which he faces tortures and death but the constancy with which he repeats himself, the patience with which he suffers and reacts, the pride with which he hides his sufferings and flings them back in the face of the one who has ordered them. Not resigning himself is his secret, not considering himself a victim, not showing others his sadness or despair.

Exploiting whatever psychological weapons are at his disposal, the author added. I smiled when I read the author's words.

■ ■ ■

Aspects of mental toughness:

Courage
Intensity
Competitiveness
Consistency of focus
Confrontational attitude
Aggressiveness under control
Relentlessness
Responsibility to do what the situation requires
Responsibility for own behavior
Honesty
Self-sacrifice—a commitment to the team's agenda
Self-trust
Ability to make necessary adjustments
Ability to compete with pain
Positive approach to task and circumstance
Ability to cope effectively with adversity
Indifference to opponent's presence or posturing
Ability to "do what needs to be done—always"

Not all inclusive, to be sure. But just as surely, an athlete who checks off all of the above as being representative of his own makeup qualifies as a mentally tough individual.

Motivation

*(He was) one of those rare persons who heighten your sense of
human possibilities.*
John Updike,
about fellow writer John Cheever

All that we do is done with an eye to something else.
Aristotle,
Nicomachean Ethics

Why do coaches coach? Because they want to teach? Because they love
the sport? Because they enjoy competition? Because winning drives
them? Whatever their needs are, they are motivated to satisfy them.
This is true of their athletes, as well. Sometimes coaches forget about
their athletes' needs.

The coach who identifies and understands his athletes' needs will be
better able to direct and monitor his focus and behavior.

Research has indicated that the two most significant needs of young
athletes are "having fun" and "feeling good about myself." The stimulation of practice sessions and the excitement of competition provide the
fun. The feeling of competence—successful execution of tasks—provides
the self-worth. So does winning, of course.

The coaches who are the best motivators know how to keep their
athletes interested and involved. This happens during practices. Competition does not, in itself, motivate *every* athlete, but it is a far easier task
for the typical athlete to "get himself up" for a competitive event than
for a practice session.

Some of the keys to maintaining motivation during practice are:

- Keep drills short and crisp. Attention spans vary in individuals,
  but better to leave a drill too early than too late, after athletes
  have reached the point of diminishing returns and the drill does
  more to *erode* motivation and inhibit execution.
- Vary drills run for a particular fundamental purpose.
- Try to involve as many athletes as possible and to avoid as much
  as possible having them standing around watching others.
- Avoid breaking the continuity of physical performance during
  practice by *constantly* interrupting it with criticism. Obviously,
  instruction is essential, but the coach should be discriminating in
  terms of "picking the moment" he can be most instructive.
  Players hear a voice when it is always "on," but they don't
  necessarily hear the message. No message, no positive stimulus;
  just a hands-on-hips posture that says, "C'mon, let's go."

- Save critiques of individuals for another time. One on one is best. Stopping a drill for it is worst.

Motivating the Individual

Everything written in this book can be linked to the coach's ability to help his athletes' mental state and mental game. And, I'd hope, to help the coach in the same respect. The communication between two individuals who understand the needs of each is the ideal.

Let me present an illustration of the coaching approach that is at the other end of the continuum. The following is a segment (there was *much* more) of a letter I received from the mother of a high school athlete. I have counseled her son, now a college student. At this point in the letter, the mother is speaking of the experience of a player other than her son.

> The kid, a senior, made the varsity team, as of this past Saturday. On Monday, this coach told him that he barely made the team, that he wouldn't get to play during the season, and that he's more like a "caddy" on the team. There was no hope given that if the kid did well at practice, that if he really performed, that he could ever get to play. No hope. No chance. No way.

The kid (later) went to (the coach), who was somewhat conciliatory, but the kid felt beat and he quit the team—feeling devastated, devoured and defeated.

My question to you: Should we just sit by and let this go? Is this "just how it is on the higher level" and that "if you can't deal with it, get out"?

I believed the letter to be true, because a friend of mine is a college coach in the area and has shared similar stories about that coach with me. Presuming the truth of the content, the letter speaks for itself.

■ ■ ■

Pat Murphy, head baseball coach at Arizona State, told me he used to think motivation came from screaming and hollering. "I stomped on guys. I raved; I ranted. I really feel bad—sad—now, that the experience for my players wasn't as good as it should have been," Murphy said. "I just tried to beat it into them. I thought that's the way I could get the job done."

■ ■ ■

One of the ways an athlete learns to fear failure is when the coach attaches any failure to the individual. Instead of working *with* the athlete to correct mistakes, he works *against* the athlete by identifying the person *as* the mistake. The issue then becomes the person, rather than the execution. It is not an effective motivational tool.

If the coach is a teacher, his emphasis should be on learning. If the coach is exclusively motivated by winning, and motivates his athletes accordingly, then the value of the learning process is diminished. It logically follows that the athletes' focus will be on the end, not the means to the end. On winning, rather than on learning what it takes to win.

Is an athlete appropriately motivated if he is taught to interpret mistakes and poor execution as failures, rather than part of the learning process? Skills *can* be acquired. This is more easily accomplished when the focus is on the technique for enhancing the skill, not the deficiency of the athlete.

■ ■ ■

Former big league manager Don Baylor was a major league player before he was a manager. When criticized for his team's apparent lack of energy, Baylor responded defensively, "No one ever had to motivate me." It was true. But it seemed that few Baylors were playing for the Cubs.

When I was with the Oakland organization, we had a minor league player who had played basketball at Indiana. He was the blue-collar type that coaches love. And Knight had loved him. He played with all-out effort and intelligence.

During an Instructional League program, this player almost cost the team a run because he didn't hustle running from second base to home plate. I asked him three questions the next day. "Did you ever do that on Coach Knight's watch?" He said he had not. "Are you *too* comfortable here?" He said he was. "Are you motivated to play professional baseball to the same degree you were motivated to play college basketball?" He said he wasn't, but he'd like to be.

"Then you'd better learn to develop internal motivation, because the external here is obviously not the same as it was at Indiana." He wasn't a Don Baylor.

Motivating the Team

To begin with, I do not trust the collective consciousness. Speaking to a group doesn't get the same results as speaking to an individual. In college, I had a coach who regularly delivered pregame and halftime "motivational" talks. Most of the team members responded as they were expected to (Rah! Rah!). That was in the locker room. On the field they were unresponsive. Poor performers.

Same sport, different year, different coach. Different approach: this coach very rarely talked to the team as a group. (I actually can't recall that he *ever* did.) Instead, he communicated with players individually, talking more about adjustments and strategies. Teaching, in other words. Quietly, encouragingly, "heightening many of the players' sense of human possibilities." Mine, for sure. His team became a national co-champion.

Pep talks are too often much "sound and fury, signifying nothing." High in decibels, low in content. Some talks are attempts to motivate through anecdotal inspiration. Before a World Series, I listened to a clubhouse talk that had players giving sideways furtive glances to see the responses of others. After its completion, one player came up to me and said, "What the hell was that all about?" I didn't respond.

Item: (*Associated Press*, January 27, 2001): "East Carolina coach Dee Stokes resigned Friday, less than a week after she was removed from the bench for what was described as a 'personal matter.'

"Stokes had locked players out of the team locker room earlier this season—prompting players to dress in a classroom at Minges Coliseum in Greenville."

The act apparently had an immediate motivational impact on school administrators.

■ ■ ■

Item: (*New York Times* on the Web, January 28, 2002, regarding Mike Krzyzewski's "talk"): "'I wish I could tell you what came out of the coach's mouth at halftime, but I don't think it's proper for television or a family newspaper,' said Duke guard Jason Williams. 'But that's good. That's why he's such a great coach. He knows all the ways to motivate us.'"

Some coaches have effective group motivational capabilities, some do not. Coaches, like athletes, should know what they are capable of. They should know when and how to best apply their skills. And to whom.

Still, a coach's most effective communication will have him coming eyeball to eyeball with his athletes. Individual contact most effectively motivates the individual.

Negativism*

Optimism supplies the basic energy of civilization. Pessimism is a waste of time.
Norman Cousins,
Human Options

It is nothing short of a miracle that the modern methods of instruction have not yet entirely strangled the holy curiosity of inquiry.
Albert Einstein,
scientist

With resounding inefficiency, coaches have attempted to teach their athletes with the operative words of "no," "don't," "wrong," and "can't." Those are the negative terms I have heard most frequently. There are more, of course. Words that address what was not, is not, and what should not be.

A coach who aspires to teach the mental game must consider the power he has to instill a picture in his athlete's mind when he talks about him and his performance. If it's a negative picture, he is saturating the athlete's soul with gloom and doom. Does he really expect that to help performance?

Some coaches believe that negativism is a motivational weapon. It might work for some, but the coach had better be sure who he's aiming it at. It kills the spirit of most people. One college coach told a pitcher who was preparing to compete that day that his past performances had been "disappointing." Just before the start of the game, he told the pitcher, "You won't last two innings."

The pitcher "lasted" two and a third innings. Not an effective tactic. The frustrated coach, drowning in the pool of his own negativism, pulled the player in with him.

A self-fulfilling prophecy is a point of view that becomes so strong in its influence that it encourages (assures, sometimes) that view to become a reality. Athletes are either victims or beneficiaries of their predictive points of view. They very often—very often—have negative anticipations regarding their performance. They do not need further provocation from the coach. (See NEGATIVISM/POSITIVISM*, section 3.)

■ ■ ■

A distraught Division I college pitcher called me on the phone. His pitching coach told him during a one-on-one meeting, "You have the best stuff but the worst mental makeup on the staff." This was offered to the athlete as he prepared for his sophomore season.

The disparity was probably well defined. The communication was absurd, if the intent was to teach, to develop the pitcher, to motivate him to learn and improve. The "compliment" before the "but" in the statement was barely heard. It certainly didn't register in the pitcher's psyche. What came after the "but" did. Emphatically. And the pitcher was left with a pronounced negative impression of himself, rather than an aspect of his mental approach that needed work. Needless to say, no plan on how to improve it was presented.

■ ■ ■

Item: (*New York Times*, May 6, 2002): "The pitching coach, Charlie Hough, came out, telling (Al) Leiter to forget the chaos around him. Leiter's next pitch, a sharp cutter, hit Brad Asmus's jersey, loading the bases." We should tell people what to remember, rather than what to forget. "Chaos" will be particularly tough to forget, because it's a pretty dramatic and disorienting perspective of one's predicament.

■ ■ ■

I made a reference to a mother's letter earlier (MOTIVATION, section 2). In it she speaks about a high school coach's treatment of a player, who was *not* the son of the woman writing the letter. Broke his spirit with negative badgering and humiliation in front of others. Did that to a number of members of team. Then told the player how much he needed him to perform. *He* needed him. The player quit. Now in college and despite having been courted by the college coach, this player has turned away from the game he used to love.

■ ■ ■

Coaches occasionally feel the need to vent. Our emotional outbursts are attempts to free ourselves from vexation, frustration, anger. (And sometimes, discovery—attempting to use our apparent anger to distract onlookers from our apparent screw-up.) The venting may serve the coach at the expense of the athlete, who, if he thinks himself to be the object, may misinterpret the coach's need, motive, and feelings, even if all are meant to be helpful and constructive. (Which is doubtful.)

A coach who vents after every play or circumstance that displeases him creates a distraction for his athletes as he attends to his own negative feelings. They may learn to turn the coach off, after having come to the realization that he is turning them off.

But what if athletes *are* the real objects of negative venting? What might be the cost? If the act of venting comes before the coach's thought of consequences, then he'll have to resort to damage control shortly thereafter. When the coach's passion preempts his prudence, the athlete doesn't profit from it.

Kareem Abdul-Jabbar said of his UCLA coach and mentor, John Wooden, "I never remember him yelling on the court, but there was no need because he never had trouble getting his point across. I remember a close game in my sophomore year against Colorado State. During timeouts, his instructions were clear and precise. I had never doubted him before, but when the game ended, it was obvious he had been thinking three moves ahead of us, calm and cool as always."

■ ■ ■

We don't always act out the positive, appropriate behavior we know will be helpful to the athlete. We're not perfect. Perfection, after all, is an imaginary state. Better to pay attention to what state the athlete is in.

Are most young athletes able—or willing—to properly apply the message about how to execute their task when negative language and splenetic outbursts are the methods of communication? Coaches usually know the answer; they just forget it when they feel the need to express their negative feelings—even if it's at the expense of efficacy.

■ ■ ■

Item: (*New York Times* on the Web, January 28, 2002): "I'm not big on wake-up calls or sleeping pills," Duke Coach Mike Krzyzewski said. "We just got beat at Florida State. But I think we've played a lot better since then. These kids are human beings, so there are times when they're excited, nervous, unbelievably confident, unbelievably down. My job is to keep things as consistently positive as I can."

Nice Person*

Nice is for losers.
Spoken by actor Brian Dennehy,
playing the role of Bob Knight in
ESPN's "A Season on the Brink"

I'd like to offer a few qualifiers for the remark above:

Nice at the wrong time is for losers.
Nice in the wrong place is for losers.
Nice for the wrong reason is for losers.
Too nice is for losers.

The implication of the overstatement in the epigraph is usually understood by everyone, including the speaker. Of course, one can always say a remark is taken out of context, and if this is indeed the case, the context merits examination.

In semantics, the statement attributed to Knight qualifies as an either-or-orientation. If nice is for losers, not nice is for winners. The remark is actually meaningless, unless the speaker defines his terms. The terms in this case would be *nice* and *losers*.

I'm reminded of Leo Durocher's now-famous remark, made when he succeeded Mel Ott as manager of the New York Giants in 1948. Durocher, a notorious not-nice guy, was alluding to Ott when he made his signature statement: "Nice guys finish last."

At the time the remark was made I was happy to believe in anything that might lead my beloved Giants to the hallowed ground of winners. And for a change, they did win.

Now that I'm a lot older and a bit wiser, I know that nice guys who are effective leaders can win, and *not-nice guys*, who are clueless about leadership and coaching, inevitably are losers.

■ ■ ■

I am a proud supporter of nice people. I am a staunch supporter of effective leadership. The persons who combine *both* traits are surely good for others and even better for themselves. It is faint praise, if praise at all, for coaches who are called "nice people" when the operative meaning of the remark is actually, "He's a nice guy, but a poor coach."

A coach's niceness—his kindness (caring and compassion)—can degenerate into a lack of principle. A certain philosophical (principled) balance must be struck. The coach should be compassionate without being weak; strong without being insensitive.

Coaches should be on guard against any tendency to act out behaviors based on a desire to be popular with the athletes. To be liked. Fair, firm, caring, and intelligent leadership gains respect always. And just as inevitably, the athletes like the person who provides that kind of leadership.

■ ■ ■

I'm reminded of a story that made a strong impression on me when I read it as a child. It is about a young boy and his father, who are bringing a donkey they wish to sell at a market three towns away from their home. They begin the trip with the father walking, as he holds the rope around the animal's neck. The son rides the donkey. As they go through their town, the father hears people say, "Look at that; the old man is forced to walk by a selfish son with young legs." The father and son switch positions.

They walk on and soon hear the townspeople of the adjacent hamlet say, "Look at that; a small young thing forced to walk, while a strong man rides." Father and son mount the donkey and both ride into the next town.

There they hear, "Isn't that inhumane! Two people burdening that poor, dumb animal. What insensitive cruelty." The father thinks for a moment. He then purchases a long bamboo pole and a length of heavy rope. The father and son tie the donkey's legs to the pole, then lift it onto their shoulders.

They walk into the next town carrying the upside down animal. "Look at those fools, carrying a donkey."

The most certain way to ensure failure in this world of ours is to try to please everyone.

■ ■ ■

Nice guys tend to be pleasers. They may have different motives, but their agenda is not to ruffle anyone's feathers. I have found three distinct differences among coaches who want to please. Some just seem to want to be liked too much. They tend to have low self-esteem; their acceptance by others is their validation of self.

Others have been criticized excessively as young people. They too suffer from poor self-esteem and wish to prevent criticism by catering to, rather than confronting, those who have any chance of giving it. Like the surly waitress in a restaurant. Or an electrician who botched the job in the coach's home, but whom the person will not call to hold accountable. Or an inept, perhaps dishonest, auto mechanic.

Still others simply have been raised to be very nice sons and daughters by very nice parents. Nothing wrong with that. Until the child becomes an adult. (I often ask such people, "What was the last thing your mother said to you when you left the house when you were a child?" The answer is usually: "Be careful." Or "Be good." Or both, in excess.)

Most of the aforementioned coaches tend to have difficulty converting "civilian" niceness to coaching competitiveness. They coach "carefully" and are "too nice."

Many with whom I've worked are concerned that if they are not acting like a Mr. Rogers, they will appear to be Attila the Hun. Not true, but if it were, Attila would be the more likely of the two to get the job done during competition.

■ ■ ■

New York Knicks coach Don Chaney had a rough 2002 season. Many observers (and some players) said he was too "laid-back." Players quit in a number of games and Chaney's job was said to be in jeopardy. Chris Broussard wrote (*New York Times* on the Web), "Chaney is not getting the maximum effort out of the players, and he could soon be replaced."

Chaney was said to be "staying positive" after players' remarks that there was no discipline. Positivism is often used as a smoke screen for those who are reluctant to be confrontational. They act as if everything will be all right. Essentially, they are enablers, avoiding the tough issue by mouthing easy platitudes dressed in positive terms, rather than the constructive criticism that is essential in order to coach athletes effectively.

When matters finally reach a point of saturation for the coach, he expresses his frustration through an angry outburst. He loses his temper well after he loses his players. Then he loses his job.

■ ■ ■

Competition is confrontation. Coaches should realize that an aggressive competitive approach may require them to reconcile any conflict they have between a personal desire to be liked and a professional competitive spirit. If efficacy comes from aggressiveness, and caution or timidity assures ineffectiveness, their choice should be clear to them.

The coach should consider the following before addressing "the right way" of approaching competition:

- That some of the finest, "nicest" people, away from the competitive arena, have been the fiercest, most confrontational individuals when it's time to compete.
- Whether he has as an agenda the need to please others.
- That, if this is the case, he should examine his attitudes, behavior, and motives—as a person and as a competitor.
- That adapting to the conduct required in any given environment, without compromising his own values, is one characteristic of a self-actualized person.
- That self-assured behavior is a major attribute of every successful competitor.

- That it might be helpful to set specific goals related to behavior during competition that address his being aggressive and confrontational in a self-controlled manner, rather than being timid and a nice person.
- That he should live and perform from the "inside out," rather than from the "outside in," meaning, he should act upon what he knows is right and appropriate, rather than what he feels would satisfy and please others.

■ ■ ■

New York Yankees pitcher Burleigh Grimes performed in the mid-1930s, when someone asked him why there were so many nice guys in baseball. Grimes said he didn't know the answer about nice guys, but he knew about himself as a competitor. Said Grimes, "I'm a bastard when I play."

Officiating

*A mistake in judgment isn't fatal, but too much
anxiety about judgment is.*
Pauline Kael,
I Lost It at the Movies

*Justice! Custodian of the world! But since the world errs, justice
must be custodian of the world's errors.*
Ugo Betti,
The Gambler

Officiating should not be a preoccupation of coach or athlete. Kael's words in the epigraph apply: too much anxiety about officiating is fatal.

Officials can go unnoticed, which is good. Or they can be distractions, which is bad. Bad for a coach's focus; worse for an athlete's. When a coach keeps talking about the officials, he provides a great excuse for his athletes.

Officials have been easy excuses for irresponsible athletes (and coaches) for a long time. Fine officials do their jobs consistently and effectively. Others are inconsistent. Still others are consistently ineffective. The same is true of athletes, coaches, and auto mechanics.

A poor official is an unpleasant challenge to the athlete and coach. Their responses to his officiating test their ability to recognize what they can and cannot control. Bad calls test their ability to control themselves—their emotions, their focus, and their poise.

Officials will be right more often than they're wrong. In either case, my attitude toward them was shaped by having remembered my father's words to me when I was a boy: "Hope for justice, kid. But don't expect it."

■ ■ ■

God and Satan get together to form a football competition, in order to "liven up" the afterlife. Satan, as is his nature, is bragging, expressing his certainty that his team would defeat God's team.

"You can't be serious," God replies. "Don't you know what kind of running backs I have? Among other outstanding backs on the team, I have Red Grange, Jim Thorpe, Doak Walker," says God. "And now I have Walter Payton."

"And *I* have the officials," answers the devil.

■ ■ ■

The devil, it has been said, is in the details. And an important understanding coaches and athletes should have is that officials are external details, therefore irrelevant to performance.

The problem posed by officials is based on coaches' and athletes' *responses* to them, as it affects their next approach. I have witnessed those who lost their focus, because they were so affected by officials they thought were "doing" them. Not making the right calls—the calls they "deserved to get."

"He [the umpire] took me out of my game," more than one major league pitcher has explained to me. My response used to be, "You allowed him to take you out of the game." After a time, my more accurate answer has been "You took yourself out of your game."

■ ■ ■

A few reminders might be helpful.

- Understand that ideals in this world, in this case an official's judgments being consistently "accurate," are not to be expected.
- Understand that an official's call is one of the many things neither coach nor athlete can control.
- Realize that the response of frustration over a call will impede the effective mental set that helps the coach "stay in the game"—and the athlete execute the next task.
- Remember that nothing or no one can "take one's focus away" without one's consent.
- Remember, as well, that efficacy as a coach and competitor is evidenced by self-discipline, not by self-destructive behavior.

■ ■ ■

I admit to having been an official long ago. A good one, I will be audacious enough to say. I umpired high school and college baseball for eleven years—on Long Island and in Vermont. I was the home plate umpire in state championship games, so I know I satisfied someone.

But there was one coach I could never please. I only remember his name as Frank. He coached baseball at West Rutland High School in Vermont. He was never happy with my judgments. And some strange happening always seemed to develop in the games I officiated for him, disturbing him further and apparently giving him the impression that these circumstances were a result of my presence.

After a few years of our stormy on-field relationship, Frank took the opportunity of coming over to me after a game. With calm sincerity he said, "Harvey, you're a good guy but a terrible umpire." He then turned and walked away.

Was I a terrible umpire? Apparently not, insofar as the many coaches who kept nominating me for the playoffs were concerned. But for Frank. . . .

Well, that's the way it goes with officials. Not evil, really. But necessary.

Old School

Habit is stronger than reason.
George Santayana,
Interpretations of Poetry & Reason

If by "old school" one means the habit of doing something a particular way, without a reasoned examination of its effectiveness—or ineffectiveness—then that school should not be accredited.

Habits don't have to be bad to be comfortable; they just have to be habits. And the comfort of something believed in or done the same way for a long time, good or bad, makes many people all *too* comfortable. When a coach's beliefs and actions are inappropriate and ineffectual, his comfort comes at the expense of the athletes' discomfort. The coach's comfort will also get in the way of his honest evaluation and growth, which is what Thoreau was driving at when he called feelings of comfort "hindrances to the elevation of mankind."

The comfortable ideas being taught within the walls of the old school should have the same burden of proof as those inside the new school. The test of an idea is not its age or continuous application. It's in the judgment of whether it's right or wrong. Whether it works or doesn't.

"I'm old school" is a remark often made with an air of false pride, expressed by people who are rationalizing their resistance to learning. It worked yesterday, so it will work today, tomorrow—and forever, it seems to say. (Did it *really* work yesterday?)

The staunch, self-proclaimed old-school coach, if given a choice between changing the way he's done something all his life or trying to prove that there is no need to change, will get right after searching for the proof, as exhausting as the search may be. That attitude is, as A. S. Byatt put it, an example of the supremacy of habit over occasion.

Some coaches will learn only at gunpoint. (If your reading has taken you this far into the book, you're obviously not one of them—unless someone is beside you with a gun held to your head.) Old-schoolers tend to have a predisposition for being overly opinionated. Their thinking is often based on ego needs and semantic inflexibility. An anxiety induced by the unknown—or the unclear—is a characteristic response to anything different.

Even when new information or approaches are presented, this type of old-school coach can't seem to change the mind-set and break out of this self-limiting prison, which is more comfortable than the pains of growth. Though the ability to change one's mind is a mental skill, these coaches only hold their athletes accountable for developing it. Perhaps not *developing* it; just changing their minds to believe what the coach believes.

■ ■ ■

In 1999, a few minutes before speaking to the entire coaching staff of a professional sports organization, I was chatting with one individual on that staff. He mentioned the "players of the '90s." (Now, these are the players of the new millennium.) As an "old-schooler, I'm not real happy with them," he said to me. I asked him to be specific, after first inquiring whether *all* the players he had to work with displeased him. He corrected his generalization. "I'm talking about those kids with nipple-rings and such, who call everybody 'Dude.'"

"Do any of these guys respond to on-field coaching?" I asked. He said nothing. He seemed displeased with me now. I figured I had nothing more to lose. I told him his contract was dated to indicate that he's a *coach* of the '90s. "Not of the 50s or 60s or 70s," I said. I didn't get a chance to elaborate the obvious implication to him, aside from the fact that some of these players were given substantial signing bonuses, regardless of where they wore their jewelry. I was called to the front of the room to begin the seminar, which included a reference to the issue, though I said this had come up at another time in another (unnamed) place.

I'm not Generation X. I'm in my sixties. *Late* sixties. But I have to work with athletes who are different from those I used to work with. That's my professional responsibility. And if I want to be effective, I'd better not be that kind of old-schooler, because it means I won't be able to adjust or learn, now that *that* school is out.

■ ■ ■

On the other hand, if by old school one means enduring universal values, then, once again, our terms had better be appropriately defined. In other words, a phrase doesn't necessarily convey meaning. Definition does (usually). (See VALUES, section 2.)

P

Parents

I should probably tell you I support my son's tennis because he gets so much out of it, that it improves him mentally and physically and teaches him so much about life. All that is certainly true, but the real reason is because it adds drama to my life.
Anonymous tennis mom
to writer Emily Greenspan,"Little Winners,"
New York Times Magazine, April 26, 1981

So many articles have been written about parents of young athletes, so many books written on the subject. So many disturbing recent events that point to parents with distorted agendas: a father files a lawsuit against a school because his son was put on the basketball junior varsity, rather than the varsity—"affecting the son's future income"; a parent stabs another parent in the head with a down marker at a youth football game; a hockey father beats another father to death at a rink.

Item: (Kathy Bunch, "Angry Grownups Are Real Spoilsports," *Web MD Medical News,* April 2, 2001):

> Last August, El Paso began mandatory parent-training classes for those whose children play sports. The three-and-a-half hour program includes videos of parents acting up at games, essays, and artwork from children explaining why they like sports, a review of how each game is played, and a psychotherapist and child crisis counselor talking about problem behavior and child abuse at sporting events.
>
> At the end, parents must sign a code of conduct that calls for suspensions—even lifetime bans—for breaking the rules.
>
> "It's made a big difference," says Powell, adding that not one of the 6,000 parents who have taken the course has had to be disciplined.

■ ■ ■

Sports Illustrated found forty cases of parental violence when they did research for a piece they were doing on the subject. They also found that 70 percent of kids involved in organized sports quit by the time they were thirteen years old and said they quit because of parents. By the age of fifteen, 90 percent of those who had quit had done so for the same reason.

■ ■ ■

Where does a coach start with all this in today's society?

My view is that it starts before each season—at a scheduled meeting with the parents. At that time, the coach sets his agenda—by establishing a healthy program for his athletes and himself and conveying it in no uncertain terms to the parents.

The parents should be presented with the specific philosophies and values (or credo) of the coach and the program. Parameters should also be set for the parents: lessons in appropriate behavior at events; lessons related to proper communication lines with the coach; lessons about the appropriate interaction with their sons and daughters—who happen to be athletes.

The coach should also spell out his specific expectations in regard to the student/athlete's grades; about promptness; about behavior in general—about discipline and consequences.

By "putting it on the line" the coach is telling the parents not to be surprised. They know what the program represents; they know what is expected of their children—and of them.

■ ■ ■

An article in *USA Today* (July 26, 2002) told of parents hiring skills coaches to enhance their children's athletic performance. A number of parents were quoted. Two particular fathers spoke effusively of how they had shaped and/or orchestrated their sons' athletic careers.

Not mentioned in the article: One son stopped speaking to the "overbearing" parent. The other, upon meeting me for the first time, asked, "How do you get a father off your back?"

■ ■ ■

It's been understood by many coaches that the toughest thing young athletes have to face is the unfulfilled lives of some parents. The epigraph speaks to that point. My experiences with *professional* athletes shout to the point.

I've dealt with fathers who made their sons call home every night to detail their performance (results, of course, and a few of the athletes lied when they did poorly); a father of a major league baseball player who would stand, during big league batting practice, behind the batting cage as he "coached" his son, humiliating the son and disgusting witnesses. (How did the organization *allow* this?); mothers and fathers who "would not let" a son marry, because "it would distract him" from his focus on the sport he played. (I scripted a telephone call one athlete made to ther from a restaurant, while his fiancée and I waited at the table. F. proposed when he returned.)

Almost all of the athletes I've come across are embarrassed by the obnoxious behavior of a parent. The athlete usually gets it, even though the parent doesn't. Yet many athletes don't. And whether they get it or not, almost all are adversely affected by the parent. One professional player I approached, after having watched and heard his father during a game, said to me, "Now you can understand what I have to deal with."

Coaches' backs have also been weighed down by parents. They shouldn't be. A coach should be steadfast in his belief in the athletic program's appropriate aims and values—and in his own presentation of them. And he should be willing to confront those parents who are making it difficult for their children to enjoy the experience of athletic competition.

■　■　■

Oh, yes, as every coach knows, there are *great* parents also. Great for their kids, great for the coach, great for the entire program. What more can a coach do but appreciate these people—and convey that appreciation? It isn't a coincidence that, with very few exceptions, their children are also great to coach.

I've used great parents as conduits to not-so-great parents. It saved me time, when that approach got results. When it didn't, I took care of the situation myself.

■　■　■

Sometimes, a parent may know something the coach doesn't—at least, about his or her offspring. In 1962, I put up a list of those players who had made the final cut for the high school freshman football team I was coaching. The name John Schultz did not appear on the list. That night I received a call at home from the boy's mother. She was polite and gentle in manner.

Mrs. Schultz told me how important it would be for John if he could be on the team. I remember her words still: "I know I have no real power, but I hoped I could persuade you." The appeal was based on the boy's past health and self-esteem. It hit my button. I had been there. A coach had given me an opportunity I probably hadn't deserved on merit (without parental intervention). I was fortunate that he had looked beyond my physical skill. I hadn't looked beyond John's.

His name was added to the list. He was our starting linebacker and center. And the varsity's for three years. And he went on to play in college. And came to believe in himself even more than his mom or his first coach had.

Patience

*[Coach Wooden] handled us with patience. I was his
slowest learner.*
Bill Walton,
All-American, NBA All-Star

Because Bob Knight has been considered such an effective teacher, and because of one of the responses he had to an interviewer years ago (*Scholastic Magazine*, December 1982) (see later), and because of Walton's remark in the epigraph, I thought it necessary to include this topic—this word—patience. Before my effort to interpret the word and apply that interpretation to coaching, I must say that I see no real conflict between what Knight and Wooden would believe, despite the manner in which they expressed themselves. In other words, I do see a semantic difference, not a difference in teaching or coaching philosophy.

The first requirement of semantic discussion is to define and examine the term. My favorite source, *The American Heritage Dictionary*, offers some terms that should make it clear why the meaning of "patient" is unclear to many.

Here are some of the offerings:

Tolerant
Understanding
Persevering
Constant
Capable of calmly awaiting an outcome or result, not being
    impulsive
Capable of bearing difficulty, provocation, annoyance

Now some examination.

- Tolerant: Should a coach accept mistakes or screw-ups in execution? No. Is accepting and tolerating the same? If one means will I allow mistakes to go unattended, the answer is, "No." If it means "Do I tolerate the athlete's attempt?," the answer is "It depends." It depends on whether the athlete is making an honest effort, whether his focus is directed at execution or elsewhere. Whether the inability to execute is based on a lack of understanding. The reader can provide other possibilities. Coaches shouldn't tolerate mistakes, but they should be smart enough to understand human imperfection.
- Understanding: See previous sentence.
- Persevering: The coach has athletes work over and over on technique and execution until "they get it right." Question:

Doesn't the impatient coach do the same? (Persevering: "persistent adhering to a course of action." That's "patience," says the dictionary.)

- Constant: Consistent. Good, but "patient"?
- Calmly awaiting an outcome, not being impulsive: As a patient coach, I did not *calmly wait*; I energetically and aggressively voiced criticism—and *immediate* instruction. But I wasn't *impulsive*. Meaning, my words and actions were based on rationality, rather than *my feeling* of the moment (frustration, anger, disappointment). (So here is a seeming contradiction within the definition itself.)
- Capable of bearing difficulty, provocation, annoyance: Mental toughness is a good thing and so, we should presume, is this aspect of it: patience.

■ ■ ■

INTERVIEWER: Beyond being adamant and adamantly clear, what else do you see as characteristic of your teaching and coaching?

KNIGHT: Intolerance. A teacher who is tolerant and has great "patience" is not going to get the results that someone who is demanding and intolerant can get. I think kids are satisfied with what I tolerate.

Knight then explained what he does tolerate and what he doesn't. So, he is tolerant, in some cases. A contradiction: one that points to the difference between a coach's meaning and a coach's attitude.

■ ■ ■

One part of patience is trying to find a better way to get a message across; the other is in allowing a particular amount of time for it to be assimilated. All-Star pitcher Kevin Brown once asking me how many times I'd have to tell him the same thing before it would kick in didn't indicate a resistance that would wear out my patience. It indicated an inability to integrate knowledge into behavior. Brown went to Georgia Tech on an academic scholarship. He *knew* what he wanted to do. My responsibility was to be sure he wouldn't keep losing *his* patience with himself. He made such urgent demands on himself that his emotions got in the way of his brain.

Different athletes learn at different rates. Is a coach to lose patience with a swift runner who's a slow learner? Patience is just a matter of working to press the right buttons, not in accepting lower standards of behavior or performance.

The patience of effective coaches allows them to ask the question "What can I come up with that will help this kid get it right?" The impatient—might we say the truly intolerant?—coaches ask "What's wrong with this kid?" And usually, they don't even take the time and effort to uncover the answer to *that* question.

*Positivism**

(See NEGATIVISM*, section 2 and NEGATIVISM/POSITIVISM*, section 3)

Positive views of truth and duty are those that impress the mind and lead to action; negation dwells mostly in cavil and denial.
Richard Whately

If I didn't know how to properly drive a nail into a piece of wood, and I wanted to learn how to be a carpenter, I'd seek out a carpenter, someone who knew how to *do* what I wished to do.

"Let me see what you've got. Here's a hammer and nail; there's the wood. Drive the nail into the wood," he might have said to me. Despite my not really knowing how to go about the task, I gave it my best attempt. The nail went in sideways and bent, because of my inept attempt at driving it. "Good grief!" the carpenter exclaimed. "You can't do it that way. Don't bend the darn thing; don't swing the hammer sideways; don't come down with it from so far away. Can't you do it right?"

He didn't tell me how to accomplish that. He knew how to *do* the task, but he couldn't *teach me* how to do it. He certainly told me what I shouldn't do.

I sought out another carpenter. The nail looked the same after I demonstrated my lack of skill to this fellow. "OK," he responded. "Let me show you what to do. To begin with, you held the nail at an angle; hold it straight up and down. Good. Now, keep your hammer stroke short and come right down over the nail head. You hit too rapidly and lost control of your stroke the first time. You want to use short, deliberate swings over the top. There you go."

It would take a while for me to become a master carpenter, but I would know what kind of teacher I needed. A "positivist." One who would teach me what to do and how to do it, rather than berate me for what I did wrong and implore me to do it right—without further instruction or demonstration.

■　■　■

Those are two approaches to coaching. It's obvious which is the more positive of the two, but it should be just as obvious which one is ... get the individual to successfully execute a task.

The battle to express all thoughts in a positive way must be fought—if it needs fighting. An athlete grows by what he feeds on. Positive language allows him healthy growth. He's more likely to be successful if he hears a coach instructing and affirming, rather than berating and degrading. The positive coach examines possibilities, rather than pronouncing impossibilities. He seeks ways to get his message across to an athlete who "doesn't seem to get it," rather than taking the easy way of judging the athlete poorly. He expects the best execution from the athlete and the best teaching methodology from himself. He relentlessly seeks solutions, rather than pointing out problems and believing them unsolvable.

On Praise

Item: From *The Sporting News*, June 24, 2002: Scotty Bowman, after wining his tenth Stanley Cup Championship as a coach and then retiring, said, "One of the regrets you have as a coach, when I had a really big team in Montreal, you never really get a chance to tell those guys how good they really were." Never took the chance, he might have said.

Bowman went on: "I am going to tell my (Detroit) guys the same thing, not just the Hall of Fame players. I am going to tell all of them that it's a wonderful feeling."

■ ■ ■

Edgar Watson Howe wrote, "The greatest humiliation in life is to work hard on something from which you expect great appreciation, and then fail to get it."

Positive reenforcement is a teaching tool. And while the absence of it should not cause humiliation, its abundance should be expected to produce better performance in athletes. The distinction I make between positive reenforcement and praise may seem inconsequential. I believe the athletes should know when they've done something right—something the coach approves of. That approval should be expressed, even if it's simply "That's the way we want it." Or "Now you've got it." Short, yet sweet enough.

Frequent and exaggerated ravings I have always avoided. They are inauthentic, and the athletes see through them and soon can't discriminate between what is legitimate praise and what is a motivational affectation.

I looked through a scrapbook my wife put together from the year I coached a high school women's state championship team. One of the players, interviewed by a reporter after the final game, was asked about

...pproach. This was one of her remarks: "He doesn't over-... compliments, so when he does give you one, you know

...akes people feel good, and it should—when they deserve it. ...-ESTEEM, section 3.) Praise offered with the exclusive inten-...making us feel good is very often inappropriate, because, though ... ...lieved to be useful, it may not actually be deserved. Such expressions should be avoided. That kind of praise is condescending.

I'm reminded of story I heard many years ago about Lou Gehrig, whose disease (MLS) had been worsening as he continued to play first base for the Yankees and extend his record consecutive game streak (now held by Cal Ripken Jr.).

No longer able to move well at all, Gehrig fielded an easy ground ball at the bag and stepped on first base for the third out of an inning. As he came off the field, two teammates ran by him and patted him on the backside, saying, "That-a-boy, Lou."

Gehrig took himself out of the lineup the next day, breaking the streak and explaining that when he received praise for essentially picking up a ball, he knew it was time to quit.

Though well intentioned, false praise is counterproductive.

■ ■ ■

Some points to consider:

- The best coaches instruct by revealing and reinforcing strategies that help the athlete accomplish his goals and tasks.
- The coach should instruct by using positive language and directives.
- The coach should be persistent in the pursuit of positivism in thought and expression—and hold the athletes responsible for doing the same.
- Be very careful to distinguish between messages of encouragement and praise. Offer encouragement always, praise when it is appropriate and deserved.

Q

Questions

There aren't any embarrassing questions—just embarrassing answers.
Carl Rowan,
New Yorker, December 6, 1963

An answer is always a form of death.
John Fowles,
The Magus

In response to Fowles's remark above, I would say that a question, then, is a form of life. It is the basic tool for examination, for understanding, for personal and professional growth.

Socrates, as I mentioned in earlier pages, was considered to be the greatest teacher in Athens. His primary skill was in making students justify everything they said. "Why?" was his favorite question. Eventually, Athenians tired of his challenges and persistence. He was given hemlock for their relief.

Athenians trumped up the charge that Socrates was corrupting the youth of Athens by having them question institutions and long-held beliefs. The people in power didn't appreciate having to answer for their policies. They still don't.

That possible attitude notwithstanding, the problems many coaches have with questions usually arise from their uncertainty of the motive of the questioner.

■ ■ ■

Parents Have Questions (Review PARENTS, section 2.)

If parents aren't expert on the sport their son or daughter is participating in (though many seem to believe they are), they're very confident in their belief that they're expert in their understanding of their offspring. (I've found many to be wrong in this belief also.) They "know what's best" for that young person.

If a coach's policies or views are not compatible with the parents' un-

191

derstanding, they question the coach. The manner and motive identify how the coach should respond. Coaches who have a "knee-jerk" emotional response can fan embers into a raging fire.

The preseason meetings strategy mentioned in the PARENTS entry is helpful for reasons noted in those pages, particularly answering questions before they are asked and establishing policy before its implementation is questioned.

Some parents' questions are innocent; others are based on a selfish and calculated agenda. The coach must be rational enough to make the distinction and controlled enough to answer with respect (though perhaps not deserved) and confidence.

Media People Have Questions

People who report on athletic events also believe themselves to be experts on the sport they are covering. They have paper credentials, at least. For many of them, those credentials are all they bring to the coach's room. Their questions may be irrelevant to the circumstances within the event and their interpretations erroneous. A media person will often "beg the question," meaning ask a question that directs the coach to respond to a slant on a play, behavior, or circumstance, the answer to which has already established in the mind of the question asker.

The coach must understand his obligation to the media but also understand what he is not obliged to do. (Review JOURNALISTS, section 2.)

Athletes Ask Questions

The athlete is the coach's primary concern and responsibility. In helping the athlete value learning, the coach should himself value intelligent questions asked for the right reason, in the right place, at the right time. These appropriate aspects of questioning should be presented to the athletes at the beginning of each season.

I've been around many question askers. Any fault I've found has not been in the question but in the motive of the questioner. Examples:

Questioner 1 seeks clarity and understanding. He's not sure how the coach wants him to execute a play or a technique—or even a broader aspect of the sport.

Questioner 2 isn't able to accept the obvious and simple. His inquisitiveness leads him to quibble about irrelevancies and to seek information about matters that go beyond what is necessary to know.

Questioner 3 asks questions because he is a contrarian or an agitator or one who wishes to challenge authority. His questions are meant to provoke or threaten.

Questioner 4 thinks he knows more than the coach. His questions are motivated by this belief and his style is one of an interrogator.

Questioner 5 seeks attention. He asks questions to which he already knows the answers.

Questioner 6 also seeks attention, but he wants a particular kind of attention. He wants to please the coach by showing how interested he is in the topic or in self-improvement. He is an apple polisher.

Questioner 7 acts like a pompous ass who is in love with his own voice.

It's easy to respond well to Questioner 1. But how a coach responds to the other six examples will determine how or if those athletes change their agendas—their mental agendas. An athlete doesn't separate himself from his needs and instincts. The motives of a questioner reveal him and, in the revelation, the coach has information he can act on.

Coaches should encourage all athletes to be Questioner 1.

Coaches Ask Questions

They address them to the athlete—to gain insights and certainty of the athlete's understanding. They ask colleagues.

Item: Newly hired New York Jets coach Herman Edwards (*New York Times*, May 17, 2001): "My philosophy is do less strategically and become more fundamentally sound. I'm not smart enough to think I know everything, but I am smart enough to ask questions when I don't know how to handle a specific situation."

Item: Bob Knight (*Scholastic Magazine*, December 1982): "I think it's extremely important to talk to kids and ask them questions. You're always going to be surprised at the answers. One of the important things I have learned in teaching is never to make assumptions."

And coaches can learn by asking questions of themselves—as reality checks, not as second guesses. The questions should be related to a coach's decisions, approaches to everyone and everything, responses to everyone and every circumstance, teaching technique, and his leadership and communication skills. And questions such as "What can I do to help this kid that I haven't been doing?" The virtual "ball of wax."

If the coach doesn't have good answers—or any answer—he'd better ask himself a question that *is* deadly: "Why not?"

R

Respect

*I attach more importance to a team's respect than any other phase of
my relationship with them.*
Paul Brown,
NFL coach, Hall-of-Famer

*It's a respect that [the manager] gives us that we end up
giving back to him.*
Wally Backman,
major league infielder

Sustained respect can't be gained because of authority. The leader has
power, but not necessarily the skill to be a teacher, a mediator, a confidant, a supporter, an encourager, a counselor—a mentor. The Icelandic
sagas call people who have that ability and function "peaceweavers." I
call them outstanding coaches. Their ambition is to help individuals to
appreciate each other and work effectively together, even when not in
complete agreement. As a team. An effective team. The team members
respect what the coach is trying to do—and how he or she goes about
doing it. This respect is for the coach's personal power, not position
power.

Respect requires reciprocity. The coach who gives it is more likely to
get it. (See epigraph 2.) In thinking about this topic, I took myself back
to my youth—and what I would want from an "ideal" coach. In recognizing that this ideal came from a deep feeling rather than any formulated understanding of the subject, I nevertheless was able to come up
with most of the characteristics listed below. Once again, this list is not
all inclusive. But it's inclusive enough for those of us who hold ourselves
accountable for being effective—and aspire to be even more so. (See
chapter 4.)

The coaches who get respect from their athletes are likely to be:

- Aggressive
- Authentic/Honest
- Balanced
- Caring/Concerned

- Communicative
- Compassionate
- Competitive
- Consistent
- Courageous
- Creative
- Dedicated
- Demanding
- Disciplined
- (A) Disciplinarian
- Emotional (Appropriately)
- Encouraging
- Energetic
- Enthusiastic
- Fair
- Flexible
- Goal-oriented
- Knowledgeable
- Open
- Optimistic
- Persistent
- Poised
- Prepared
- Rational
- Responsible
- Strong (Mentally)
- Trusting
- Trustworthy
- Understanding
- Willful

■ ■ ■

Item: (*Associated Press*, December 29, 2000). The Headline: "Haslett and Saints Get Respect." It refers to the arrival of New Orleans' coach Jim Haslett. Saints lineman Norman Hand spoke about his new coach. "He earned respect from Day 1. . . . He took control of this whole organization from the first day. Now we play like he played. We're not going to back down from anybody."

Haslett sensed complacency in the players when he arrived (tardiness, missing a doctor's appointment). He sensed a losing attitude. He suspended and fined a Pro Bowl lineman, who responded with respect for Coach Haslett. "He is what this organization needed. We needed a hard-nose, disciplined and enthusiastic coach, and that's exactly what we have."

Response*

If you leap into a well, Providence is not bound to fetch you out.
Thomas Fuller, M.D.,
Gnomologia

He who hesitates is a damn fool.
Mae West,
actress

An emotional response has no hesitancy. A well-planned rational response has no hesitancy. But one of those two responses is likely to be more appropriate than the other. The other is more likely to put us at the bottom of a well.

Mae West knew what she was doing. She was calculating and followed up on her calculations. So history seems to indicate. She was no damn fool.

But we make fools of ourselves when our needs are not met and we become frustrated, angry, disappointed, hurt, distraught, resentful, jealous. These, quite obviously, are emotional states that can lead to emotional responses. Better to get to our brain as quickly as possible, before we act out of these states, rather than out of our rationality. Better, in other words, to hesitate, to think—and *then* to act. (Review chapter 7.)

Athletes are asked to respond intelligently, with poise and understanding of what is required of them next in competition. There is no distinction, in this regard, between athlete and coach. Aside from the coach being a model, he is a leader—and effective leaders know how to deal with whatever comes at them—or whatever they're going at.

A coach's response during competition will be one of the most important factors in determining his next decision. His brain should not be eclipsed by his emotions.

■　■　■

A young minor league manager in the Oakland organization had a mouth that operated much quicker than his brain when adversity set in. Head shaking and negative remarks were clearly heard by players in the dugout. The manager might criticize, in a very negative manner, a play one of his defensive players had just made—or, more likely, had not made. He talked angrily about the player and, when the fellow came off the field and into the dugout at the end of the half inning, his teammates were only too willing to report the manager's ripping response.

Whatever a player's needs might be, he certainly doesn't need that— especially because the manager only talked behind his back.

After having observed this behavior a few times, I spoke t⁄
ager—an intelligent and generally responsible guy. Our s⁄
this, when I was in town: I sat next to him in the dugout, an⁄
an inappropriate response was just getting off the laur⁄
quickly grabbed his wrist. It was a reminder and a key for ᵤ⁄
wrist, close mouth. Pavlov's dog couldn't have responded bette⁀.
learned to give himself the right mental cues and to be a more effective
manager.

■ ■ ■

A coach's irate response to every incident that displeases him reveals a
lack of poise, among other things. Getting overheated is an indication
that he doesn't have the right temperature for poise. He doesn't have ice
in the bone marrow.

Athletes will take a coach's lead; they always do. The coach who has
poor responses is telling his athletes, "Don't do what I do, do what I say."
It doesn't work that way, though the coach might like to believe otherwise.

Simplicity*

Pete Newell described two groups of coaches: those who believe in simplicity and execution and those who believe in surprise and change. Obviously, he and I are part of the simplicity and execution group.
Bob Knight,
Scholastic Coach, December 1982

I'd better keep it simple. First, what Knight meant by surprise and change was trickery and inconsistency. And he was referring to change for the sake of change or because of a lack of confidence in any solid belief.

Simplicity and execution: the one strikes at the heart of how something is most effectively done, the other at the repetition required to *get it done.*

Simplicity says, "Less is more." It allows athletes to have a sense that there are specific techniques and strategies that are basic for their success—the success of the team. They gain confidence because of their familiarity and consistency of purpose.

Simplicity demands execution. If every athlete knows what to do, and every opponent knows what will be done, the anticipation is one of predictability. This is comforting for those who execute and seemingly comfortable for those who believe themselves ready to respond. Unless, when trying to react, the opposition finds that it cannot deal effectively with what they know is coming, *because it is executed so well.* That's very disheartening.

The coach who uses complex strategies and trickery cannot expect his athletes to execute them with any consistency, because, by nature of definition, they are not easy or familiar. The opponents may be initially fooled by the deception but relieved to see that the surprise was wrapped in a poor execution.

Simplicity says, "I will eliminate the unnecessary so that the necessary can be perfectly expressed." Well, as close to perfect as can be possible. Certainly the incorporation of the unnecessary so as to confuse the opponents will bring athletes closer to confusion than perfection.

The greatest truths are the simplest. So are the greatest coaches.

Again, Lombardi's sweep right, sweep left—simple and executed precisely right into Super Bowl championships. Perfect simplicity, as George Meredith wrote, "is unconsciously audacious."

Item: (From *The Sporting News*, August 12, 2002, regarding current South Carolina coach Steve Spurrier): "He is a demanding technician. He believes in specific mechanics that guide his quarterbacks until they release the ball; they do it his way, and it wouldn't matter if it's Brett Favre or Danny Wuerffel. Receivers run distinct routes. . . . Breaks are executed at specific spots; if you are to cut at a certain place, you better do it. Nor does he have a ton of plays. They just are run so precisely and executed so well, they work."

Simplicity is an indication of trust in what a coach believes. No garnishes, no garbage. The desire to be clever sometimes overwhelms the understanding of how to be effective. Ralph Waldo Emerson had it right. "To be simple," he said, "is to be great."

T

Trust

(Review RESPECT, section 2)

Trust men and they will be true to you.
Ralph Waldo Emerson,
writer/poet

Trust ivrybody—but cut th' cards.
Finley Peter Dunne,
"Casual Observations" (1900)

When, as a boy, I was questioned about my comings and goings, I responded quickly to the grand inquisitor, my father. "Don't you trust me?" I asked. "I trust you," he said, "but I worry." He wasn't a worrier; his message was clear. And when we played cards, he always cut the deck before the hand was dealt.

"To be trusted," wrote George MacDonald, "is a greater compliment than to be loved." Emerson (see epigraph), unlike my father, trusted that the offering of trust would make other men trustworthy. Coaches should be inclined toward his view, rather than Dunne's—or my father's. But whether we're naïve or skeptical, we should *value* trust. And in the valuing, a coach should extend it to his athletes. He can watch and be wary or he can offer it with great faith, but it should be offered.

Athletes may be compliant to a coach's wishes or demands because of the nature of their relationship with an authority figure. But to an athlete, the trust of a coach is, indeed, a great compliment. It's also a great asset for him, as he attempts to master the mental aspects of his sport.

Item: An article about then Kansas basketball coach Roy Williams, who had taken much criticism in the media for having had wonderful won-lost records during the regular season but "disappointing" NCAA tournament results (Review CRITICISM, section 2) (*Associated Press*, March 25, 2002): "'[Coach Williams] has had so much confidence in this team all year,' [point guard Keith] Langford said, 'and we've trusted him back.'"

An even greater asset is the trust an athlete has *for* his coach. Given tangible evidence that the coach is trustworthy, the athlete will then allow himself to accept the coach's beliefs and edicts beyond *further* evidence. That's *faith*. It's been said that faith can move mountains; it surely can move an athlete's psyche in the right direction. Faith and trust in the coach are synonymous with *assurance, confidence, certainty, credibility,* and *unshaken opinion*. Those are powerful mental tools for an athlete to have at his disposal. And they're all kept in the coach's toolbox.

Item: A column by Harvey Araton about Jim O'Brien, who replaced Rick Pitino as coach of the Boston Celtics (*New York Times*, May 19, 2002): "Walter McCarty, a graduate of Pitino U., is one of three former Kentucky players on the Celtics. . . . 'Right now, the great thing about this team is how much we all trust each other,' said McCarty. 'We've got the coach's (trust) back, and the coach has ours. There's more focus on what you can do instead of what you can't. There's no more of, "If you don't do this, I'm going to leave."'"

■ ■ ■

But probably the most important trust given is the trust an athlete gives himself. If he doesn't trust his talent, if he doesn't trust his muscles during competition, if he doesn't trust that he knows how to execute the required task—all other trust is inconsequential, and his performance will reflected that consequence.

Self-trust is self-confidence. (See CONFIDENCE, section 3.) Both athlete and coach will be well served if the coach can help the athlete to develop and enhance his confidence.

An eighteenth-century cardinal wrote, "A man who doesn't trust himself can never really trust anyone else." That may often be the case. But I've come across many athletes who, because they didn't trust themselves, trusted *everyone* else. Whichever view is *right* in describing a particular athlete, the athlete's performance will be *"wrong."*

Urgency*

I didn't sense any anxiety or desperation. Determination, yes, but not desperation.
Green Bay fullback Chuck Mercein,
talking about the final Packers' drive
in the famous "Ice Bowl" game vs. Dallas

The secret of success is constancy of purpose.
Benjamin Disraeli

Often, without making a conscious choice, a coach employs a particular term about the game or moment his team faces, and that word works in a counterproductive way. (Review BIG GAME/EVENT, section 2.) The term I refer to is *urgency*. It's a very popular one with coaches, athletes, and media types. Lately, I've heard the word *desperation* used in the same context. I choose not to use either term when speaking with athletes. The words are too easily interpreted in such a way as to encourage tension and anxiety—in the athlete—and in the coach.

The constancy of purpose coaches should want from their athletes is to perform with a relaxed, intense, directed focus. The point has been made many times: the focus should be directed toward the task at hand, rather than the result. The athlete should perform aggressively, with his muscles relaxed.

Unfortunately, the term "urgency"—now a very popular and frequently used word—sends messages to the athlete that inhibit the kind of performance both he and the coach are looking for. The sense of urgency placed on a particular game or play can distract the athlete from the immediate task and cause him to think of the importance of outcome. Nothing good comes from such thoughts. Lest the reader think that urgency is never interpreted in such a way, let me refer to *The American Heritage Dictionary*. The word is *pressure*. Definition #6 states: "urgent claim or demand."

The words urgent and pressure can have a negative relationship. The athlete should not become part of a triangle with those terms and meanings.

What coaches mean when they use the term urgent is that a game or moment has the weight of importance to the extent that it is a "must-win game." Or a play that "has to be made." Essentially, the idea is correct. But invoking such language before the athletes approach the task at hand is to take the risk of having them internalize a point of view that tightens their muscles, focuses their minds on consequences rather than approach, and may get in the way of the very result the coach (and athlete) wishes to achieve.

The real intention behind a coach's use of "urgency" is to get everyone connected with the team to pay attention, to appreciate, for example, how important a game is. Should they pay more attention to this game than they have been to past competitions? If the answer is "yes" then the "constancy of purpose" has not been developed within the framework of the team's mental approach. The goal is *always* to focus with intensity on the moment. On the present. On the immediate function. On the proper approach. To point out the urgency of a game is to make a distinction. "This game *really* matters" is what's being conveyed. But every game should matter, every pitch, every play, every shot, every stroke.

There may be special significance to an event, but the special athlete brings his consistent approach to the arena. The coach should remind the team to take care of business the way they're always supposed to compete: by intelligently and aggressively approaching the execution of the task in front of them.

■ ■ ■

Quite often, the coach who talks about urgency is talking about his own need and anxieties. He would serve them better by asking the athletes for energy, intensity, zeal—and a sense of purpose. Always!

V

Values

If athletic competition does teach, then what more valuable lesson is there to learn from time to time than that we have a responsibility to stand up for what is right.
Pete Dawkins,
Heisman Trophy tailback, West Point, Colonel, U.S. Army

We have a commitment to competition, but we have a greater commitment to values, integrity and academic quality. . . . While we do have an occasional problem because these are young people, we simply do not tolerate unacceptable behavior. If you stick to that, the program builds a reputation over time.
Carol A. Cartwright,
president, Kent State U.

The words of President Cartwright were reinforced after her school re-hired football coach Dean Pees after a 1–10 record for the 2001 season. The program had one winning season in twenty years. "You don't hear of too many extensions after 1–10," Pees said.

You also don't hear about strong commitments to values beyond winning that are backed up when winning doesn't take place. That's the reality in many academic institutions. "Ultimately, every school has to police itself," Cartwright told a skeptic.

Every coach must make a decision and then a commitment to what he thinks is right. While all seem to pay lip service to the importance of teaching and representing values that are honorable, some do not put their money where their lips are.

■   ■   ■

Athletes who come into a program or organization bring their own backgrounds, interests, and sets of values. These values influence the meaning the athletes take from the environment around them. Each individual's world is shaped by his self-concept and he behaves accordingly.

Each coach, then, in understanding this, seeks to shape his team by initially establishing a collective set of representative beliefs. Whether it's called a value system, a credo, or a mission statement, the members should all recognize what specific aspirations and behaviors are valued and expected.

At both the amateur and professional level, I tried to present the attitude toward these values in a manner similar to the mothers of a particular Native American tribe, who said to their misbehaving children: "That is not the Hopi way." I came at it in the positive, for example, "This is the such-and-such way."

■ ■ ■

Rex Wells has more than 300 career wins as a high school wrestling coach. His teams have won two state championships and a number of conference titles. After a 13–2 season and a career record of 304–71, he told me (January, 2003): "I'm proudest of the things I can teach them that they can carry on in life. They're going to remember the ideals and principles they learned in practice."

One of his senior wrestlers told the local newspaper, "[Coach Wells] is always trying to teach us some life lessons. He teaches us how to fold clothes and take up after ourselves. To him, that is more important than teaching us any move."

■ ■ ■

Item: A column written by Bob Herbert appeared when Tyrone Willingham was hired as the new Notre Dame football coach ("An Unlikely Coach," *New York Times*, January 24, 2002): "'When I started to develop my fondness, or my love, for athletics,' (Willingham) said, 'it was because athletics was a powerful way to influence youngsters to be better people.' He said that while his goal at Notre Dame was to win championships, he always felt that the ultimate goal of athletics 'should be to help mold young people to be our leaders.'"

First, they must follow. And where that leader takes them will determine, to a great extent, the direction they seek when they're on their own.

What does the coach want his team to represent?

- Commitment: the enthusiastic devotion to individual preparation and team practices.
- Relentless execution: all-out effort from start to finish, regardless of score, significance or insignificance of event.
- Self-discipline: the control of emotions, thoughts, and focus.
- Good sportsmanship: respect for the opponents as his team tries to beat their brains out in competition. Showing up an opponent is unacceptable behavior. (See Items following.)
- Playing the game right: the application of knowledge and respect

of and for the specific sport and the nature of competition.

- Responsibility: to academics, to family, school or organization, community, and self.
- Courage: aggressive, competitive behavior—always, particularly in the face of adversity.
- Individual sacrifice: for the sake of collective goals.
- Concern: for what the uniform represents, as stated above; for the well-being of teammates.

■ ■ ■

Item: (From *The Sporting News*, August 5, 2002): "New York Yankees manager Joe Torre scolded [outfielder] Raul Mondesi recently for showing up the Devil Rays. After Mondesi hit a home run, he carried the bat nearly to first base and then flipped it aside. Mondesi told Torre that he had a history with the Devil Rays that went back to his days with the Blue Jays. That response didn't satisfy Torre, who does not want anyone to tarnish his team's reputation. Mondesi is trying hard to blend in with his new team, but such behavior shows his attitude doesn't fit with Torre's team-first mentality."

■ ■ ■

Item: Robert F. Kanaby, executive director of the National Federation of State High School Associations, had this to say about relative values (*Charlotte News & Observer*, July 28, 2002): "If we produce a high school quarterback who passes for 300 yards and leads his team to the state title, but who robs the convenience store that night, then we have failed."

Values, like journeys, are roads not destinations. High roads make for safer travel and rarified air—for the coach and the athlete.

Winning

I like to train. I enjoy challenges, but most of all I like winning.
Sugar Ray Leonard,
world champion professional boxer

What is there more of in the world than anything else? Ends.
Carl Sandburg,
The People

Winning is, of course, more fun than losing, and the desire to win is nothing to be ashamed of. But when the desire to win becomes the sole source of gratification from a sport, then we are as impoverished as if the sole value in food was its taste and not the nutrition we also receive.
Thomas Tutko,
Sports Psyching

Winning is a result, of course. A result of preparation, dedication, concentration, attitude—all the mental and physical aspects athletes and coaches are aware of but not always attentive to.

For some coaches, winning is the sole object in the big game of power and advancement. (Review ASPIRATIONS, section 2.) But most know that the striving is what a coach and his athletes will spend most of the time and energy on. And that their controllable behavior will provide their regular reward, assuming they behave appropriately.

■ ■ ■

There are means to the ends that Sandburg speaks of in the epigraph, and they are what the coach should focus on—and have his athletes be attentive to. The means are what an athlete should be attentive to when he's preparing and performing. The task in front of him. The now. The how to. The singular execution of a strategy or play. The ends come *as a result* of the physical behavior. The mental approach to the task will greatly determine the result. That approach is within the athlete's control. The result, as has been said *many* times in this book, is not.

Athletes can hear it many times, but they are often not resourceful enough to "find a winning way" on their own. They require a coach who will teach them how to go after the outcomes they want.

A key to achieving a desired result is in knowing *how* to succeed. For example, we can talk all we want about winning, but do we know how to win? What it takes? Well, to be repetitive, it takes commitment, preparation, focus on task, relaxed muscles, trust in one's talent, aggressiveness, self-control, insistence, persistence, and so on. All these are the ingredients for success. The *process* through which it's gained. Not today, necessarily, but with consistency and perseverance, tomorrow—or the day after.

All the topics in sections 2 and 3 are spokes that lead to a hub—the center, the *way* to be a winner. (See appendix D.)

■ ■ ■

Thomas Edison once said, "I have not failed. I've just found 10,000 ways that it won't work." But he did find a way, a favorite phrase of coaches. And the way to find a way is to *focus* on a way—a means of getting the job done. We must trust that an appropriate approach will provide us with what we want. In fewer than 10,000 attempts.

Well, Lombardi, Wooden, and Knight, and others like them, would have no problem with 10,000 repetitions. It would get done. The right execution, that is.

But let's consider the attitude these three coaches had about winning. John Wooden never referred to the word. His UCLA teams won regularly, and consecutively.

Bob Knight had this to say (*Scholastic Coach*, December 1982): "You can keep winning and losing in perspective by never thinking about either one. The ultimate objective is neither to win or keep from losing. I can tell people how to win some games, but I don't think many coaches know how to think about winning. The way you win is not by striving to just 'win the game,' but *by striving to play as well as you can*." (Emphasis was Knight's.)

And now for the words of Vince Lombardi, who bellowed them out on a particular day: "Winning isn't everything; but it's the only thing." Oft quoted, oft misunderstood. Lombardi had many one-liners referring to winning, but that one followed him to his grave.

These words he spoke at a later time, relating to the infamous remark, are rarely heard: "I wish to hell I'd never said the damned thing. I meant the effort. . . . I meant having a goal. . . . I sure as hell didn't mean for people to crush human values and morality." (*What It Takes To Be #1*, by Vince Lombardi Jr.)

He probably wished he had said: "Execution isn't everything; but it's the only thing." But his players knew what he was talking about. They knew that winning was really "a state of mind."

Losing, as well as winning, plays an important role in an athlete's personal growth and development. (See RESPONSE*, section 3.) Without experiencing both, he will find it difficult to objectively measure his performances and his skills. To test his persistence and courage.

But some athletic programs declare that winning is unimportant. It's been my experience that those who make the declaration are people connected with losing programs. They rationalize their program's weakness by saying that winning doesn't matter. Only losing does?

Winning does matter—to an appropriate extent. When winning is valued and appreciated, the attitudes of coaches and athletes are healthier. The practices are better organized and more meaningful. The competitive atmosphere is a positive stimulant.

Winning just shouldn't matter to an extreme. I recall the words of former NBA player, Marquette basketball coach, and CBS sports analyst Al McGuire: "Winning is overemphasized," he said. "The only time it's important is in surgery and war."

Another overstatement, perhaps. But it serves to remind me that coaches walk on a balance beam of glory. They must always watch their step.

Xs and Os

Wait a minute, let's remind ourselves, let's remind the world. Let's use that language [of being a teacher] all the time so it doesn't escape us that you have some job beyond Xs and Os.
Michael Josephson,
president, Josephson Institute

Mr. Josephson's words in the epigraph imply that the chalkboard is important, but that there is, for the best coaches, a "job beyond" it.

For the coach who wishes to effectively address the athlete's mental game, Xs and Os can be but one aspect of his total responsibility. He must approach the athlete directly and individually and help him to interpret, understand, and improve his thinking patterns—and put a harness on his emotions.

As has been previously noted, some athletes will not learn because their internal insecurities prevent them from hearing anything but the dull, insistent, internal buzzing of their insecurities and unmet needs. The coach may paint a picture of what the game should be but the athlete is unable to see it clearly.

When an athlete keeps repeating the same mistakes, the coach should see the "red flag" of someone whose mental game is deficient. Going back to the drawing board will not stop that flag from being waved. Xs and Os are part of the *analytical aspect* of preparation. The *human aspect* must not be neglected. The teacher-coach may know his subject but he'd better know his student-athlete.

Asking, probing, encouraging, motivating, clarifying, reiterating, reinforcing, disciplining: the coach helps enhance the athlete's mental game through the use of these approaches and responses. They are directed at those who are called upon to integrate the coach's teachings into behavior. It's sometimes hard to remember that it is *others* who must *apply* all our profound principles. Theory must become practice. For many athletes, the leap from one to the other is wide and threatening.

John Dunning, expressing a view in opposition to a popular saying, wrote, "A magnificent picture is never worth a thousand perfect words.

Ansel Adams can be a great artist, but he can never be Shakespeare. His tools are too literal." I share Dunning's belief.

Xs and Os are literal. They paint the picture of what's there, on the surface, so to speak. Shakespeare's words indicated what is hidden—in the recesses of a Hamlet's psyche, preventing him from acting on his theoretical plan. Anyone coaching Hamlet would not initially spend time diagramming plays. Not if he wanted the guy to perform.

Yes-People

*We love flattery, even though we are not deceived by it, because it
shows that we are of importance enough to be courted.*
Ralph Waldo Emerson,
"Gifts," Essays: Second Series

And yet, Emerson's view notwithstanding, I have seen men and women
who seemed to have been deceived by the yes-people surrounding
them. They acted on a bobble-head subordinate's professed agreement
of their own views—with poor results.

Many leaders say what I've had some of my own bosses say: "I don't
want yes-men around me." It's the smart thing to say. It's the smarter
thing to believe. It's the smartest thing to encourage assistant coaches to
express opinions, even though they may be in opposition to the head
coach's point of view. It's not what most frequently happens.

The agenda of those who tell the boss he's right all the time is a simple and clear one: self-preservation. Constant and indiscriminate agreement is not a relative of sincerity. Yet many people in positions of power
are duped by it, because their own agenda is as insincere as that of the
yes-man.

In order to have assistant coaches operate at their best, a head coach
needs to establish a trust that subordinates' opinions and ideas that run
contrary to those of the head coach are appreciated always, even if
rarely implemented.

Players should also be encouraged to provide input, if they have
something they think is worth offering. Some coaches don't appreciate
hearing players' opinions. The environment suffers, but a concern of
mine is the internal environment of the coach himself. Stubborn? Is he
dictatorial? Do his ego needs preclude an ability to have anyone else
know something he doesn't know or hasn't yet thought of? When the
answer to any of these questions is a "yes," most often it indicates a sign
of insecurity or an arrogant arbitrariness.

The open-minded coach is healthier than the close-minded one. The
healthy coach is not threatened by opinions, advice, or criticism. Or by
the candidness of others.

The coach who is aware and secure recognizes flattery that originates from the insecurities or hidden agendas of others. Knowing what's true and what's best, he encourages those around him to act out of the healthy motives. He courts creative thought and honesty, motivated by the desire to do whatever helps them achieve their common goals. No matter who originally owned the thought.

Z

Zapped
(Burned out)

But he was used to switching off, to living his life in separate compartments. He'd learnt early, in his first few months of practice, that those who take the misery home with them burn out and end up of no use to anybody.
Pat Barker,
Regeneration

"Taking it home" is not good for a coach. Nor is it good for whoever is at home, waiting for his return. The youngest and most energetic coaches can best conserve their mental energy and exuberance by compartmentalizing. By having a perspective that allows them to recognize the existence of a world other than the world of the sport he coaches.

By "leaving it in the locker room"—or his office—the coach gives himself an opportunity to regenerate his vitality, enthusiasm, brain cells. His wider perspective also allows him to better handle the frustrations and difficulties of the job. To better handle the issues the athletes have. Having himself "together" allows him to put some of his athletes back together. The suffering leader makes everyone around him suffer.

■ ■ ■

Earlier in this section, a reference was made to Temple basketball coach John Cheney. (Review ADVERSITY*, section 2.) He was so distraught at one point during the 2002 season that he spoke of retiring. A poem he recited for the reporters before stating, "I could probably quit somewhere in this season," indicated how mentally fatigued he must have been.

The prelude to the poem was a statement that "I think the Lord is against me." His recitation follows.

> The world is against me he said with a sigh.
> Somebody stops every damn scheme that I try.
> > The world has me down and is keeping me there.
> I don't get a chance. The world is unfair.

Does that not sound like burnout? It can happen to anyone. This plaintive expression about the plight of the poor expressed Chaney's feelings at the time. Was it at all relevant to his own lesser plight? It seems that he felt it was. And what one feels can be very a compelling agent for what one says and does. He did not retire, apparently after reconsidering the reality of circumstances and the state of mind he had when he recited the poem to the press.

Also, his team performed much better.

■ ■ ■

George Welch, sixty-seven years old, meant it. He announced his retirement as head football coach at the University of Virginia. A former quarterback at Navy, Welsh had been a coach for nearly forty years, including tenures at Navy (1973–1981) and Virginia (1982–2000).

Welch wrote in the *New York Times* (December 17, 2000):

> In weighing my decision to retire, I didn't think I had burned out, but almost. I had started to get more nervous, I didn't have the energy to do what I used to do. . . . And I was getting so tired at night; I couldn't work those extra hours it took for a head coach to do the job the way it should be done.
>
> I don't know why the pressure became greater for me in the last couple of years. It's hard to explain. Some coaches—I'm sure Joe Paterno of Penn State is one of them—don't feel that kind of pressure. But I did . . .
>
> When Joe Gibbs quit as coach of the Washington Redskins . . . I read that he was shaking a little bit during the season and maybe after the season. That's the way I felt. I didn't want to go through another year with that stress, not being able to sleep most nights. And I would wake up in the middle of the night until I started taking some sleeping pills. It didn't seem to be worth it anymore. Not because of the level of expectation I had set for myself, but the losses became harder to take; we were 13–10 during that time, so we weren't setting the world on afire. It was as if some guy said, "You ran out of gas." And I was afraid it was going to affect my health.

A couple or so years earlier his wife gave him an ultimatum: quit coaching or I quit the marriage. He kept coaching. She must have seen what was coming before Welsh himself did.

■ ■ ■

My personal zapping experience came while I was a member on the staff of the Tampa Bay Devil Rays in 1998. An expansion team, the Rays had more difficulties than the people in the organization could manage. Some in the organization created more problems than they solved.

A serious family illness issue at home concerned and distracted me, and the daily working environment frustrated me. I had some anger and resentment about the way players and the front office were going about their business.

My sense that I had not been doing my own business very well was confirmed when one of the players, an affable pitcher named Scott Aldred, said to me in the clubhouse one day, "Harv, are you ever going to talk to us again?" We both laughed, but I knew my decision would not be a laughing matter. Many truths are said in jest.

It was time to change. My inability to respond well in an adverse environment provided the answer. It was time to leave. I did.

■ ■ ■

My father once told me that everything in my body was working hard. But the total you, he said, is not. "Force yourself." As much as we may love what we do, we sometimes have to force ourselves to do it. Especially to do it *right*! Losing seasons, athletes in trouble, badgering parents, adversarial administrators. It ain't always easy for coaches. The fight they have is similar to what was addressed in chapter 7—referring to resistant athletes. A coach must formulate and entertain every strategy he can think of, and think hard, rather than feeling hard. He should do as much as he can to combat all recognizable issues.

When all has been done, and if all has failed, he should then consider moving on. The discomfort of change, for me, has always been better than the ease of becoming ineffective, stagnant, and cynical—harmful to myself and to others. Zapped.

Section 3

The Mental Game, A to Z

Athletes' Impact Terms

Section 3 Contents

Adversity*

Fire is the test of gold; adversity of strong men.
Seneca,
On Providence

It is difficulties that show men what they are.
Epictetus

Shakespeare thought that the uses of adversity were "sweet." That's because his thought process led him to think of it as something one could learn from, rather than something one would be threatened by—used by. The point of view is not uncommon; the point of action is. Confronting adversity and responding to it with courage and energy allows us to use it instead of being used by it.

It should be mentioned here that, at one time or another, all of us meet with adversity in and away from the arenas and fields of athletic competition. The serious illness of a family member, for example, can be a terrible burden and distraction. My advice to athletes when that is the case has been simple and direct. First, it must be determined whether he should be elsewhere. Is there something he can do to remedy the situation or solve the problem? If so, then I encourage him to stop agonizing about what to do and fulfill his responsibility. Do what needs to be done.

If there is nothing that can be done—that is, no immediate control the player can exert over the adverse circumstance to improve it—I try to help that player concentrate on what he *should* be doing at the field: functioning effectively during a complicated time. Easy to say, hard to do.

An athlete may feel ill himself—or tired—before and during competition. The best competitors are effective even when they are not at their physical best. Actually, the body most often will provide the athlete what he asks for if he wants to "win the war." The body's sympathetic nervous system kicks in as compensation for minor fatigue or illness. A "battler" will get an extra adrenal charge. Everyone who has ever competed can remember a day (days!) when, though he felt terrible, his performance was wonderful.

When facing adversity, a choice must be made. Will it be fight—or flight? Tough-minded athletes will last longer than tough times.

Facing adversity down elevates us—shows us the best of what we are. Anything that can provide such a strong effect doesn't come easy.

■ ■ ■

Mike Jarvis, coaching the St. Johns University basketball team, said about his players, "We're tough, but what I want to emphasize is that we're mentally tough. What I look for are players who have not just won all their lives, but who have been through some type of adversity and who have found a way to come through it." Good for him. Better for the players.

Finding the way often requires assistance—a someone to give directions leading to that right way. The coach should consider himself responsible for being such a person. It's fine for a coach when he has an athlete or athletes who show up in his program already mentally tough. It's a rarity, however. A college coach recruiting athletes can look for that toughness; a high school coach is much more likely to be a first instrument.

■ ■ ■

The coach addresses the mental game by:

- Helping the athlete to recognize that people will inevitably be faced with adversity in their professional and/or personal lives, rather than ignoring or denying that eventuality.
- Teaching the athlete to consider, philosophically, that an adverse circumstance is a challenge, rather than a threat.
- Encouraging the athlete to be self-assertive, rather than self-pitying.
- Helping the athlete to think of possible solutions, rather than dwelling on the problem.
- Directing the athlete, during competition, to think about what to do (execute the task at hand), rather than give in to how he is feeling.
- Teaching the athlete to recognize what is happening; to gather his thoughts; to coach himself with positive self-talk—"C'mon, execute (whatever the task)," or utilize whatever mantra the athlete chooses. All this, rather than forfeiting his internal control to adverse external factors of the moment.

Aggressiveness

No absolute is going to make the lion lie down with the lamb; unless the lamb is inside.

D. H. Lawrence

I was twelve years old when my father told me, "You're going to be either the hunter or the prey. Make up your mind which one it's going to be." It was overstated, of course—the semantic either–or orientation. But the picture painted by the metaphor was perfectly clear to me.

One of the synonyms for "aggressive," as noted in *The American Heritage Dictionary*, is "assertive." The term will serve those well who wish to understand what aggressiveness should mean to an athlete.

In order to be assertive, an athlete must put himself in an attack mode. Success for him, whether it's going down a ski slope or hitting a tennis ball, comes from adopting that philosophy and putting it into action.

By being aggressive the athlete increases the personal likelihood of success. He competes to succeed, rather than being tentative or submissive, playing to prevent failure, which many do. (See FEAR OF FAILURE, section 3.)

To be aggressive is to be proactive, rather than reactive. An opponent will recognize the difference quickly, perceiving the athlete to be aggressive or passive—or, worse yet, submissive. When an athlete's approach is nonaggressive, he forfeits whatever edge he may have had because of talent or circumstance. Aggressors have usually been victorious throughout history, because they intimidated through confrontation. The nonaggressive participant will most likely be the vanquished, not the victor.

I haven't met an athlete who hasn't understood this point—or who argued it. They know. Intelligence and understanding are there. What is missing? Trust, courage, discipline—and, inevitably, assertiveness.

■ ■ ■

The step from being tentative to being submissive is not a long one. Having taken this step, an athlete will feel himself far removed from the confidence he values and needs. A person who is nonassertive needs to change his behavior before he can gain or regain that feeling of confidence. He must learn to act aggressively, even though he is reluctant to do so. It does not happen over night; it is a challenging process. The more ingrained the bad habit, the more challenging it is to change it.

■ ■ ■

It *is* possible to be too aggressive. Remember, the Greeks said it 2,500 years ago: "Nothing in excess." Balance is required—control. Overaggressive athletes try too hard. They become the proverbial bull in the china shop. They "try" to attack wildly, like a frantic boxer who swings his arms without regard to his target—or his overexposure.

Aggressiveness is not a frantic behavior. It is controlled, methodical, relentless. A number of the many athletes with whom I've discussed this issue have responded to my initial critique of their out-of-control aggressiveness with "But I'm a COMPETITOR!" An ineffective one, I answer. It's one thing to want to win; it's another to know how to win. Overaggressiveness doesn't get the competitor what he most wants—success. (See COMPETITOR, section 3.)

The athlete who is too aggressive accelerates his thought process, which speeds up and tightens his muscles. Execution suffers as a result. Too much becomes too little.

Years ago, I told a minor league pitcher in the Oakland organization that he pitched like a linebacker. "I AM a linebacker," he replied. I reminded him he was supposed to be a pitcher. He had, in fact, been a linebacker at the University of Arkansas, but he learned to harness the energy and competitive spirit he had brought to football and control his emotions on the pitching mound. He got to the big leagues and is now a major league bullpen coach. He advocates an aggressive, controlled approach, I'm certain.

■ ■ ■

Finally, as major league pitcher Kevin Brown says—and now backs up with behavior: "If you make a bad pitch *aggressively* [his emphasis], you have a much better chance of getting away with it. However, if you make a pitch tentatively or cautiously, that's when you get nailed."

The athlete in every sport will "nail" his nonaggressive opponent.

■ ■ ■

The coach addresses the mental game by teaching the athlete to:

- Gain an advantage physically and psychologically in competition by being aggressive.
- Use the advantage by relentlessly competing.
- Understand that just as a racecar has an accelerator, it also has a brake, and the athlete keeps aggressiveness under control by knowing when to use the brake—not by shifting into reverse.
- Express this "braking" by controlling thoughts, emotions, and physical movements.
- Recognize when aggressiveness becomes extreme and make an adjustment by coaching himself calmly with positive, functional

directions. And deep breathing.

- Trust his aggressive approach, knowing that the results will not always be favorable.

Aloneness

[Loneliness is] the central and inevitable experience of every man.
Thomas Wolfe

One of the experiences of aloneness is founded on the belief that what an individual is going through, in terms of his inner workings and issues, are exclusive to him. No one else shares such traits or difficulties. That belief reduces the sense of self-worth at the same time it increases all kinds of self-camouflage.

The initial feelings expressed by athletes I've worked with have been related to the relief they have that their sufferings are not exclusive to them. "I thought I was a weak act, and everybody else had his stuff together," said one player. The mental agenda is a hidden agenda, and when it's revealed it can be threatening to the person who opens himself up. How nice to know that his state of being is part of the human condition. "I'm not a freak," as one fellow put it.

■ ■ ■

When working with professional baseball teams, I'd speak at spring training before the players stretched. They'd have their minds stretched first, and then they'd stretch their muscles. The talks would be short and on a variety of topics aimed at enlightening the players about themselves, the game they played, and life, in general—occasionally, in very specific terms.

One day I remember speaking to the Oakland players about dragging the child we were with us for the rest of lives, instead of keeping what we wanted and jettisoning the rest. The players stood in a semicircle facing me. As I spoke I surveyed my audience. I saw tears running down the cheeks of a big outfielder standing to my left. "I hit his button," I thought to myself.

The next day I spoke about courage. Again I saw tears running down that same long face. I can't recall the following day's subject, but the picture of those tears running down again is vivid. "What's going on here?" I asked myself. I soon found out.

As the team broke to move to the area where they did their physical stretching, the outfielder walked next to me, put his arm around my shoulder, and said, "Harv, that's great shit. But do me a favor; tomorrow talk about somebody else." (One of my very favorite *true* stories.)

I turned to face him. "Dan, do you really think I'm talking about you?" He did. When told him these were universal themes about the human predicament, he was much relieved. And, it should be noted, this guy was—is—a very intelligent person.

■ ■ ■

Precocious athletes, like ordinary people, are comforted in their misery by company. More so, because their talent is relatively exclusive to them, so they think their inner worlds are as well. They are relieved to know that they're not the exclusive possessor of troubling issues. A coach, knowing this, can relieve many pressure valves. (Or he can unwittingly create the pressure by addressing his athletes as if they are the only ones who screw up, or can't remember plays or tactics, or clutch up in tight situations.) Better to help than to hinder.

■ ■ ■

I spoke at a coaches' convention a couple of years ago. A big one. After my talk, I was escorted to a smaller room. There I entertained questions of specific interest to members of the audience who followed me into the room for the purpose of having those questions answered. That session took two-plus hours.

Many questioners left after a time, but one young man remained until everyone else was gone. He had been a demonstrator for a coach in a presentation given before mine. He was a high school catcher and his coach brought him there to teach the technique of blocking balls. He did this admirably.

Just the two of us remained in the room, and he took the opportunity he'd waited for to reveal how unhappy and adversely affected he was by the coach's treatment of him. Of how there was no joy in playing anymore (and, in fact, there was some dysfunction). I responded to him and told him we'd stay in touch with each other. Before he left, he handed me an envelope. It contained an essay he had written for his advanced placement English class. I won't reveal what its contents were, but I will include an excerpt from my letter of response to him.

> Dear Joe,
> I read your essay on the plane flight home. I enjoyed it and appreciated it. . . . It is articulate, intelligent, honest and direct. I expect it was well received by your audience (teacher? class?).
> At the [convention], I spoke to the coaches about "the universality of human emotions"—and how players think they are the only ones with fear, etc. I told the anecdote about the player who thought I was talking about him every day when I addressed the team before stretching. Well, your line about

Robin Yount, "who struggled with these fear issues just as I was," speaks to that point. As does your next sentence: "Feeling as if I had a partner in this situation I no longer felt as if I struggled alone." In that regard, none of us struggles "alone."

The most important company we have is our selves. During my early years I was most often alone, bedridden—without peers or friends, since I rarely attended school. But somehow I developed a sense of self, so that despite the physical weakness I perceived in myself, I somehow managed—with the help of books—to understand that the self is the most important company and that it is not a platitude to say that no one is alone.

■ ■ ■

One of Stephen Sondheim's wonderful songs is entitled "No One is Alone." Bernadette Peters sings it in a way that can make anyone believe it's true, which it is.

■ ■ ■

The coach addresses the mental game by:

- Teaching the athletes that circumstance may be unique to the individual (may be!) but the internal responses to it are shared by many, if not most, people.
- Creating an environment in which players feel comfortable communicating their athletic and personal concerns to the coach.
- Responding to the athlete's concerns in a calm and controlled manner, thereby giving the athlete confidence that the issue he has is neither unique nor unmanageable.

Anger*

> Anger, resentment, envy and self-pity are wasteful reactions.
> . . . They sap energy better devoted to productive endeavors.
> **The Honorable Ruth Bader Ginsburg,**
> associate justice, U.S. Supreme Court

The angry athlete's brain systematically sounds an alarm system for the automatic nervous system. Adrenaline pours into the bloodstream. Blood pressure increases, breathing become abnormal. The athlete is ready for a "fight," rather than "flight." Yes, he's willing, but unfortunately, he's not able. An angry performer can't think, can't focus, can't control his muscles, and can't execute his task. Even an aggressive football lineman must have a significant degree of emotional control. The anger may provoke him, but it cannot control him.

It's difficult to control muscles (the application of skill) when thoughts (the execution of strategy) aren't being controlled. The athlete isn't going to put up much of a battle against an opponent when he's so preoccupied with whatever has provoked his rage.

And yet, I've had some athletes tell me they like being angry. These fellows are most often sensitive, nonassertive, inhibited and self-doubting, who finally explode, externally or internally, as a result of "the straw that breaks their back," as they've explained it to me. The anger frees them from their self-consciousness. From feeling, as they invariably do, that they are so terribly responsible for so many things. They like the freedom that anger seems to provide. "I just don't care any more," they've said. That's only natural, since they have been caring too much about too many of the wrong things.

Those concerns "just don't matter," when they're angry. For them, the prospect of failure and always wanting to please others (what they "care" about) is washed away in a raging torrent of adrenaline. They pay a dear price, however. Because it rarely, if ever, works for them. And it can't be sustained if it does. (See AROUSAL and NICE PERSON, section 3.)

Anger can work for an athlete only if it is very brief in duration. It may "clean the blood," and then be used as an attention-getter for a wandering focus; it must subside before the athlete gets back on task. If anger continues, distraction from that task continues. The athlete, as noted, will be preoccupied by whatever provoked him—usually frustrated expectations. Being mad is not being prepared. He must deal with his anger before he is able to deal with the immediate future: before the execution of the next task.

The athlete will not be able to fix what has already happened, and if he doesn't fix himself, he can look forward to further problems. He'll be punished, not so much for his anger, as by it.

■　■　■

The coach addresses the mental game by helping the athlete:

- To understand his personality and emotional tendencies.
- To recognize the degree of anger he expresses, the timing of it, the causes of it.
- To understand that anger is a strong emotion that can preempt rational response and interfere with controlled thoughts, breathing, muscle movement, and vision.
- To develop an understanding of the importance of making adjustments as quickly as possible, of recognizing anger during competition, and separating himself from it quickly.

- To learn, using this recognition, to use anger, rather than allowing it to use him, by motivating him to "pay attention to business."
- To then direct himself to calm down, breathe deeply, and get ready to focus on the execution of the next task.

Approach

Perhaps the most valuable lesson of education is the ability to make yourself do the thing you have to do when it has to be done.
Aldous Huxley

When talking with athletes about their performance, I make certain to lead the discussion toward how they approach it: their general preparation, that is, their daily regimen—eating, sleeping, conditioning habits, and routines. We then move down to the bottom rung on the ladder of abstraction. We talk about the very specific matter of an athlete's approach during the actual competition, about his identifiable behaviors—internal and external—during competition. Essentially, it's the litmus test for an athlete; his approach will determine how successful he will be.

■ ■ ■

One of the meanings of the word *approach* is: "the method used in dealing with or accomplishing something." *Method* is the key word here, indicating *how* one goes about trying to accomplish whatever it is one sets out to do. As Huxley says, doing the thing the athlete has to do in competition. And employing the effective methods to accomplish it.

Making shots, *scoring* goals, *getting* hits are about results. Effective execution of task is about *behavior*. That is what I talk about first with athletes, making the distinction between approach and result, then addressing the hows.

How to eat properly, how to regulate sleeping patterns, how to get in shape and stay in shape are usually very obvious to players. (Whether or not they apply what they know is another matter.) Less obvious, and more difficult to apply even when understood, is how to mentally prepare between performances—and how to think and act during competition.

■ ■ ■

As a youngster in elementary school, I was taught in arithmetic lessons that large fractions are unwieldy and unmanageable. It is, I was told, too difficult to add, subtract, multiply, and divide them. For example, how, as a fourth-grader, could I be expected to divide 160/48000 by 8000/24000? I was not, and I could not. (We had no calculators then.) But I could manage 1/30 divided by 1/3. By reducing to lowest terms— by getting those fractions to be as simple as they could be—I could effectively deal with the example and get the answer: 1/10. (The lowest common denominator was the vehicle for approaching the addition and subtraction of the large fractions.)

■　■　■

Now, let me specifically and simply apply this lesson to an athlete's approach. The lowest common denominator every performer shares is the execution of the next task. What has happened and what might happen will vary with each athlete and each circumstance. But the next task must be made: a block, a tackle, a pass, a pitch, a stride, or a stroke. It is a universal truth within every game. That is how the competition progresses. One manageable task at a time. That is the focus of the moment—for observers and participants. That is the action reduced to its simplest term: the moment, the task at hand.

But does this moment exclusively hold the athlete's attention? If not, the approach suffers. The performer cannot expect the result he desires. The more complicated and scattered his thoughts, the more unmanageable his task. His distractions will force him to think big, rather than think small. His focus on whatever task he must execute will not be intense. This one "small" deficit becomes the athlete's biggest inhibitor to performing effectively.

■　■　■

The athletes I've been with over the years have revealed any number of different intrusive and distracting thoughts. It is the human predicament to have conflicting thoughts and impulses. "Isn't that normal?" I've been asked many times, after having admonished an athlete for his poor approach. It is, yes, but to be "normal"—ordinary—should not be the goal of any competitive athlete. Exceptional is the goal; normal is the excuse.

"Keep it simple," I say constantly. It should be a performer's mantra. Big thoughts, many thoughts, conflicting thoughts all divide the athlete's attention, thereby corrupting his approach. A task is not done well if not approached well. It is critical for athletes to understand and embrace the simple approach noted below.

■　■　■

The approach leads to a result. A good approach has a much better chance of producing the desired result. However, that is not an inherent guarantee in competition. An athlete may execute a fine shot, a great pass, a perfect pitch. But other factors cause a bad result: the wind takes the ball off its path; the great pass is dropped; the hitter flails at the perfect pitch and hits a lame duck just over the infielder's outstretched arm. Results *cannot be controlled.*

But the performer can control the approach. Always. He can't control what happens after the task has been executed. He executed effectively; he should repeat his effective behavior instead of concerning himself with what the result was.

I tell every athlete that he defines himself by the way he approaches his competitive task. His plan, his poise, his intensity, his aggressiveness, his focus. His breathing pattern, his tempo, his body language. That is behavior. That is approach.

Directly related, and as important, is the athlete's response. (See RESPONSE, section 3.)

■ ■ ■

The coach addresses the mental game by helping the athlete to:

- Understand that the manner in which he approaches his goals and tasks identifies him to his teammates, his opponents, and, if he is paying attention, to himself.
- Examine the quality and extent of his preparation leading up to performance—his habits regarding sleep, nutrition, workouts, and routines.
- Recognize his past behavioral tendencies during competition, especially in difficult times and situations.
- Recognize that his approach is comprised of thought and deed; it is entirely his responsibility and within his control. (Results are not.)
- Understand what an approach to competition actually means. (See above.)
- Be aware of thoughts and behaviors that are not conducive to peak performance and make the necessary adjustments as quickly as possible.
- Remind himself to reduce performance to its most manageable form—one task at a time.
- Hold himself accountable for asserting the mental discipline of an incorruptible approach.

Arousal

The "fire in the belly" is the metaphorical flame of the competitor. But just as every competitor is different, so must every flame be different— adjusted to the level of intensity and control that will allow the athlete to be effective in competition.

We each have a different capacity; we each have a different need.

■ ■ ■

Many of the athletes I've been associated with, when asked what "arousal" means, tell me "being psyched-up—let's go!" Others have related the term to anxiety: having heightened feelings (heart palpitations, sweaty palms, diarrhea), they say, stimulated by a negative anticipation of the performance ahead. According to those responses, a performer, then, may be "worked up" for better or for worse. And so it is.

Research has shown that athletes typically experience physical symptoms before competition in which they invest meaning. The best competitors I know invest the meaning of "challenge" to each performance. Bruce Bochy managed Kevin Brown in San Diego during the 1998 season and was impressed by the challenge Kevin saw before each outing— "the fire and intensity that he [Brown] brings to every game he pitches," Bochy said.

Some athletes view competition as a "threat." Then there are those who invest minimal meaning to each performance and still others whose assessment is reliably unpredictable. While each athlete's arousal level is influenced by his interpretation of the event or situation he is to face, it's also influenced by the degree of trust he has in himself.

The most effective competitor knows himself; he manages whatever physical indicators exist prior to his performance. He knows whether he has too much energy ("I'm hyper." "I'm out of control.") or too little ("I can't get up for this." "I can't get my mind on business.").

■ ■ ■

When an athlete and I talk about finding an appropriate arousal level, we first examine the type of personality he has. For example, some people are introverted, others extroverted. Some are hyperactive, others laid back. We then consider the differences in types of activity and the particular arousal level for each. If he's a football lineman, high-energy, high arousal serves him because that gross motor activity involves strength, stamina, physical contact, and bursts of speed. Pitching requires fine muscle movements, precision and control, balance, and intense concentration on a small field of attention (the target). During competition, a pitcher is more likely to require calming mechanisms (as would a golfer) than those requiring more power (as would a weightlifter).

And personality? Many sports psychologists believe that individuals have distinctive biological differences affecting arousal. An extrovert tends to produce a slower and less pronounced stimulus than does an introvert. For the extrovert, there is a need for more intense input from an external stimulus. The introvert, often the "more sensitive" person, tends to produce a stronger internal sensory signal and so requires less external input to become aroused. A coach need not motivate him to play.

Many athletes (many *people*) see the opposite as being true, because of outward appearance. They don't see inside the athlete, however. They see fire in a Kevin Brown's eye, perhaps, but not in Jamie Moyer's. But each of these personality types can have a competitive approach. And they have developed their own methods for optimal arousal, based on how they're predisposed to feel before performance. The fact is, a high-energy personality needs a greater input to generate his greater need for excitement, more fuel to keep that motor running. He has a higher threshold for arousal and uses external sources of stimulation (a particular opponent or race, etc.). Introverts don't require those outside signals. And they tend to have more developed fine motor skills. They are usually control (command) people, not power people.

Both coach and individual athlete can work together to determine the most effective arousal level.

Most important is the ability of an athlete to properly *adjust* and channel whatever level of arousal he's feeling during competition. To psyche up or psyche down, according to need.

Item: This about Lleyton Hewitt's victory in a tennis match at Roland Garros in Paris (*Associated Press*, May 30, 2002): "At that juncture, Hewitt was playing shakily and without emotion. At the ensuing changeover, though, he ripped off his white headband. Suddenly, it was as if he flipped a switch on his racket from 'Off' to 'On.' The transformation was amazing. . . . He punctuated winning shots by beating his chest with his palm, pumping his fists, and exhorting himself with yells of 'Come on, Rock!'—he watched the Sly Stallone sequel in the morning—'Fight! Fight!'"

■ ■ ■

The metaphor I use is the flame of a kerosene lamp. "If it flickers, it will be of no use," I tell the athletes. "At the other extreme, you don't want to burn the house down! Heat and light, that's what we want. Heat and light. The same with arousal."

■ ■ ■

The coach addresses the mental game by teaching the athlete to:

- Understand his individual predisposition toward anticipated competition.
- Make distinctions between what level of arousal one position or sport requires and what another requires (Example: A linebacker vs. a quarterback) and determine what is appropriate for his needs.
- Determine the level of arousal he has had when his performances have been positive, as well as the level when they have not been satisfactory.
- Recognize the possibility that he may need to heighten his pregame arousal—turn the flame up. If so, he should concentrate his thoughts on his game strategy and visualize past performances when he has dominated in order to get adrenaline flowing early.
- Recognize the possibility that he may need to lower his arousal— turn the flame down. If so, he should sit in a quiet place, breathe deeply in a consistent pattern, relax his muscles, and employ self-talk in a calming and low-key manner.
- Make the same adjustments during competition, though for a shorter duration. (Self-talk example to heighten arousal: "Let's go! Get focused." Perhaps, even, "Fight! Fight!" Self-talk example to lower arousal: "Be easy now. Right to the target." Etc.)

Attitude

If you look at life one way, there is always cause for alarm.
Elizabeth Bowen,
The Death of the Heart

Attitudes are shaped early in our lives. We are all taught by parents, teachers, and peers. We interpret our experiences through these teachings. The glass that is perceived as being half empty or half full serves as an example of how different people can look at the same thing and identify it in different ways, in this case, both being correct.

But sometimes, we're not close to being correct. And that false perception—that "one-way look"—will influence the attitude we carry forward. It doesn't have to.

■ ■ ■

Viktor Frankl, in his profound book *Man's Search for Meaning*, speaks of our ability to be self-determining. "Man does not simply exist," Frankl writes, "but always decides what his existence will be. . . . Every human being has the freedom to change at any instant. . . . The last of the human freedoms is to choose one's attitude in any given set of circumstances, to choose one's own way."

In other words, we aren't bound to be tomorrow what we have been today; we are not bound to act tomorrow as we have acted today. We have the freedom to make a choice about our attitude.

Athletes I've come across who were considered to have bad attitudes are, as their teammates so directly put it, "clueless" about all this. The ones with good attitudes act like "free" people, and they are healthier and happier—and greatly valued by their teammates and coaches. And they play to their peak far more consistently than "bad apples." They *always* contribute to the team—by their example alone.

The major point, for me, is that they are free. Athletes with poor attitudes are unhappy—victims of their own weakness, quick to blame circumstance or other people when confronted about unacceptable behavior. They have forfeited their freedom. They wait for the world to make them happy. It does not happen often, and when it does, it doesn't last very long.

Almost all of the athletes I've had a working relationship with have understood the difference between a good attitude and a bad one. I would further say that *almost* all appreciated the benefits of having a healthy attitude. Some just did not have the personal strength and self-discipline to work on changing. They are victims of the bad habits their attitudes have created.

■ ■ ■

An athlete doesn't have to be a troublemaker on a team to qualify as having a bad attitude. He is a troublemaker for himself. Negative expectations burden him and inhibit his performance. His perspective on his performance, and on life in general, is clouded to such an extent that he can't make necessary changes. He just bemoans his fate and/or disparages himself. His self-talk works against him. And on it goes.

That individual doesn't recognize the possibility of making a choice to honest about what he sees and having the freedom to change what he sees and does not like. Some encouragement from the coach would probably be necessary and would definitely be helpful. But personal commitment and determination on the athlete's part will ultimately be responsible for whatever change of attitude results.

■ ■ ■

A few words about the term *attitude* as used by those who say a performer "has an attitude" when he competes. The extensional meaning in that context defines the athlete as tough-minded, aggressive, and insensitive to irrelevant environmental conditions—conditions that would distract someone without the attitude. Such competitors give no quarter; they are pit bulls who have to be dragged off the field or course. Their attitudes get respect from their teammates, their coaches, and the people they sink their teeth into. (See COMPETITOR, section 3.)

It's also "all about" perspective, enthusiasm, aggressiveness, self-respect, and commitment. Attitudes point athletes in the direction they will go and, at the same time, identify the person making the journey.

"Where do you start?" Davis said when he arrived in Cleveland. "I told the team in the locker room that it's amazing what a football team can accomplish when everybody is committed to each other."

Attitude is about trust, as well. It is the state of mind with which we approach our surroundings, our performance, our teammates, our opponents, and our lives. The athletes who most fulfill themselves have healthy attitudes; those with bad attitudes have what Chesterton called "a bad smell in the mind." Coaches should keep a disinfectant at hand.

■ ■ ■

Coaches address the mental game by holding the athlete accountable:
- For making himself aware of his existing attitudes through honest evaluation.
- For making the effort to understand why and how these attitudes were developed.

- For recognizing the freedom of choice he has to change an attitude, rather than feeling he is destined to stay the same because of genes or circumstance.
- For identifying what attitude changes, if any, he would like to make.
- For exerting the consistent energy to form and reform desired attitudes through self-awareness and persistence.
- For identifying the many choices of attitudes that exist. Choices between attitudes include being:
  1. Pessimistic or optimistic
  2. Cooperative or uncooperative
  3. Open minded or close minded
  4. Responsible or irresponsible
  5. Selfless or selfish
  6. Committed or indifferent
  7. Realistic or unrealistic
  8. A problem solver or a problem causer
  9. Relentless or yielding

And so on.

B

Body Language

By the husk you may guess at the nut.
Thomas Fuller, M.D.,
Gnomologia

An athlete should ask himself this question: "Do I want to be perceived as a focused and relentless competitor?" If the answer is affirmative (if it isn't, the coach has an agenda established for himself), then he must know how to look the part before he can play it. A performer who gives off signals of vulnerability will not act out appropriate behavior. Furthermore, opponents and teammates will recognize these signals. The actual perception of the athlete will fall far short of the one he values and desires.

Wearing one's heart on his sleeve is dangerous in competition, if it is not the "heart of a lion" or, more appropriately, the heart of a warrior. I speak here of body language, a language understood by anyone who is paying attention. Why would any athlete *want* to project, through his posture and movement, the language of frustration, uncontrolled anger, self-pity, fear, or complacency? He would not, I believe. That the athlete may be speaking through his body in any of these ways is an indication that he has been distracted and disturbed. He cannot effectively compete. He's not fit for combat.

It's hard for many to believe that the athlete himself is most often not aware of the signals he's giving off. But consider this: if he's distracted from attention to task because of his frame of mind, then he is focused on his major concern or anxiety of the moment. It follows that, as absorbed as he is, he is inattentive to all else—including his appearance.

■ ■ ■

It's natural enough for people to want things to go their way. It is just as natural for them to be affected when they do not get what they want. The test of each individual is how he responds to such a circumstance. He can rise above his disappointment, or he can sink below it. An athlete's body language indicates whether he is in the process of elevating himself or burying himself. (See RESPONSE, section 3.)

The nature and degree of disappointment will vary, but the appearance of an athlete during competition should not vary, for consistent behavior leads to consistent performance. Poor body language leads to poor performance. It is already poor behavior—and not consistent with the athlete's physical actions when things are going well for him.

■ ■ ■

In the late 1980s, a young pitcher came up from the minor leagues to pitch for the Oakland Athletics during the second half of the season. He pitched aggressively and effectively as a reliever; his rookie season statistics pleased him. He had a 1.93 era, a strikeout-to-walk ratio of almost 2 to 1. He gave up only 45 hits in 72 innings pitched. The next season, however, he seemed a changed pitcher. He was tentative, behind in the count quite often, and the batters had much better swings at his pitches—and better results—than they had the previous season.

His body language told the story. The year before, I had referred to him as "a stalker" during our conversations. His posture was firm and strong looking. His manner said to the catcher, "Hurry up and give me the ball; let's go." He looked as if he wanted to get back on the rubber and attack—again and again. And he had done just that, the way all aggressive competitors so.

But now, his performance was a different story; his body told a different story. And watching him was like watching a different pitcher. He clearly was not a stalker. Instead, he appeared to be the one being stalked. He looked as if he didn't want to throw the next pitch; his tempo was excruciatingly slow. As he seemed to want to avoid the next delivery, he also tried to avoid contact. He "picked," was behind in the count regularly, and the quality of his pitches diminished. The hitters took advantage of it.

All this was rather evident to the pitcher. What wasn't, I felt, was how he looked out on the mound—the indicator of every bad thought and feeling he was internalizing. I asked him if he had tapes from the previous season; he did. We took a few recent tapes from the current season and went to his apartment. The format was to view them without comment. Just watch. He was astounded. He was disgusted with his current body language—the signals he was giving off. "This is what my teammates see?" he asked rhetorically. "This is also what opponents see," I said. "You're enhancing their self-confidence because they see you don't seem to have any."

We then discussed the importance of a pitcher's appearance to a hitter. That hitter has perceptions of the pitcher, to a great extent based on what he sees. I told the young man that what I would want, if I were the pitcher, would be to intimidate the hitter in any way possible. The first way would be to show myself on the mound as a relentless and aggressive competitor. If I looked vulnerable, I'd allow the hitter to be comfortable facing me. More confident. It can be a subtle difference in an opponent's mind, perhaps at a lower level of consciousness. But it will be there.

As a tough competitor, I would not allow him to see me suffer. If I'm in command of the game, it's easy to act out superiority. But if I'm struggling, it's more difficult—and more important. By expressing negative thoughts and emotions through body language, I'd hurt myself. Not only couldn't I make an adjustment, but I'd be forfeiting my advantage to the hitter. All this, I told him.

"This is exactly the garbage I've been bringing out there," said the real pitcher.

The reason his behavior had changed from his rookie season and the process he went through to address his issues are irrelevant here. It is important to reiterate that the display of negative emotions while performing is not the behavior of effective competitors. Whether the body speaks in assertive or submissive language, it is speaking. And speaking is behaving.

■ ■ ■

Finally, this: In 1976 I coached a high school women's basketball team for the first time. Our first game was against a top-division team, one that imposed a humiliating loss the previous season (a 60-point deficit) on the kids who were now my seniors. Our players had worked hard to prepare for the season—this opener on the road.

Very early in the game, one of our forwards missed an easy layup off a hard-fought offensive rebound. She was shaken and distracted by the miss and slowly moved down to the defensive side of the court, her head bowed.

I shouted out, not in anger but with force, "Keep your head up!" I wanted to snap her out of her funk. She responded with language that was silent but with a message that was petulantly, haughtily clear. She thrust her chin the air in an exaggerated head's-up pose as she swiftly ran down court.

At the next whistle, a substitute took her place. Carol (now forty-five years old!) went to the end of the bench, as far away from me as she could get. She sat alone and unattended for a long period of time. When I did go down to pay her a visit, I knelt in front of her and asked, "Do you know why you're here?" The vigorous up-and-down shaking of her head threw tears onto my tie.

Her body language never again expressed anything but aggressive determination. Some people learn faster than others.

■ ■ ■

The coach addresses the mental game by helping the athlete to:

- Understand that his posture and gestures constitute what is called "body language."
- Understand, as well, that it is the tendency of people to express their internal thoughts and feelings through body language.
- Pay attention to his own body language during performances, through the use of tapes or by having others observe and report.
- Recognize that tough-minded competitors show themselves to be that, in part, through their physical presence during competition.
- Establish the habit of acting out, through body language, who he wants to be, rather than how he may feel, knowing that acting the warrior will help him to be the warrior.
- Know that when faced with difficulty, an aggressive internal adjustment should include the physical posture he presents to the opponent, to his teammates, to the world—and to himself.
- Know that body language that indicates disrespect to a teammate or coach will not be accepted, even if it is reflexive rather than intentional.

Breathing

I just wanted to breathe.
Serena Williams,
before her final serve, defeating sister Venus for the
2002 Wimbledon Championship

People are always talking about "relaxing" during competition, and yet I've heard those who don't understand the term. Coaches have said, "I want my player intense, not relaxed," as if relaxation is a sign of disinterest or nonaggressiveness.

Relaxation is about the muscles being free, rather than restricted, in their movements. An aggressive mentality sends the signals to the muscles that they should "go for it." A relaxed physical state allows them to do just that. Therein lies the distinction.

Certainly a poor perspective can greatly inhibit kinetic freedom, so that is a topic that merits attention. (See PERSPECTIVE, section 3.) But philosophy and outlook aside, proper breathing at times of heightened arousal during competition is essential.

"Breathe or die," I warn athletes. They don't need the literal warning. It is simply a verbal key, reminding an athlete to pay attention to the "when" of breathing and the "where." The athletes know how, and they know why. Yet some tend to forget everything they know in the heat of battle. It only seems to happen during periods of tension—when the relaxation technique is most required.

Anyone who has ever been to a movie thriller has had a chance to understand the relationship between tension and inhibited breathing patterns. For example, during a Stephen King film, an ax is held high, the killer poised to strike. Down comes the ax; off comes the head. . . . The scene ends abruptly. Cut away to a pastoral scene now, quiet, peaceful. An audible gasp by the audience. People had been holding their collective breath. The cutaway relieved the tension; they could breathe again.

■ ■ ■

I've seen performers hyperventilate during competition, the result of racing thoughts and a general disorientation. The hyperventilation (shortness of breath) has mental causes and physiological effects. Muscles tense up; the arm does not have a fluid function. The delivery breaks down: coordination, range of motion, balance, timing, power, and accuracy are adversely affected. All this is triggered first by what the mind has focused on (danger) and, then, the unsatisfactory ratio of carbon dioxide to oxygen in the bloodstream.

To use the racecar metaphor once again, carbon dioxide acts as a brake; oxygen acts as an accelerator. Carbon dioxide slams down on muscles; oxygen propels them smoothly. When exhaling deeply, pitchers release carbon dioxide from their blood stream and allow oxygen to take over.

The last act of downhill Olympic skiers, before they push off for their run, is to exhale deeply. Most basketball players do the same before taking foul shots.

Athletes often forget. They breathe, for certain. But during crisis, many think about "the falling ax," and their breathing either becomes shallow or it stops. The skiers and foul shooters are not in the midst of action. Their breathing precedes it. And that, too, should be the case whenever there is a break in action. When whistles blow, before the center snaps the football, between tennis points. As with every other good habit, the more consistent the breathing pattern, the more consistent the total approach.

How, specifically, can breathing help a performer's approach? First, it relieves muscular tension and enables the athlete to maintain his typical physical/mechanical behaviors. Second, it will aid the athlete in calming himself. In slowing himself down. The tendency of someone in trouble during competition is to rush. To speed up his tempo and force his muscles. He will jump out, rather than be fluid. But the major loss will be in his ability to slow down his thoughts. He'll have no chance of making appropriate adjustments because his mind is racing. He has forgotten to breathe, and he will forget to gather himself.

Deep breathing patterns during competition will be enhanced by exercises incorporated during progressive relaxation exercises. In his chair, the athlete can work on specific breathing exercises, inhaling and exhaling regularly and slowly—counting from one thousand, eyes shut, mind clear. (Especially good for inducing sleep at night.) He should create a consistent breathing pattern, wherever and whenever used during competition.

It's easiest to create a pattern, a habit, of breathing if it is practiced. And it is easy to practice. It can be done in the athlete's room at home and should be done during practices.

Effective breathing is not gasping. It is not necessarily a discernible action. It should be a regular one. A number of athletes have involved themselves in martial arts training, the better to regulate and develop effective breathing patterns. Former major league pitcher Dave Stewart was a prime example.

Each year, it seems, more athletes are learning to incorporate patterned breathing into their approach. It becomes obvious to them that random breathing is not as helpful to them as regulated breathing. Or no breathing at all.

■ ■ ■

The coach addresses the mental game by encouraging the athlete to:

- Understand that breathing patterns—or no pattern, at all—have physiological effects on him during performance.
- Recognize what these effects are.
- Realize that breathing will involuntarily change during times of crisis and/or tension.
- Experiment during practice sessions, until he is satisfied with his technique.
- Create a consistent pattern of breathing during practice sessions in order to relax his muscles and himself during competition.
- Stand in front of a mirror in his room to see what seems to be best for him, and to feel what seems to be most natural.
- Use it regularly, in order to integrate it fully into his performance approach.
- Check himself regularly when making adjustments during the game and when reviewing behavior after the game.

Competitor

A minor league pitcher came up to me after a poor outing during which he'd stormed around the mound, his anger and frustration very obviously having taken control of him. I spoke to him about this "antic disposition."

He was adamant as he shouted his response (read excuse): "I'm a competitor!"

"Yes," I said calmly, "a horsebleep competitor."

He was silent, so I continued. "You mean you want to win badly—for the team, for you? Well, everybody wants to win. To do well; to succeed. Wes, I never had a guy come up to me and say, 'Harv, help me to fail.' But not everybody knows *how* to succeed. You showed that lack of knowledge out there today. *My* definition of a competitor is someone who *knows* how to compete—and then *does* it!"

That conversation has been "replayed" many times, with many different competitior-wannabes. Some think that the madder they show themselves to be, the more likely it is they'll qualify as competitors. Others don't think at all; they just react to their unhappiness when things go wrong. Overreact, actually. And then tell the world how badly they "want it."

So much for the pretenders to the throne. Real competitors qualify as athletic royalty. No matter what their skill level, they know how to go about their business—and they take care of that business. Consistent in what they put into their efforts; consistent in how it's put in. When? Always.

■ ■ ■

Athletes who express admiration for other athletes tend to identify that person as "a tough competitor." Though I share the object of their admiration, I believe the term they use to characterize it to be a redundancy. To my mind, an athlete who is not mentally "tough" is not an effective competitor at all. That toughness is prerequisite.

It seems that many people hold an image of a tough competitor to be someone with fire flaming from his nostrils. He scowls, he kicks at the air, he swears, he sweats. Sort of an unpleasant dragon in a china shop.

The term *killer instinct* is frequently used, and aptly so. That instinct is admirable and necessary, if one is to be a tough competitor. But a "calculated cool" must accompany the instinct if the job is to be "executed," so to speak. I would not consider an athlete to have an "assassin's mentality" if he always seems to destroy himself.

■ ■ ■

One of the measures of an athlete's competitive tendency is how he performs when he's not at his physical best. Ineffective or poor competitors panic, try to do too much (overkill), or give in by declaring, "It's gonna be one of those days" (surrender). A true competitor recognizes the need to compensate with intelligence, intense concentration, and persistence. Courage. It's a legitimate competitor's instinct to stick to his battle plan, rather than succumbing to disorientation or losing his spirit (heart *and* soul).

The true competitor holds himself even more accountable to employ all his mental resources on those days when his physical skills seem to be unavailable. *Seem* to be. His sympathetic nervous system will help, if he gives it a chance, providing adrenal rushes, as needed. Many players have said—without being aware of that physiological backup system— "Funny, I've had my best performances when I've felt my worst."

■ ■ ■

A notion some athletes have expressed to me is that in order to be a fierce competitor one must be an arrogant, ignorant, and obnoxious person. This view is most widely held by intelligent, sensitive, often deferential people. (See NICE PERSON*, sections 2 and 3.) Intelligence is an *asset* during athletic competition. Sensitivity and deference are not. A fierce competitor's concern is with knowing how to go about his task and battling to give his team and himself a chance to win. He has no other concern; he is insensitive and unyielding. He is not a terrible person. Nice guys might identify him as such, because they feel incapable of competing fiercely and use personality as an excuse.

Rick Honeycutt, to name a favorite person of mine, is a gentleman, a nice guy—*out of the competitive arena*. He pitched for twenty years in the big leagues, not because people liked him, but because whenever he was given the ball, he competed. He reminded me of an old English sea captain Thomas Fuller wrote about. Fuller noted that Captain Somers, a veteran "of many Atlantic voyages" in the late 1500s, was "a lamb on the land, a lion on the sea." Rick Honeycutt and other athletes like him are sensitive, caring people who become fierce competitors. They know how to win battles.

■ ■ ■

One of the wonderful aspects of sport is that warrior metaphors—battles and infantrymen and sea captains—can be used when speaking of great competitors, athletes who "take no prisoners" yet cause no fatalities. Because intense competition, in the words of William James, is just "the moral equivalent of war."

■ ■ ■

The coach addresses the mental game by helping the athlete to:

- Understand that behavior, rather than appearance, is the determining factor in becoming an effective competitor.
- Understand that the mentally tough competitor responds to fear, frustration, or inadequacy by being able to direct and maintain his thoughts and focus on what he can control—his behavior.
- Remember that the intensity of a competitor is directed to executing the next task, rather than thinking about outcome.
- Remember that aggressive behavior must be controlled. A proper balance must be struck.
- Develop a consistent, persistent approach, one not related to score, circumstance, or "meaning" given to the event.
- Learn that during every performance, he should "run through the finish line." Battle to the end of his performance. Every pitch, every play, every shot, stride, or stroke.
- Be unyielding, even when he does not "feel physically comfortable."
- Develop his concentration skill to a level at which he can be oblivious to irrelevant external cues and aware of relevant internal cues.
- Understand that the opponent is an irrelevant, external cue. Focus intensely on the task at hand.

- Remind himself of the difference between being a gentleman off the field and being a fierce competitor on it.

Concentration

The question people ask most is what I think about when I line up for a kick. They want to know if I feel the pressure, but I never think of that. Instead, I concentrate on looking at the spot where the ball will be put.
George Blanda,
former NFL kicker

To prove that wise men can be wrong, I concentrate on you.
Lyrics by Cole Porter,
songwriter

Cole Porter knew that concentration is prepotent. Tiger Woods knows it. Most athletes wish to have that kind of potency, that ability to concentrate so intensely that nothing can distract them. Few work at it.

I've heard a sport psychologist refer to concentration as a fortress. I prefer to use "weapon" as a metaphor for effective concentration. A fortress, it seems to me, protects; a weapon challenges. One is reactive, the other active. The more aggressive a performer is, the more likely he is focused on the appropriate aspects of his performance.

The stronger and more sustained an athlete's ability to concentrate, the better he'll consistently execute his task aggressively and effectively. Athletes know what they should focus on, but don't always know how to maintain that focus. It takes practice.

As a young boy, I remember reading a number of books by the French aviator/writer Antoine de Saint Exupéry. One, in particular, seemed to speak to me specifically. (I was twelve years old; the book was *Flight to Arras*. I have it still.) In it was the following: "The field of consciousness is tiny. It accepts only one problem at a time. Get into a fist fight, put your mind on the strategy of the fight, and you'll not feel the other fellow's punches."

■ ■ ■

Being prepotent, concentration is the first and, arguably, the most essential skill of a performer. Because of that skill, no circumstance, no problem, no possible distraction comes into to an athlete's highest level of awareness during his competition. Even words that wise men might have said. The athlete's concentration leaves no room in his mind for any irrelevant, intrusive thought. That may seem to be an ideal, but it is an ideal truth—and attainable.

So the development of concentration skills should be at the top of the list of goals for every performer. And it requires regular attention. The most skillful athletes can still improve. The more skilled an athlete is, the more likely he is to take his concentration for granted—until he begins to struggle, when his focus becomes broad and undisciplined.

A struggling athlete will think of all matters except the task at hand while he's competing. That's a loss of focus, due to a weakened mental discipline. Anyone who has ever sat through a boring lecture or read a dull book understands this perfectly. If it's important to listen to the lecture, you must discipline yourself to concentrate. If it's important to read and understand the book, you must discipline your eyes and mind to be attentive to the material. It can be a daunting task. But those who persist in attending to task can develop and intensity of concentration that has "a hunger to it."

■ ■ ■

It's very common for athletes to have several thoughts before and during their preparation to perform. But when they get to the "moment of truth," they must limit their thoughts and change their focus to a narrow, external one. This is a habit to cultivate. It should be an important behavior goal.

The better an athlete is performing, the more naturally his concentration skills are able to serve him. An athlete who is "going good" will say to me, "My mind is clear; I'm not thinking about concentrating." And that's why he's going good. He shouldn't concentrate on concentrating; he should concentrate on task, which is simple and immediate. Hence the clear mind. ("Uncomplicated," he might have said.)

His highly effective behavior is more often than not rewarded by desired results. But when athletes begin to get poor results, they tend to change their approach. Their head fills with distracting thoughts. Their attention becomes divided. Their thinking becomes too broad, very often thinking about results—consequences. The future, rather than the moment. Too complicated.

■ ■ ■

Item: Bill Russell, known as a single-minded competitor when he played for the Boston Celtics, was recently interviewed by a writer for the *New York Times*. The writer asked about a player being subjected to boos and taunting by crowds. Russell, named as the greatest player in the history of the NBA in 1980 by the Professional Basketball Writers Association, had this to say: "You know . . . my youngest child asked me one time, 'How do you handle people booing you and saying unkind things about you?' I said, 'Me personally, I never accepted the cheers, so I didn't have to worry about the boos.' When I was playing, there was nothing outside the lines."

"Nothing outside the lines." That's taking care of business. That's appropriate focus.

■ ■ ■

When a child is behaving well, a parent doesn't have to discipline that child. The discipline must be applied when the behavior is unacceptable. The same is true with an athlete. His "parent"—his rational mind—must step in and assert itself, disciplining the hitter, so as to stop him from operating out of his feelings (frustration, self-doubt, etc.) and get him back to focusing on the execution of task. How the performer responds to adversity—whether it's the boos of a crowd or the burden of his responsibility—will say a lot about his concentration skills.

The more disciplined an athlete is, meaning the more able he is to focus on the task exclusively, the more successful he'll be over time. This doesn't always come "naturally." A persistent effort must be made. A concentrated effort, so to speak.

■ ■ ■

An athlete must understand a few basic things if he's going to improve his concentration skills. First, he should understand what is possible to control and what is not. It's possible to control one's thoughts, feelings, and behavior. We can't control external events, other people's thoughts and deeds, and consequences beyond our behavior.

- The athlete can tell himself what to do in positive terms.
- The athlete can focus on the immediate, rather than past or future. (The next task—"the now"—is all that can be acted upon.)
- The athlete can focus on his approach, instead of results—past or future.

These simple understandings should be reiterated regularly, so they become a working philosophy for concentration. Athletes practice physical skills on a daily basis, but they usually just expect mental skills to develop themselves. They don't. The athlete must practice effectively to perform effectively—physically and mentally.

It's often easier for an athlete to practice mental skills than physical. He doesn't need a physical environment. He can work on some concentration skills away from the field or arena, sometimes just by sitting in a chair at home.

A few suggestions and practice activities will help the athlete to develop his ability to concentrate effectively and consistently. They can be varied or improved upon as the athlete becomes a more skilled practitioner.

But first consider this: *mental toughness* is the term used as an ultimate compliment to an athlete. The degree to which you are able to fully and intensely concentrate on your task is a major component of that "toughness." If it's worth having, it's worth the effort it takes to develop it. The persistent effort to improve is also part of the toughness. It will enhance the athlete's ability to concentrate on the task during the toughest of times.

For years now, Jamie Moyer has used the grid mentioned below. A few years ago he was struggling a bit. We discussed some of the possible reasons. One discovery he made was that he had stopped using the grid drill that had meant so much to him in the past. He resumed the practice; the struggle ended.

Item: From *The New York Times Magazine*, July 14, 2002: Tiger Woods' father "tried every trick he could to disturb his son's calm. While Tiger was in midswing, he would push over a golf bag, jiggle keys, throw pebbles at his ball. Pressure corrodes the swings of even the best golfers, but not Tiger's. 'Everything builds to a crescendo,' Tiger has said. 'Your senses are heightened, your awareness of where the club is and what the situation is, and that's when you execute the shot.'" Prepotency at its most powerful.

■　■　■

The coach can address the mental game by addressing with the athlete the material discussed above. The coach should also encourage the athlete to do work on his own to enhance his ability to concentrate effectively. Following are some concentration exercises. The athlete should:

- Be an observer. Notice everything, especially details. This will bring him to be attentive to things he'd never paid attention to before. It is a constant exercise in disciplining your mind and his eyes.
- Look at pictures hanging on the wall (or advertisement billboards at the ballpark). Start by taking in the entire image, then keep narrowing his focus until he's centered on a very particular part of the picture/ad. *See* it completely, noticing every detail. Stay on it with his eyes until he has committed the details to memory.
- Play the old kid's game (abbreviated version) of Concentration, using just a few cards from a deck of playing cards. Include one card for each number from two to ten. Have someone place the nine cards face down in random order. Then turn them up and view them quickly. Turn them face down again. Distract himself

for one minute. Then attempt to turn the cards over in order, starting with the deuce. As he becomes better able to this—and decrease the time required to do it—add numbers from different suits, so he then has to turn two number 2s over, and so on. Be patient with himself. He'll get better if his discipline is stronger than his frustration. (And that should be one of his goals during competition, as well!)

- Make up a grid of 100 squares on a sheet of paper. (Make a bunch of photocopies.) Have someone else fill in the blanks of a grid randomly with numbers 00, 01, 02 . . . through 99. The athlete takes the grid and goes through it, using pen or pencil to cross out the numbers in consecutive order. When he becomes stuck—seemingly unable to "find" the next number, he stays with it. No quitting! He works through to completion. He repeats this exercise as many time as he wishes, having the person fill in the numbers in different spaces, of course. He will see improvement.
- Using the same exercise, he times himself, keeping a record of his times. He doesn't expect a continuous improvement. He'll have good days, and not-so-good days, just as he will on the field. The key is to be persistent, rather than giving in to a bad attempt. To stay the course. To focus on task, not on difficulty. (A terrific exercise, because it serves many purposes.)
- Using the same exercise, the athlete turns on a talk radio program while he's working on the grid. He raises the volume as he becomes more skillful. This provides still another possible intrusion and distraction.
- The athlete or the coach can invent his own exercises. Diligence is always a requirement.

Confidence

Confidence is that feeling by which the mind embarks in great and honorable courses with a sure hope and trust in itself.
Cicero

I was not confident at all, but learning to be good at something, getting better at something, helped me a lot and not just in sports.
Sharonda Johnson,
N.C. State H.S. track champion,
Southeast Raleigh H.S., Class of 2002

William Hazlitt wrote (*Characteristics*), "As is our confidence, so is our capacity." A lack of confidence can shrink a person to a diminished expression of his capacity as a human. It shrinks an athlete to a fraction of his capacity as a performer.

Confidence doesn't "*come* to you"; an athlete must *take* it. He has a better chance when a coach offers it—encourages the athlete to reach for it.

The confident attitude the athlete can take on will be tested throughout his life, on and off a playing fields, courts, rinks, tracks, and pools. Even exceptional people will fail the test occasionally, but they'll step back and assess themselves—and adjust their attitude so that it becomes an asset, rather than a liability.

Self-doubt is part of being human. A person who continues to doubt himself often does so because he thinks he "always ought to be confident" as one athlete told me. He's wrong. "Always" is not typically being human. We all have self-doubt. It's a matter of degree and determination.

Confidence comes to those who fight through their self-doubt, rather than giving in to it. The more persistent the fight, the more likely the victory. The more an athlete wins those battles, the greater his self-confidence becomes. The more confident he becomes, the more capacity he'll develop to perform well. It is, as already noted, a lifelong ordeal. Most things that have value require great and sustained effort.

And that's a key to understanding "confidence." An understanding that the individual must work on it, not wait for it. That the fight itself, the resolve, will enhance his self-esteem and, therefore, his confidence.

■ ■ ■

If an athlete seeks enhanced confidence, he must *understand* that he can control only that which he has the capacity to control. Below is a checklist of those elements of his being that can be controlled.

- Daily physical and mental preparation requires time, effort, and consistency. A prepared athlete will already have appropriate preparation to be confident in.
- Thoughts: having a plan helps direct them.
- Focus: know where his attention should be.
- Emotions: his feelings will get in the way of his thinking. He should get thoughts focused on the task at hand; what he wants to do and how he wants to do it.
- Responses: responding by addressing next approach, rather than past outcome.
- If unhappy with his previous approach, he should ask himself the three questions: What was I trying to do? What went wrong? What do I want to do next time?
- Execution: Bring that plan to the next task.

- Action: He should act with assertiveness, and he'll enhance his confidence because of that behavior.

In exerting the control spoken of above, the athlete "has it together." That will better allow him to maximize his talent and increase his capacity. Not every athlete can claim this achievement; it isn't gained with ease. But if he can achieve it, the athlete will be a warrior armored in self-confidence.

■ ■ ■

Mamie "Peanut" Johnson played for the Indianapolis Clowns from 1953 to 1955. She was one of three women to play Negro League baseball. Before throwing out a first pitch at a Norfolk Tides minor league game in August 2000, the licensed nurse and former engineering student at New York University gave attribution to her remarkable capacities. "If you don't have no confidence in yourself, there's no use trying," the sixty-four-year-old "Peanut" said.

Well, Peanut, I believe the attempt is important. But patience and persistence are required. The athlete must make a choice to be dedicated to self-improvement and to thereby move onto and along the path to confidence. The hallmark of confident athletes is that they take control, rather than being at the mercy of fear or fate—which can be merciless.

■ ■ ■

The coach addresses the mental game by teaching the athlete that:

- Confidence ebbs and flows; it's not a constant.
- Self-doubt is normal, but exceptional people don't give in to it.
- Life-threatening consequences will not result from a poor performance.
- Failing at a task is not the same as being a failure as a person.
- His reach is more important than his capacity.
- Self-discipline is more important than talent, because talent has already been established.
- His approach and response are more important than results, which you have no control over.
- Responsibility encourages confidence; excuses encourage cowardice.
- Taking risks will stretch him; being careful or fearful will limit him.
- Self-coaching during competition, using positive, functional self-talk, will build confidence; criticizing himself and being negative will erode it.

- Focusing on what he wants to do will prepare him; worrying about what the opponent might or might not do will distract him.
- *Acting* confident helps develop an attitude of confidence. If he acts it enough, he'll believe in it. Belief in himself *is* self-trust—confidence, in other words.

Consistency*

After watching Greg Maddux for [many] years,you come to appreciate the consistency in performances, the consistency in his work between games, the consistency in his thought processes, the consistency in the excellence of his innings, his games. It is amazing, just amazing to watch. It just never varies.
Bobby Cox,
manager, Atlanta Braves

Consistency is habit formed by repeated acts. "Consistent behavior will get you consistent performance." I've said that to players many, many times, and written it a few times in this book. (See HABIT, section 3.) All of the teaching theories based on repetition indicate that the constancy, the reiteration, the over-and-overness of behavior allows it to become second nature.

Second nature. An instinct that is first nature is called a natural instinct. Coaches will rave about an athlete's instincts, commending an individual for being born with the gift. And that is so. But instincts can be acquired, as well. They're acquired by being repeated. At first uncomfortable, not graceful—awkward, perhaps—they are not natural. But with constant repetition, the behavior becomes more fluid—more natural looking. Eventually, the behavior is second nature. Naturalness acquired—learned.

No one was amazed by Greg Maddux's consistency during his first stint with the Chicago Cubs. He was good, but he acquired the ability to be great. Through consistent approaches—mental and physical—to his craft. To competition.

■ ■ ■

The coach should set up practice routines, meetings, travel behaviors, and so on that are patterned. Not obsessively so, but consistently so. It will provide order, security, and direction for the athletes. They need it, whether they know it or not. And they specifically need to develop consistent patterns for the performance approaches.

The coach should help the athlete to know what he's doing right— and what he *should* be doing but isn't. The athlete's goal is to think the right thoughts, make all the right adjustments. To relentlessly approach his execution—in practice and in competition—with a functional focus. Successful execution comes when technique becomes habit. Habit is developed through the consistent repetition of thoughts and movements.

■ ■ ■

Change is inevitable. The ability to change indicates an open mind. But when speaking of a behavioral approach to performance, an established and appropriate approach, the athlete will value consistency. He values it because he has defined and established his performance approach; he has reached an understanding of what it takes to be an outstanding competitor, and so on. He learns more about the sport and himself as he continues to perform. And he adjusts—changes—accordingly. But as he goes about performing, he trusts his behavioral plan—and sticks to it. His consistency is an indicator of his mental discipline.

The athlete should be rational, rather than emotional. It is a sign of trust, which requires courage. It is a focus on what to do, rather than how one feels. Consistency reinforces what he knows is appropriate, and this behavior becomes a habit. By having consistent thought patterns and reenacting appropriate behaviors, athletes will, to use Greg Maddux's wry statement to me, "have a hard time doing the wrong thing." And the behaviors will be proactive, rather than reactive.

In competition, the athlete strives to be unwavering, indiscriminate, methodical, (meaning having a method and sticking to it) reliable. He practices with the same consistent intensity and focus. He always applies his mental energy to his purpose: to being a "winner." The striving for excellence must be consistent, the execution must be consistent, and then only can the performance be consistent. A winning performance.

■ ■ ■

The coach addresses the mental game by teaching the athlete to:

- Realize that consistent performance is the result of consistent behavior, and that consistent behavior requires a consistent pattern of thought.
- Understand that consistency is developed through mental discipline—repeatedly doing the "right thing," irrespective of circumstance or consequence.
- Reiterate on a regular basis his plan (i.e., approach, behaviors, techniques, keys, etc.).
- Hold himself accountable for the consistent implementation of this plan on the practice field and on the playing field.
- Evaluate the consistency of his behavior on a daily basis—his work habits and game habits.

- Be aware of the factors that tend to "throw him off the beam" and work rationally so as to be able to quickly "climb back on."
- Remember that consistency also results from an unwavering trust in his own appropriate thoughts and behaviors, as they are reinforced through repetition and reinforcement. And that inconsistent views expressed by media, fans, opponents, and so on are irrelevant.

Courage*
(See FEAR OF FAILURE, section 3)

It is courage, courage, courage, that raises the blood of life to crimson splendor.
George Bernard Shaw,
Back to Methuselah

"Courage tastes like blood," the character Leander Wapshot writes to his sons in John Cheever's *The Wapshot Chronicle*. Shaw (epigraph) refers to courage as life's blood. Bold blood. Of crimson splendor.

When courage goes, the blood congeals. We shrivel and dry up without it.

■ ■ ■

The Latin *cor* means "heart." To have courage is to have heart; that term is heard often enough around athletic arenas. To many, it implies fearlessness. But that is *not* the point of courage. To have courage is to *act bravely in spite* of the existence of fear. Hall-of-Famer Dennis Eckersley has exemplified courage for as long as I have known him. The Oakland As outstanding closer for many years, "Eck" was a pitcher—a man—who fought and won the battle against alcoholism and who announced to the world that he was terrified of failure. Of public embarrassment and humiliation should he perform poorly.

Essentially, he would say to himself, "If I don't want to fail, then rather than acting out what I *feel*, I'll act out what I *know* will help me to succeed." And he did; he was consistently aggressive as a pitcher. And courage was evident in that consistency, which he expressed regardless of circumstance. As a recovered alcoholic, Eck recognized that a person abandons himself when he acts out of his fears.

■ ■ ■

Courage is facing fear and "spitting in its eye." Trying to avoid danger, as so many athletes do, is not an effective performance strategy. Nor does it bring the safety the athlete seeks. Rather, as has been said in other pages, it almost guarantees failure. The feeling of vulnerability is reinforced by the lack of courageous behavior. Dennis Eckersley's behavior preempted his feelings. As a result, fear dissipated; courage prevailed.

Courage allows the athlete to express all his other qualities; acting out of fear suppresses them. Stifles them. Challenging fear elevates behavior and elevates the individual.

■ ■ ■

To *not* have fear is to not require courage. But many, if not most, athletes have some fear or performance anxiety, whether it's hidden or exposed. Since his emotional system is the source of his fears, the environment and activity is less significant than the personality and perception of the fearful person. Sport may just be entertainment for the spectator, but it is considerably more to the participant.

■ ■ ■

Courage is more than acting against fears. Courage is often required to act against fatigue. Performance that reflects a "feeling" the athlete has of being tired also reflects a giving in. If "fatigue makes cowards of us all," as Vince Lombardi suggested, it behooves an athlete to be in shape. But well-conditioned athletes may still work hard enough to become tired. A courageous competitor does not let a decrease in his level of physical energy diminish the level of his mental energy. Tired muscles should not be allowed to surrender because they are being led by a tired mind. "Sucking it up," as athletes and coaches say, is an expression of courage. Satchel Paige used to brag that the more tired he became, the more effective he became. Self-indoctrination such as that makes bravery easier to come by.

As discussed in an earlier section, battling through adversity also requires courage. Losing one's heart is really "giving one's heart away." Certainly not an act of courage. Having everything seemingly going wrong during a performance tests a athlete's mettle. Officials' calls, teammate blunders, lack of physical "rhythm," general bad luck—all can be included in the test. The strong of heart fight through it. They pass the test. (See RESPONSE*, section 3.)

Whatever the circumstances may be that might "threaten" an athlete, whether it be a "big" game, facing an imposing opponent, or coming into the game in a crucial situation, the resolution to stay with his aggressive approach and the courage to act it out will make a winner of the performer, whatever the results may be.

All the qualities of an athlete are better able to express themselves when courage clears the way. Talent armed with bravery becomes a formidable combination, as I tell those I meet for the first time.

Unfortunately, I've seen too many athletes disappear because they could not so arm themselves. The words of Sydney Smith apply exactly: "A great deal of talent is lost in this world for want of a little courage."

■ ■ ■

Here are some essential understandings related to courage:

- Courage, by definition, allows for the existence of fear.
- A person's attempt to avoid confrontation or "danger" is focused on fear and will most likely produce whatever it is he or she is trying to avoid.
- Fear has an emotional basis, whereas a plan or strategy has a rational one.
- The integration of a rational, aggressive plan into a behavioral approach can preempt fear.
- The ability to identify the situations or circumstances that challenge one's courage acts as a forewarning. By being forewarned, a person is forearmed—and better prepared to face up to and attack these fears or worries.
- One of an individual's freedoms is the freedom to change—to work at being more courageous in work environments and in social environments. This first step, in itself, is a courageous act.
- Behavior is entirely within an individual's control. Courageous behavior is a winning choice.
- Courage is not measured against the behavior of others. It is measured against the degree of fear or reluctance to confront what is perceived to be unpleasant, uncomfortable, threatening, or dangerous.
- The more a person avoids confronting weaknesses, fears, and reluctance, the more these undesirable traits are reinforced. The individual is "feeding the monster." The monster grows.
- Conversely, the regular enactment of courage by the faint of heart "starves the monster." The monster is weakened and eventually dies. The regular facing up and enactment of courage can be considered an ordeal. One's ability is enhanced and the ordeal made easier through the consistency of behavior. Self-confidence increases exponentially.
- Courage is self-discipline and the assertion of will to do what is right, appropriate, and theoretically or practically necessary. It is doing the difficult and challenging because one knows the value and benefit of the act—beyond yourself and, at the same time, for yourself.
- Habits cling. Shed yesterday's uncomfortable garment and what is

then worn will be worn again—and again. The habit of efficacy is the suit; the habit of courage is the undergarment.

- Your pronouncements identify your wishes; your courageous behaviors identify you.

■ ■ ■

Though as human beings we often don't have freedom from all conditions, we do, as Viktor Frankl points out, have "freedom to take a stand toward conditions." We are free to confront those conditions—and respond to them intelligently—and courageously. Or not.

■ ■ ■

The coach addresses the mental game by helping the athlete to:

- Understand the definition and nature of courage.
- Integrate a rational, aggressive plan—approach—into behavior so that fear is preempted by the courageous act.
- Identify the situations or circumstances that challenge his courage, so, forewarned, he is forearmed—and better able to face up to these fears or worries.
- Understand that courage allows talent to express itself.

Dedication

*I'd like to say that the quality of any man's life is a full measure of
that man's personal commitment to excellence and to victory,
regardless of what field he may be in.*
Vince Lombardi,
Hall of Fame NFL coach

Although every athlete proclaims that he wants to succeed (I've never
had one ask me to help him fail), not everyone wants to do what it takes
to reach that goal. Yet a vast majority really does *want* to do "whatever it
takes." Many of them do not know what it takes, but I'll defer that point
for a moment.

As a star at the college level, as an Olympic champion—a world-class
soccer player—and as a professional star, Mia Hamm has been one of the
most visibly dedicated athletes in this country. She has written (*The
Right Words at the Right Time*): "Being the best is a simple decision. . . . It's
not glamorous. It's not about glory or God-given talent. It's about commitment, plain and simple. But saying you want to be at the very top of
your field and doing it are two different things. . . . Sometimes deciding
to be the best feels great. Sometimes it's discouraging, and almost always
it's exhausting. The bottom line is, if I don't go into it every day consistently committed, I won't get results."

Many athletes have lapses in their commitment, to be sure. It's part
of being human. One recurring tendency I've noticed is the neglect of
their mental game. It is an arduous task to be regularly introspective
and accountable for thinking, saying, and doing what is appropriate. As
noted, athletes I've worked with have called it "Harvey's ordeal." And it
can be that. Mental laziness is not about lack of desire; it is about lack of
self-discipline. (See WILL, section 3.)

Those athletes who aspire to excellence in their mental game are
willing to sacrifice "comfort" and ease. By making that sacrifice, they el-
evate themselves to a level of extraordinary behavior, separating themselves from the ordinary. They ask more of themselves, within reason,
rather than allowing less of themselves. They shun instant gratification,
the easy pleasure of mass man.

Instead, the exceptional individual opts for behaviors with a long-term payoff. A payoff that moves him toward his long-term goal through short-term focus on daily achievement. Such acts require and further develop trust, courage, discipline, intelligence, responsibility, focus, and such. The process is not an unappealing one for the truly dedicated athlete. He learns that whatever enhances his ability to do well becomes a joy to do.

The daily pursuit of excellence indicates a commitment to personal and athletic growth, which, in turn, helps build and reinforce self-confidence. If it were easy, everyone would do it. It isn't; they don't.

■ ■ ■

The athlete who wishes to be an exceptional performer must learn to be an exceptional "behaver." To begin with, as suggested above, he must know what it takes. This attitude does not come naturally for most. But attitudes are choices, and any athlete who is dedicated to excellence makes unnatural good choices that, over time, become second nature. Good habits are as hard to break as bad ones. (See HABIT, section 3.)

■ ■ ■

Years ago, major league catcher Rich Gedman, a former Red Sox teammate of Roger Clemens, told me about Clemens's now well-known commitment to his physical conditioning. Clemens seems to be as good as he ever has been, and it is almost twenty years since Gedman shared his thought with me. That would be the mid-1980s.

While Clemens and all those who work so diligently on their physical conditioning are to be admired, it takes mental conditioning, as well, to become a peak performer. The ordeal involved in this process is a hidden one; the person on the outside cannot admire Clemens's mental preparation the way he can the physical. He cannot judge it—until it's time for competition. And though the observer cannot see inside the competitor's head, he can see the expression of the athlete's thoughts and feelings—his preparation or lack of it—through the behavior in the heat of battle. How he competes, how he makes adjustments, how he responds to adversity—how he executes his task.

And that is a big part of "what it takes." Physical preparation *and* mental preparation are the ingredients for success. After his trade to the Yankees in February 1999, an executive of the team that traded him and that traded for him called Clemens "a warrior." The Toronto and New York general managers alluded to both of the aforementioned ingredients.

■ ■ ■

Athletes who are diligent in their running programs, who work on their lifting program regularly and appropriately, and whose sleeping and dietary habits are impeccable are indeed preparing for excellence. However, the mental and the physical must complement each other. Extra running or physical "conditioning" of any kind the day after a poor performance (and I have witnessed this form of self-flagellation numerous times) will not help an athlete to learn how, for example, to replace negative thoughts with positive ones during competition.

Perhaps the athlete is not aware of his actual needs. That is one problem that is easier to solve than his flight from doing what he knows he needs to do. I have had to address this issue with a significant number of athletes over the years. Their reactions in words have often been much like their reactions in deed (the extra running). It is a form of denial, as A. S. Byatt says, a "shrink[ing] of reality to a single pattern." Run more, lift more, curse himself or his fate more, run more, lift more. . . . Understand less.

The coach is in a position to help or hurt the athletes' mental game. Needless to say, he should be inclined to help.

Item: After a very tough New Jersey Nets loss against the Boston Celtics in Game 3 of the NBA playoffs (*USA Today*, May 5, 2002): "[Coach Byron] Scott decided not to run the Nets hard. He said they needed psychological help, not physical punishment."

Extra physical work neither compensates for nor corrects an unacceptable mental approach. For many, running is an easier task than: (a) confronting his mental/behavioral inadequacies, (b) having the self-discipline to make his "psyche sweat," by working on the improvement of the mental part of his game. Unless the athlete and the coaches address (a) and (b), neither can consider himself to be "dedicated" to maximizing the athlete's ability to perform optimimally.

An athlete's total dedication is measured, after all is said, by what is done.

■ ■ ■

The coach addresses the mental game by helping the athlete to:

- Learn "what it takes" to succeed, so he can be dedicated to doing what it takes.
- Understand that any dedication to success includes the sacrificing of instant gratification for long-term achievement.
- Develop an attitude that reflects an appreciation of whatever process helps him develop into a more effective performer.
- Understand that physical conditioning is one factor of that development and mental conditioning is another—and that they are not mutually exclusive.
- Be aware of his possible tendency to react to an ineffective performance by "working harder" at physical conditioning,

though the cause of the ineffectiveness has been his mental approach.

- Identify the elements of the "mental game" so he may dedicate himself to their development and improvement as regularly as he does to physical enhancement.
- Understand the strengths and weaknesses of his mental game, that is, the specific behaviors and thought patterns that enhance his game and those he needs to improve upon.
- Be determined to hold himself accountable on a daily basis for improvement of these mental skills. (See GOALS, section 3.)

E

Excuses

One unable to dance blames the unevenness of the floor.
Malay Proverb

With the help of an "if" you might put Paris into a bottle.
French Proverb

As a young boy, I was fond of the use of the word "if." It seemed to protect me from my own self-image. I was the only one fooled. This my father pointed out one day. He had his way of helping me out: every time I said "if" or "if only" he'd respond, "If frogs had wings they wouldn't bump their ass on the ground." I was eventually cured.

■ ■ ■

When the Spanish explorer Cortez landed in Vera Cruz in the sixteenth century, the first thing he did after unloading his equipment was to burn his ships. He then gave his men a pep talk.

"Men," he said. "You can either fight or you can die."

He took away the third alternative, the excuse for not fighting: going back to where they came from. Cortez and his men won the battle.

Coaches should not allow their athletes to go back. No excuses. Burn the ships and fight.

■ ■ ■

To make an excuse is to transfer responsibility. We try to teach our athletes to be responsible, but sometimes the manner in which a coach offers criticism is threatening. The athlete who is not self-assured—weak, perhaps—will defend himself with an excuse, weakening himself further.

Athletes should be taught that mistakes are meant to be learned from, and that excuses get in the way of that process. They should be taught that responsibility is power; it is part of the glory of self-fulfillment. Athletes have asked how a person gets that power. "You don't get it, you take it," I answer. "But it's easier to give it away than to take. That's why the first power is to make the right choice."

An excuse engenders weakness, rather than courage. The courage of honest introspection is a required first step toward the changing of negative, ingrained habits. As has been said quite often, awareness is the first step to change. If no one else tells a person about his tendency, the person is left with himself as his sole resource.

It should be noted that the coach who is hearing the excuses hears them as confessions of guilt, not innocence, as was the original intention. The only person being deceived is the excuse maker, because he has trained himself to believe his excuses, a form of denial, and/or because he wrongly believes he is deceiving his audience. In either case, he does harm to himself. He hears denial; the audience hears admission. Teammates lose respect for an athlete who makes excuses. The athlete himself has little chance to build self-respect through such behavior. The most compassionate verdict would be "guilty with an explanation." But still guilty.

The conscious acceptance of responsibility is one of the greatest indicators of an athlete's maturity and personal makeup. The immature athlete will try to attribute difficulty to circumstance, teammates, coaches, family history, persecution, or plain bad luck. He externalizes responsibility and so shuns making choices and living with the consequences of his own behavior. He waits for a lucky accident to get him what he wants—or he tries to force the luck through superstitious ritual.

The athlete must first slay his demons, before he can slay dragons. Excuses die, achievement endures.

■　■　■

The coach addresses the mental game when he teaches the athlete to:

- Be aware of any tendency he may have to make excuses.
- Recognize the damage done by excuses, including the inability to learn and make corrections because the mistake is denied.
- Understand the source of his behavior, but not so as to use that as an excuse.
- Build a positive self-image by taking responsibility for his thoughts and actions, rather than by trying to excuse them.
- Understand that mistakes are surely not goals, but they are opportunities for growth, if followed by learning, rather than by an excuse or excessive explanation.
- Understand that mistakes are important, because they illustrate the athlete's areas of need for improvement. Correction, not excessive criticism—whether it comes from a parent, a teammate, or a coach—should be the focus.
- Know the very best strategy for controlling excuses is to keep

quiet and allow the deed to represent itself—for better or for worse. And know that in either case, he is on the path to self-respect, though it may be difficult for him to believe at the beginning of the journey.

- Understand that taking responsibility expands him, while pointing to external factors diminishes him.
- Understand that taking responsibility—or avoiding it—is a choice, at whatever level of consciousness it is made.
- Understand that responsibility is forfeited when he "thanks his lucky stars," or bemoans "all the bad breaks" that went against him.
- Be responsible for his physical condition and habits, for giving a sincere and relentless effort—and for taking the consequences with proper perspective and attitude.
- Listen to himself and be determined to express the language of responsibility, thereby fostering responsible behavior.
- Look first in the mirror, with honest intent.

Fear of Failure

(Review COURAGE*, section 3)

> *When men are ruled by fear, they strive to prevent*
> *the very changes that will abate it.*
> **Alan Paton,**
> "The Challenge of Fear," *Saturday Review*

> *Oh, I thought about getting beat, especially when I was just starting*
> *out scared. After I won the title, I didn't worry about it no more.*
> *Oh, I knew that if I kept on fighting, some guy would come along*
> *and take the title away from me, but not this guy, not tonight.*
> **Joe Louis,**
> heavyweight champion boxer

> *I think a lot of athletes are really fearful of failure.*
> *I used to have some fear.*
> **David Cone,**
> major league pitcher

"Not this guy, not tonight." That is the determined expression of confidence and courage, the antidote for whatever anxiety or fear may exist.

■ ■ ■

Acute anxiety (fear) leads to a psychological paralysis—in turn, perhaps, to a physiological one. The common performance anxiety is based on the fear of failing. Failing who? The coach? The parents? Teammates? Athletes will provide their own individual answers.

■ ■ ■

Fear of failure has its causes. Athletes learn to fear failure because they believe—or are taught—that mistakes are synonymous with failure. Instead of understanding that they failed to execute a task, they personalize the failure and take it as one that identifies them. Parents, teachers, and coaches have been known to introduce and reinforce that view. The pronoun "you" is a common culprit, being used to focus (inappropriately) on the athlete, rather than on the act.

Fears can be acquired through direct and vicarious experiences. Difficult and troubling situations can have dramatic effects on people, whether they personally go through them or witness others going through them. The more dramatic the situation, the more likely the person experiencing it is to acquire a related feeling of fear. From that point, the fear may be maintained and intensified through traumatic memory and a self-defeating anticipation of meeting the situation again.

Very often, athletes set unrealistically high goals for themselves. Or have them set by coaches. Result goals particularly exacerbate an athlete's anxiety, because they can't be controlled. An athlete can behave well during competition and still have results that are perceived as failure.

An athlete can become fearful because his coach, parent, or anyone else creates grandiose external rewards for him, rather than the athlete being rewarded by achievement of his own personal goals.

A coach's tyrannical behavior can provoke fear. (See DESPOT, section 2.) Even mild criticism can create anxiety in the gentle soul of some athletes. This is a fear of disapproval.

Some athletes who lack confidence to begin with often attribute their good performances to luck. They create disclaimers when receiving praise, but are seemingly comfortable in taking blame. This attitude plants the seeds of fear.

Many times an athlete who fears failure will protect himself by not going all-out. This is a mechanism that he thinks protects him. He's essentially thinking, "If I don't try that hard, they'll blame my failure on that, instead of saying I'm not talented." If this sounds like a stretch, it isn't. I've heard it from the mouths of those who have come clean with me, professionals included. It's a fear of a commitment that will end up disappointing him.

Fear of success is related to that commitment, but the focus is usually on the judgment of others. One professional athlete I worked with had been an alcoholic. But he only drank when he did well. "Now they'll expect me to do that again," he would say, en route to the bar.

■ ■ ■

The performance of an athlete with fear is adversely affected by more than a mental distraction. The body produces an alarm reaction, created by a number of stressors. The sympathetic nervous system readies the athlete for "fight or flight." In the first case, the fighting will be uncontrolled—panicky and desperate, and ineffective. In the second case, the athlete will cave in. In either case, the performer's respiration and heart rates will increase, too much adrenaline will surge through him, his muscles will tense, breathing will shorten, his sugar level will rise, blood will move away from the skin surface. He will lose feeling in his nerve endings. So much for the bad news.

■ ■ ■

The good news is that I have seen a good number of athletes overcome their fears, and a greater number learn to cope with them so they would not interfere with performance. The very exceptional athletes, Dennis Eckersley, for example, harnessed their fears and used them to motivate themselves to succeed.

All three processes require what is called "intellectualization." The first step is "catastrophizing." An athlete and I would explore the worst possible scenario, the most dramatically "terrible" thing that could happen in his career. The core of his fear. The intent is to reduce the arousal caused by the perceived threat by distancing the player from the discomfort, through the use of his intelligence, rather than his emotions— the prevailing emotion being fear. The great golfer Jack Nicklaus used the technique successfully. Any athlete who uses the technique learns that fears tell lies. They suggest that situations the athlete will face are more difficult to deal with than they actually are.

■ ■ ■

Iris Murdoch wrote, "Demons and viruses live in every human organism, but in some happy lives never become active." But it is possible to *deactivate* the active ones. When someone intellectually examines his fears or concerns, he diminishes the impact the emotion can have on his system. For an athlete to perform successfully, a "locus of control" must be developed. People with internal control are able to cope with fears because they come to understand the fears are their response to—their *interpretation* of—external events or situations. They are not inherent in the "outside world."

Catastrophizing allows them to further understand what Shakespeare expressed centuries ago: "Present fears are less than horrible imaginings." What an athlete invents in his imagination creates more fear than any actual "threatening" situation may cause. Rational thinking helps combat all this. It is a reality check. "How likely to happen is the abysmal failure you fear?" I have asked countless times. On a scale of one to ten, ten being the most likely, athletes' responses very rarely are above six. "Then you have an excellent opportunity to take control," I suggest to those with good scores.

Working toward internal control encourages a person to recognize his own responsibility. The world at large (athletics in particular) is not waiting to attack or threaten him. He has something to say about the situation and about the fear itself. Taking responsibility is admitting to his fear, what poet Joy Harjo expressed so well: "You have choked me, but I gave you the leash." No more.

■ ■ ■

"Think about what you want to do, not what might happen to you," I advise the athlete. I tell him the brain can process threatening impulses quicker than it can develop helpful thoughts, so he must learn to give himself time—time to ensure thoughtful, rather than emotional responses being brought to the next task to be executed. By being proactive through thought, he'll help himself to eliminate reactive emotional responses. "Emotions feed the monster," I tell him. "Thought starves it."

■ ■ ■

For some, happiness is the absence of Murdoch's demons and viruses. For me, in my experience with athletes, happiness is the vanquishing of them. Facing up to fears is an initial step, and poet Lucille Clifton puts that step above happiness. "Honor," she wrote, "is *not* not acting because you are afraid. Nor is there honor in acting when you are not afraid. But acting when you *are* afraid, *that's* where honor is."

■ ■ ■

Item: By figure skater Aaron Vays, as told to Dana Shapiro, *New York Times Magazine*, August 4, 2002: "When you're out there on the ice, you're scared, scared to fail. But it's a good fear. . . . There are so many people looking at you, and all the judges. When I'm skating, I forget about everything, and I feel like Batman, as if I have special powers to get up in the air and spin." The power of *prepotent concentration*! (Review CONCENTRATION, section 3.)

The coach addresses the mental game by helping the athlete:

- To know first and foremost that fear of failure is very common in athletes, though very unpleasant.
- To understand that fear of success is just a variation on the theme of fear of failure, and that, though they are situationally different, they are psychologically the same: a problem based on self-doubt and eventual failure.
- To learn to be aware of irrational thoughts based on consequences of failure.
- To define failure, the term, as a failure to reach a goal or accomplish a task, rather than attach to himself the personal label of being a failure.

- To recognize what does and does not constitute failure in his performance, meaning that results do not indicate performance failure. Poor behavior and execution do.
- To understand that fear impedes judgment.
- To thoughtfully script out a list of rational thoughts to replace the irrational.
- To, with self-discipline, practice repeating the rational, fear-confronting thoughts, preferably aloud, if alone.
- To remember that habit is powerful, and it is therefore important to create the good habit of acting fearless, despite feelings of fear.
- To learn to focus on execution, regardless of physical symptoms of fear, thereby detaching himself from emotions and attaching himself to planned behavior.
- To adjust arousal created by feelings to a level desired for effective performance through deep breathing and by visualizing past successes.
- To develop a "will to bear discomfort" during competition by focusing on the next task, rather than on his feeling.
- To coach himself through adversity with positive, functional directives and appropriate arousal adjustment—up or down, based on a whether the system is signaling fight or flight.
- To reward himself for good behavior, despite the existence of bad feelings.

G

Goals

Setting goals is not the main thing. It is deciding how you will go about achieving them, and then staying with that plan.
Tom Landry,
Hall of Fame NFL coach

Good purpose should be the directors of good actions.
Thomas Fuller, M.D.,
Gnomologia

The most successful people in the world are known to be goal setters. The problem I have come across with athletes and coaches is that too many of them set goals over which they have no control. Team won-lost records and all statistical goals direct attention to what people want, while diverting it from what they must do. In the doing, though behavior may be exemplary, the goal may still not be reached. Many outcomes in sports competition are left to the doctrine of chance—or an opponent who flat out plays better.

■ ■ ■

And that's why I'm always so adamant with athletes about setting very specific, individualized behavioral goals. But they must be goals that are completely within their reach. The individual athlete can impose his will on his thoughts and acts. He cannot impose himself on bad fields or rinks or courses, bad weather, bad officiating, or bad teammate support. If those factors influence the athlete's behavior, he has already failed to satisfy a goal. The kind of goal that lends itself to self-assessment—from task to task. (See TASK AT HAND, section 3.)

■ ■ ■

The value of goal setting has been established by research and by elite athletes' anecdotal reports. Studies and athletes reveal that specific goals direct their attention and provoke them to physically act on this focus.

In addition, goals help to sustain their efforts and enable them to evaluate themselves on a regular basis.

Players who tend to use "I'll just do my best" as a goal fail to commit themselves to a real challenge. The goal is too high in subjectivity and too low in responsibility. It is often stated in an off-handed manner.

Self-pronounced team players have said their only goal is to help their team win. It is a pleasing lyric perhaps, but the tune cannot be carried. An athlete must first know how to help himself. Being a winning player requires specific individual achievement. An athlete should set individual goals that will address his needs, as he strives to accomplish what will benefit him, thereby helping the team to win.

■ ■ ■

Goals not immediately reached should not immediately be abandoned. They should be modified—adjusted—based on the degree of progress being made. If little or no progress has been made, the goal set was probably too lofty. There is no "failure" implied by an adjustment of a goal. One of the purposes of setting goals is to help encourage the athlete to be more confident, as a result of identifiable daily achievement. The purpose is not to frustrate effort and motivation and have the athlete become neurotic.

■ ■ ■

An athlete will bring on neuroses if he allows the expectations of others to become his goals. He must learn to distinguish the difference, and approach his goal setting appropriately. It has been said that some primitive tribes believed photographs taken of them to be a theft. The tribesmen felt their selves were taken from them through the image in the photo. The expectations of others can steal a pitcher's self. Self-image, self-assessment, self-discipline, self-control (topics specifically treated or alluded to in this book) are the ingredients of self. And an athlete's goals must be set for him and by him. The coach should contribute his thoughts, not edicts.

■ ■ ■

Some goals might be:

- *Swimmer*: Work at push-offs to improve turns.
- *Pitcher*: Improve the ability to hold runners (better move to first, varying moves, being "quicker" to the plate, etc.).
- *Golfer*: Work on improving use of sand wedge.
- *Wrestler*: Work on escape moves.
- *Basketball player*: Work at getting more arc on jump shots.

- *Hockey goalie*: Work on side-to-side movements.
- *Soccer goalie*: Work on fielding long kicks more effectively.
- *All athletes*: Improve concentration during all drills or practice routines.
- *All athletes:* Establish effective breathing pattern.
- *All athletes*: Monitor ability to maintain poise during competition.
- *All athletes*: Work at converting negative thoughts to positive, functional commands.

Execution of task comes from all the *thoughts* and *behaviors* that precede it. All are within an athlete's control, and are therefore appropriate as goals.

■ ■ ■

The coach addresses the mental game by encouraging the athlete to:

- Set goals for himself, with the input of the coach, based on specific, individualized behaviors and skills he wishes to improve.
- Understand that the expectations of others are not to be considered as part of the goal-setting process, nor should they be considered.
- Express goals in positive language, rather than in language that indicates what he does not want to do (e.g., "I want to attack the strike zone regularly," rather than "I don't want to walk guys").
- Adjust unrealistic goals, rather than abandoning them.
- Prioritize goals, according to need.
- Put the goals in writing.
- Keep a record of progress, in order to hold himself accountable on a daily/regular basis.
- Be reasonable in the evaluation.
- Understand that an unattainable goal should be abandoned, because it was inappropriate to begin with.
- Understand that goals relate to performance, not self-worth—that the failure to reach a goal does not make him a failure.

Habit

Habits are the principal magistrate of man's life.
Francis Bacon

In chapter 2 I spoke of one the favorite "games" I play with athletes. I play it to illustrate how people fall into "comfort zones." Habitual behavior produces these states of comfort. I'll reacquaint the reader with the procedure.

I ask an athlete to clasp his hands and wait for me to give him a signal to undo the clasp—to pull his hands apart. Then, after having unclasped his hands, he must quickly clasp them again, this time putting the other thumb on top and intertwining the rest of their fingers. The feeling he gets, and his expression of that feeling, indicates the power of habit. Words such as "different," "weird," "strange," "uncomfortable" drive the point home.

■ ■ ■

Creating a good habit is an act of self-discipline and persistence. Habits identify the way an athlete treats his preparation and performance. Eating habits, sleeping habits, running, lifting, his manner of practice, and event-day preparation create a pattern. If an athlete has no consistent routine, he still creates a pattern. The pattern is one of inconsistency, which represents his habits and, most likely, his performances. Order produces security; randomness or chaos leads to its opposite.

The more an athlete can develop routines, the more confidence he can have in his preparedness. (See the next section.) He will feel a greater sense of control and focus. His routines are formed through choice and consistent expression of the behaviors he understands will serve him well. These routines are the focus of his attention and help him to stay in good habits, so he does not have to concern himself with getting out of bad ones. The habits are developed in relation to directed tasks.

■ ■ ■

Bad habits are harder to break than good ones are to develop. "Winning is a habit," Vince Lombardi said. "Unfortunately, so is losing." In other words, people have good habits and they have bad habits. Bad ones are harder to break than good ones are to develop, so it stands to reason that people should work diligently at creating good habits for themselves.

But staying out does require determination and diligence. That's what the athlete must recognize and confront if he's to get to a higher level of game consistency.

Shaky confidence is a common inhibitor. So is fear. A disciplined focus on the competition is essential to combat those emotions. The will to think right even when the athlete doesn't feel right helps him to get that focus. The habit of appropriate behavior will become stronger than any inappropriate emotions he may have on event day. He "fakes it until he makes it."

For example, acting out a courageous behavior while at the same time being fearful is a form of heroism. (See COURAGE*, section 2.) The consistent enactment will allow the fear to dissipate; the habit of behavior will preempt the emotion. As Lawrence Durrell wrote, "One day you will become what you mime. The parody of goodness can make you really good." Such is the power of habit.

■ ■ ■

Every routine reinforces consistency. Without being compulsive, the athlete can create a form of ritualistic behaviors, so very helpful in that they provide him with systematic lead-ins to his regular performances. He will have his off-field, pregame, in-game, and postgame habits firmly established. Physical and mental preparations that are habituated will allow him to focus on what he wants to do, rather than on any thoughts or circumstances that are distracting. Good habits represent his plan, his adjustments, and his philosophy. Habits also represent his character.

Ritualistic behavior is not the same as superstition. Habits shouldn't control an athlete; he should control them. Without being compulsive, he can create a form of ritualistic behaviors. He should believe in this preparation, rather than in his "lucky shoes" or in his repeating the route he took to the gymnasium locker room, so as to repeat a good performance.

Effective athletes recognize that their effective performances are results of preparation and execution, rather than the benevolence of the fates they try to placate and please.

> Pisano was always superstitious; whenever anything good happened to him, he would spend the next day seeking out every possible misfortune that might result from it, on the reasonable grounds that a disaster imagined never occurs. (From *The Dream of Scipio* by Iain Pears)

A superstition is a belief that one's fate is controlled by some "magical" behavior he enacts or avoids regularly. Superstitions represent what athletes fear (failure) and what they distrust (their own ability). They give responsibility to forces outside themselves. Athletes, particularly, should hold themselves responsible.

They're responsible for their performance, for their habits—their plan, their adjustments, and their approach to their sport. That's what they should trust. That's what defines them as competitors. And that will allow you them express their talent more consistently.

■ ■ ■

The coach addresses the mental game when he helps the athlete to:

- Understand the power of habit.
- Recognize that old habits are difficult to break.
- Determine to create new good habits through diligence and discipline.
- Set up routines that will best serve him and reenact them daily, on the field and off, so as to create a ritual that is natural and effective, without being compulsive or obsessive.
- Remember that appropriate physical and mental habits are part of his "presentation."
- Understand that these habits are a form of preparation and consistency.
- Define superstitious behavior as a lack of self-confidence and an avoidance of personal responsibility.

I

Intelligence

Intelligence is quickness in seeing things as they are.
George Santayana,
Little Essays

Intelligence gives the athlete an edge. It helps him to know what the circumstance of competition requires, in terms of technique and strategy; to know what to focus on: to know how to execute his plan. Yet many athletes mouth clichés about "'thinking too much"' and so on.

Below are a few catch-phrases athletes (and coaches!) use. They're meant to imply that intelligence can get an athlete in trouble—and it can. But rather than accept the phrases at face value, the athlete—and the coach—should recognize what's misleading about them.

These catch-phrases are clever and hold elements of truth:

1. "analysis equals paralysis"
2. "no brain, no pain"
3. "ignorance is bliss"

Regarding catch-phrase number 1, too much analysis, the wrong kind of analysis, analysis at an inappropriate time can result in paralysis. On the other hand, without analysis there can be no adjustment. (How about this cliché: "timing is everything"?) The major problem seems to be that intelligent, sensitive people often "look for trouble," and, having not found any, they invent it. These inventions can become a multitude of irrelevant and/or unlikely circumstances and consequences. Life and sport then become complicated and difficult to manage. The most insignificant possibility is analyzed in the dim light of improbability. If this process goes on directly before or during athletic activity, dysfunction can result. Paralysis. The rational system (brain) is not the initiator of this problem; the emotional system is the culprit.

As for number 2, though brains may register pain, they don't cause it. Every athlete I've ever met has had a brain with enough capacity to allow its owner to function well. Poor function by the athlete comes from poor use of that brain. Or no use at all. Also, I've seen players with the most limited intellectual ability feel the pain of frustration and failure. Pain is not exclusive to smart performers. Actually, the bigger the brain, so to speak, the more able the athlete will be to understand and solve whatever issue is facing him. Yet, it's also true that the more fertile a player's mind is, the more capable he is of inventing scenarios that will cause pain. And that's why the cliché of "no brain, no pain" is invoked by so many players. ("Just kidding," many players tell me when using the phrase while talking with me. But many a true feeling is expressed in jest.) Those who hold this feeling thereby hold the brain responsible, instead of the self that uses it ineffectively.

Finally, for number 3, people tend to value comfort greatly, bliss even more, because it is much more rare. Yet the so-described bliss of ignorance—not knowing what's going on around or within you—has terminated more professional athletic careers than any other factor I can think of. Comfort, the diminutive brother of bliss, has kept more athletes at a level of mediocrity than any other factor I know. Real bliss for an athlete is being smart and using smarts to his advantage, not to his disadvantage. Most of the athletes I've encountered have not been blissful, using either of these definitions. They tend to devalue their intelligence and analytical capabilities, because they have not adequately applied them before, during, or after their performances. So they yearn for the bliss they say comes with being ignorant. I, myself, would rather take my chances with whatever intelligence I've been allowed, deal thoughtfully with whatever pain comes my way, and not create any for myself. (Or for others).

■ ■ ■

Having analytical ability is an advantage, not a disadvantage. But pitchers too often overanalyze what might happen to them—the consequences—or what they shouldn't do, rather than what they should do. That is the textbook formula for developing negative thinking, cynicism, fear. Effective athletes have better perspective. They are therefore able to convert rapid analysis into immediate plan. What *to do* next is their focus.

Example: A lineman senses he is up too high during his run-blocking. That analysis should not be an extended, disorienting process during which he's distracted by his problem and the possible catastrophe that can result if he doesn't "get things together." (Meaning get his thoughts and himself together.)

"O.K., I know what I'm doing." This thought as he returns to the huddle. The problem is understood. This is the pivotal point in determining what kind of thinker—or nonthinker—the player is. The immediate plan is simply to remind the body to "stay down and thrust." Done. That's an adjustment. On the other hand, agonizing over the past poor blocks and whatever might have resulted from them; feeling extended anger and frustration; focusing on the mechanic during the delivery—those are analyses that lead to failure.

Athletes can describe their problem as "thinking too much." My responses to them: "Trusting too little results in 'thinking too much.'" And "Wrong thoughts; wrong time."

The basic formula: analysis when not competing, simplicity during competition. Every brain can then serve its master.

■　■　■

The major demands of a coach are for the athlete to play hard and play smart. The intelligent approach gives evidence that the athlete knows what to do, as well as how and when to do it. That is keeping it simple smart, not simple stupid.

A word of warning: If the athlete's head is full of the coach's screaming directives, there is no room for his appropriate thoughts. His responses will be anxiety producing at worst, tightness and distraction from the task, at least. Even if what the coach is screaming is "intelligent."

■　■　■

The coach address the mental game by teaching the athlete to:

- Value his intelligence and understand that analysis is a process for becoming a more effective performer.
- Be a keen observer of others in the sport and all the sport's elements, including opponents—noting their strengths, weakness, and tendencies.
- Analyze how others approach performance—and identify which athletes are more effective than others and why.
- Understand that extended analysis should not take place during competition. Recognize what is going wrong, gather himself, coach himself with brief, functional directives.
- Continue to develop and reinforce that philosophy. If others (teammates or parents) are overanalyzing, help the athlete to have the self-assurance to keep it simple for himself during competition.

J

Justice

Justice is always violent to the party offending, for every man is innocent in his own eyes.
Daniel Defoe,
The Shortest Way with the Dissenters

I've quoted my father's meaningful words to me on the subject elsewhere between the covers of this book. But it's very appropriate to do so again. When, as a seven-year-old, I complained about my plight, he said to me, "Hope for justice, kid, but don't expect it."

In my later experiences, I've found that athletes' hopes for justice are related to two primary matters: their performance outcomes and their coaches.

Let's start with outcome—results. Athletes are understandably disappointed when they invest themselves in rigorous and enthusiastic preparation and participation and don't get the results they want. Those who have a healthy perspective understand that they should continue to approach their preparation and performance with the same diligence. Others, with less mature outlooks, bemoan their fate and have accompanying letdowns in their mental energy. Still others express self-pity, cursing the fates that seem to be conspiring against them. The weight of this perceived injustice leads their minds to many places—all of them far from a relentless attentiveness to the specific competitive task they should be executing.

Feelings of injustice affect the athlete's mental game. Motivation, perspective, energy, focus, and consistency are among those aspects affected. The athletes with the lowest levels of self-esteem and confidence will buckle under the weight of a perception that indicates to them that hostile fates are their adversaries, in addition to those they must compete against.

These are the same athletes who tend to turn to excuses, when the others have pointed out the absurdity of their self-pity. (To say nothing of the weakness and dysfunction it causes.) The coach will easily identify this attitude, but not as easily have it changed. It becomes a matter of how much time is available to connect with these individuals and provide them with the guidance they sorely need. Many coaches, I've

279

noticed over time, are not inclined to make that investment. It's a difficult process.

■ ■ ■

The second hope athletes have for justice is related to their coach. They hope for and seek fair treatment. By this, most mean, as they've expressed to me, not being "buried"—a fixture at the end of the bench, an also ran, a mop up. They want the opportunity to shine. "It's only fair," they say, always quite sure, as Defoe alludes to in the epigraph, that they are able to fairly assess their athletic worthiness, even when the coach cannot. Especially then.

The coach cannot please everyone, nor should he try to. But he can be sensitive to those needs of his athletes.

I called a substitute player off the bench to enter a basketball game—for the first time—with less than two minutes remaining. The player said to me, "No, thanks." I said nothing.

After the game, I expressed my sense of justice to the team by announcing, "One of the members of this team will be handing in the uniform tomorrow." The player came to my classroom during the next school day and begged forgiveness—and the opportunity to remain on the team. "It will never happen again," the player said. Reinstatement seemed like justice to us both.

Athletes want information, at least. Perhaps I hadn't communicated enough with this player. I truly can't remember that I hadn't, but neither can I remember that I had at that stage of my coaching career. By far, the one question athletes most want answered for them by coaches and managers is "Where do I stand?" To know their role. I hear this on a regular basis.

So it comes back to this: communicate with the athlete. Tell him his role, tell him why, and tell him what he needs to work on in order to get what he wants in terms of the opportunity to complete.

That's as much as a coach can do. An athlete hopes for it. A good coach provides it, whether or not the athlete expects it.

■ ■ ■

The coach addresses the mental game by teaching the athlete that:

- He can control his approach to performance and his response to it.
- He cannot control results.
- Fate is indifferent to his performance, and luck, good or bad, is random.

- Feelings of injustice based on poor outcomes will result in a weakened resolve and will erode the competitive spirit.
- A self-conscious focus will forfeit any possible competitive edge.
- Whatever his role may be, he is valued and can make a contribution to the team.
- His role is, at the particular time, _____ (fill in the blank).
- The communication process is important to the coaching staff.

Kinetic Memory

During competition, effective performers must and will forget about the workings of their muscles—their mechanics—their physical technique. They trust their kinetic memory. Kinetic memory will govern the athlete's muscles—unless there is interference from a counterproductive mental agenda. Then the muscles receive messages that cause them to tighten up ("muscle up"), lose their natural fluidity and control, and, instead, become controlled by the urgent messages imposing themselves into the performer's thinking pattern. Athletes must be taught to leave their muscles alone! To forget about them while the performance task is being executed. To trust them! They have been executing the same functions for years—since the athlete's childhood. The muscles have learned how to do what they're supposed to do. And they are at their best when the athlete's mind doesn't interfere.

Easier said than done. Athletes tend to dwell on mechanics and technique when they're struggling. They're essentially throwing gas on the fire. Their relaxed and focused execution goes up in flames.

The performer, when he's not trusting his kinetic memory, turns much of his attention to his mechanics, hoping the solution to his performance difficulties will be solved as a result. What does result is divided attention—distraction from the task. Performance is never enhanced when the athlete isn't fully concentrated on task.

Late in the 2000 season, Major League catcher Charles Johnson was asked to explain his career-high batting average (.290s). "I'm just relaxing and focusing on quality at-bats. I'm letting my muscles do what they know how to do," Johnson said. "I'm not giving away at-bats by worrying about mechanics. And I'm seeing the ball real well."

That's what happens. That simple—to understand. Trust is doing what you understand.

The coach addresses the mental game by teaching the athlete:

- To learn that practice sessions are the times to pay attention to mechanical adjustments or to refine technique.
- To learn that, during competition, the athlete must trust his muscles' memory—their ability to repeat functions because of that practice.
- To understand that if kinetic memory has not yet been properly established, continued repetition—in practice—will establish the memory.
- That thinking about mechanics as he performs will divide his attention, taking focus away from the execution of the task at hand.
- To trust his kinetic memory—even when he is uncertain it is trustworthy. (See MENTAL DISCIPLINE, section 3.)

L

Losing

We play with enthusiasm and recklessness. We aren't afraid to lose.
If we win, great. But win or lose, it is the competition
that gives us pleasure.
Joe Paterno,
football coach, Penn State

Many of the athletes I've met over the years have not taken pleasure from competition. Some have told me that their focus on "not losing took the joy out of it." I tell them it wasn't *taken*; they *gave* it away. "Your perspective is your responsibility," I've told them. The problem has always been that these athletes acquired their perspective from others.

Who? Why? The athletes themselves provided the answers for me. First, they heard more about losing than about winning from the negative and/or fearful parents or coaches around them as they grew up. The message registered in their psyche: "Don't lose." And that's the way the athletes learned to approach competition.

Second, the words of those who spoke of losing were dressed in the color of catastrophic consequences. They did not have the attitude Joe Paterno expressed in the epigraph: "If we win, great." Rather, it was more, "We'd better not lose or else."

That's a terrible message to bring into competition. That kind of thinking will keep most athletes from competing anywhere near their best—if what they do will actually qualify as "competing." The athlete is more in a survival mode. He is not to be trusted when the heat is on.

"Must-win" games are often approached poorly by coaches. "Must-not-lose" games are always approached poorly.

I've heard many solid people say, "The agony of losing is more intense an emotion that the ecstasy of winning." I've felt that myself. But how many people have I heard say, "Winning isn't a joy, it's a relief." A relief from . . . losing. Unfortunately, too many.

■ ■ ■

Playing to survive—to not lose—prevents athletes from being aggressive. A survivor, by definition, is protecting himself against something threatening. Competition shouldn't be a threat. It should be a challenge. Different perspectives right there; different approaches according to how the individual sees his athletic environment. (The same case is made regarding coaches and their viewpoint and approach to competition: "coaching to not lose.")

Usually, not much is said about losing, and that's good. But much is thought about it, and that is bad. The focus should be on competing aggressively and effectively. Coaches who do talk about losing get in the way of the very thing they covet: winning.

The best competitors don't talk about losing and don't think about it. And when they do lose, they look forward to the next event. The Roman poet Virgil wrote in the *Aeneid* the one safety the vanquished should have is to hope for no safety at all. The best competitors don't want safety; they can't wait to "put it on the line" again.

Enough said about this topic.

Mental Discipline

I believe in discipline. You can forgive incompetence. You can forgive lack of ability. But one thing you cannot ever forgive is lack of discipline.
Forrest Gregg,
NFL player and coach

Forrest Gregg learned the importance of mental discipline from his Green Bay coach and mentor, Vince Lombardi.

"Discipline is a part of the will," Lombardi said. I would say that mental discipline is the umbrella that covers "the will" and just about everything else related to "the mental game." An athlete can develop the ability to effectively and consistently direct his mind by disciplining it. Courage in battle takes discipline; concentration takes discipline; preparation, self-coaching, consistency, the breaking of bad habits through the development of good ones are all under the umbrella. Or, to use some athletes' more palatable metaphor, mental discipline is "the whole enchilada." An athlete who hopes to perform at his highest level of physical ability must develop an insistent discipline of the mind.

Scientist Louis Pasteur attributed his success not to his brain, but to his "tenacity." It is this tenacious approach that truly distinguishes a great competitor from a mediocre one.

■ ■ ■

The American Heritage Dictionary defines discipline as "training that is expected to produce a specified character or pattern of behavior, especially that which is expected to produce moral or mental improvement."

Mental discipline, for my purposes here, can be defined as the ability to sustain effective and consistent focus on task, regardless of potential external or internal distractions. This is accomplished through controlled attention to relevant information and cues, followed by appropriately controlled behavior.

The athlete knows what direction he *wants* to take and *how* to take it.

Now he disciplines himself *to take it*. He *controls* his mind; he disciplines it.

The cycle of control.

- *Control through awareness*: The control of the ability to recognize and evaluate what the athlete is thinking, feeling, and doing—and what is happening to him. This control gives him the understanding of where his attention is directed and, if it's not where he wants it to be, the reason it isn't. He is then able to follow the cues he knows that help him concentrate on task.
- *Control through thoughts*: This control is exerted after concentration has broken down or has been "given a break." These thoughts should be rational and relevant to the task of the moment. They redirect the athlete's focus.
- *Control through self-coaching (self-talk)*: If the quality of the athlete's thoughts has deteriorated, he controls the words he speaks to himself—internally or externally. These words are directives to get him back to a general positive attitude and to concentrate on positive function.
- *Control through behavior*: This control is of physical behavior, guided by rational, rather than emotional, directives; the "final instructions" provided by self-talk. Examples: "See the ball." "Be easy." "Find the open man." "Stay low." Regardless of how he feels, the athlete acts out of what he knows, what he's been reminded of. After that action, he assesses his body's behavior—and the language that directed it. He comes full cycle and anticipates greater success in the next cycle.

Of course there will be many external and internal challenges. The extent of the discipline applied will determine the success the athlete has in executing his task effectively. Mental discipline requires great effort. If it's worth having, it's worth that effort. An unyielding persistence is part of the discipline. It will ultimately allow the athlete to focus on his task in the toughest of times.

■ ■ ■

In June 1998, en route to the Chicago Bulls second "three-peat" of the decade, Michael Jordan noted that fans and critics had expressed concern about the Bulls' "physical tiredness" during the finals against Utah. "You don't become champions five times without having some type of mental advantage. Right now, we are mentally strong enough to defend what we have. . . . The mental side counts for something." It counted for plenty. It helped them become champions for the sixth time, though Jordan felt the Bulls "may not be as gifted [as Utah]." The discipline was in playing with focus on function, rather than on fatigue or the perceived "physical gifts" of the opposition. After all was said and *done*, that was playing "tough."

■ ■ ■

After having played his final hole in the Andersen Consulting Match-Play Tournament in February 1999, Tiger Woods spoke of being "mentally fried." Said Woods, "I know what I have to do, so I focus on that. But as soon as it is over, then you feel it." Those who *work on it*, feel it. Feel what the poet Dante called *"tutta spenta"*—entirely extinguished. And proud of the effort that kept the flame burning during competition.

■ ■ ■

The coach addresses the mental game by teaching the athlete to:

- Understand that by developing effective mental discipline he is learning to control the emotions, thoughts, and behaviors that would, if uncontrolled, be distractions during performance.
- Recognize that mental discipline addresses whatever distractions or behavioral tendencies may adversely affect him before, during, or after competition.
- Know that this identification is prerequisite for the process of self-improvement and includes eating habits, sleeping patterns, and conditioning.
- Be aware also of the more subtle "weaknesses" that inhibit performance, such as lax practice habits, being less attentive when his team is far ahead or far behind in score, not being mentally prepared for a game which seemingly has less or little importance.
- Understand that the process of developing mental discipline is an ongoing and demanding ordeal, requiring mental energy and stamina, as well as the expression of will power.
- Set as a goal the mastery of individual mental skills he wishes to work on daily, knowing that a goal is a promise, but self-discipline is keeping it.

Negativism/Positivism*

*What is a cynic? A man who knows the price of everything
and the value of nothing.*
Oscar Wilde,
Lady Windermere's Fan

Optimism is a kind of heart stimulant—the digitalis of failure.
Elbert Hubbard

Negativism

Cynicism, dreary attitudes, giving up, and dread of what each day brings all take the meaning out of a person's life and livelihood. Negativism rules the individual and infects the environment in which he moves.

A negative person not only takes any unhappiness he may have had in the past; he brings it—and premature failure—to his future. He's the athlete who, when things are going well, thinks it's an accident or that he's due to screw up soon.

■　■　■

Because children are initially taught the nos and don'ts of touching hot stoves or crossing streets alone or fighting with a sibling, they hear negative teaching during much of their childhood. It was written many years ago that by the time a youngster gets to high school, he has heard those two aforementioned negatives 40,000 times.

Youngsters are greatly affected by the words and deeds of the people who raise them, teach them, and coach them. Much of what they learn will comes from what they hear and see in their extended environment. Indoctrination to negativity creates excessive pressure and a distorted outlook. For a young athlete, negativity becomes poisonous food for thought. And the most pronounced thoughts in an young athlete's environment will accompany him into adulthood.

Negative thinking and perceptions do not allow athletes to have the "fun" a positive thinker has in competition. Negativism does not allow him to have a life that is uplifting.

How some negative athletes manage to function at all impresses me greatly. It is a testimony to their *talent*. But negativism gets in the way of their enjoyment and appreciation of what they possess. And some don't have what it takes to change their view of the world and of themselves. It takes honesty and trust—and an immense effort. (And an encouraging coach.)

■ ■ ■

Athletes who degrade themselves can have a number of motives, each of them traced back to low self-esteem. (See SELF-ESTEEM, section 3.)

Athletes who verbalize in negative terms tend to find things wrong with teammates, managers, coaches, and others. They focus on whatever they say is wrong with others. The effect on them is not a helpful one.

The pessimists of the world expect the worst and usually produce it.

The "blind-alley" players tend to disclaim responsibility. Blind-alley thinking leads athletes' thoughts to unchangeable past events, to unmanageable future events, jealousy, or resentment of others. It encourages remarks that put athletes in the role of victim.

Strategies can easily be formulated for such people. They can become positive problem solvers, but only if they change their thinking and speaking, in a positive and resourceful way, and reject the negative and wasteful ways of their past.

■ ■ ■

Destructive negative statements, commonly mouthed by athletes who think in negative terms:

"No way I can do well today."
"With my luck _____ ." (Completed with a self-pitying phrase.)
"This'll never work."
"We don't have a chance against these guys."
"Don't mess this up."
"He never comes through when I need him."
"This guy (a teammate) doesn't have a clue."
"I can't believe they're leaving me in the game."
"I can't believe they're taking me out of the game."
"This guy thinks he can always psych me out."
"I can't do a thing right."
"I stink."
"This stinks."

"I can never make this play."

"I'm an idiot."

"If only _____." (Whatever the wishful thought might be.)

"I've got no choice."

"It's not my fault."

"Why does the coach always do this to me?"

"Don't rush."

"I'm lost out here."

"I'm a loser."

"He's a loser."

"How can such a loser be telling me how to get it done?"

"I hope they don't expect me to get it done all the time."

"These playing conditions are brutal."

Even when things are somehow going well, extreme negativists will not be convinced: "This can't keep going so good."

■ ■ ■

Enough. The reader can add to the list, I'm sure. People who spend their time expressing such thoughts are people who, as Cormac McCarthy has written, "hold funerals before there's anything to bury."

The athlete must start to listen to himself, understanding that as he expresses these negatives each day, he is increasing the chances of negative outcome and walking around with an unhealthy point of view—diseased, if truth be told.

Positivism

The term *positivism* is not meant to be applied as a doctrine referred to in philosophy books. Rather, it is a reference, in these pages, to a thinking skill that is a countervailing force to negativism.

Nor is positivism a synonym for optimism, which is often a tendency to expect that "everything will work out for the best." The athlete should be optimistic about *himself*—about his own ability to deal with whatever he faces.

For an athlete, positivism is the utilization of appropriate thinking patterns—task-oriented directives, stated in positive language: What to do and how to do it. The "best" may not result, but the athlete will be "at his best." He will execute effectively by employing positive self-coaching techniques.

If an athlete is not predisposed to speak in positive terms, he must learn to do so, acquiring the behavior as a skill is acquired. It is bad enough that negative language reflects an unwholesome attitude. Worse is the fact that the negative thoughts an athlete may have, expressed silently or aloud, are translated into negative approaches. A performer, in telling himself what *not* to do, focuses his attention on just that—and increases the likelihood of the very behavior he wishes to avoid. Positive self-directives provide the performer with a focus on what he should do.

■ ■ ■

The battle to express all thoughts in a positive way must be fought—if it needs fighting. The first campaign is to employ general language such as: "I will"; "I'll find a way"; "I'll adjust." An athlete who tries to "find a way" looks for a positive strategy, rather than saying, "It can't be done," or "I hope it works out." The performer who employs positive language seeks excellence. The performer who speaks in negative terms seeks an escape from failure. One athlete is likely to find what he is seeking; the other is likely to be found by what he is fleeing from.

■ ■ ■

An athlete grows by what he feeds on. Positive language allows him healthy growth. He affirms himself, rather than degrading himself. He examines possibilities, rather than pronouncing impossibilities. He seeks ways to improve himself, rather than seeking ways to judge others poorly. He is grounded in reality, rather than floating in imaginative thinking ("If only . . ."). He expects the best, rather than being certain of the worst. He looks for solutions, rather than wallowing in problems.

The development of appropriate behavior is a process. It takes longer to habituate desired behavior than it does to determine the behaviors. To say "OK, I'm going to speak in positive terms as much as I possibly can" is a simple enough plan. The execution is the challenge.

■ ■ ■

The coach addresses the mental game by helping the athlete to:

- Be aware of the common vocabulary of negativism so that, in identifying "the enemy," he can combat it.
- Understand that to be a positive thinker is to think of what to do and how to do it, rather than warning himself what not to do— or thinking everything will work out by itself to his satisfaction.
- Recognize the importance of self-coaching.
- Accept the responsibility of coaching himself in a positive, constructive manner.
- Listen to himself thinking and speaking, in order to monitor his language.
- Examine how his attitude is reflected by his thoughts and speech.

- Understand that earlier negative influences do not have to continue through adulthood, if they are understood and rejected.
- Take responsibility for what he says and how he behaves, knowing that what he thinks and says will greatly influence what he does.
- Know that changing the quality of his thoughts will change the quality of his performance—and his life.
- Know that the change is a choice and requires commitment and positive mental energy.

Nice Person*

[Vince Carter] wants to be friends with everybody. You are one of the best players in the league. You don't need friends.
Charles Oakley,
NBA player, former teammate

You can't play good tennis or hit a golf ball if what you are thinking about is how other people are perceiving you.
Bob Graham,
chairman, Senate Intelligence Committee,
June 20, 2002

Even politicians understand that anyone focused on behavior intended to influence the perceptions of others is not focused on the task at hand.

Many politicians were skeptical when Senator Graham was named to lead the investigation, the inquiry into events following September 11. They felt he would be too gentle, not aggressive enough, too nice. And the senator was aware. "In this business [9/11] you have to do what is appropriate [one of my favorite words, as readers have probably already determined] with some confidence in the end that it will work out," Graham said, adding to the statement in the epigraph.

■ ■ ■

My father's brother was a loving, lovable black sheep in the family. A "street guy" (he was connected to "the fight game," ran a bar at which women were encouraged to ply the oldest trade in the world, and had other failed businesses), he was tough and soft at the same time. He had no children, but took on his nieces and nephews as his own. He was not a literary man, yet he gave me the gift of a book when I was eleven years old that opened a literary horizon for me (*Huckleberry Finn*). He also gave me a sheet that looked as if it had been taken down from a barroom wall. (It had tack holes at the two top corners.) Typed on the paper was a poem, the printing faded and faint. He told me to read the "last two paragraphs." Stanzas, he meant. "They're important," he said, and left my room.

The message, unlike the print, was clear.

The poem was entitled "The Guy in the Glass." It appears in its entirety in appendix B.

> He's the fellow to please—never mind all the rest,
> For he's with you clear to the end.
> And you've passed your most dangerous, difficult test
> If the man in the glass is your friend.
> You may fool the whole world down the pathway of years
> And get pats on the back as you pass.
> But your final reward will be heartache and tears
> If you've cheated the man in the glass.

Even a player as talented as Vince Carter had to learn that being Mr. Nice Guy is not the agenda of a fierce competitor. The way an athlete goes about his business will define him. Opponents should form their definition based on that competitive persona. Winning a Mr. or Ms. Congeniality award should not be a goal. Winning the approval of the man in the glass should be.

■ ■ ■

In 1999, while coaching at Notre Dame, Matt Doherty spoke of his great fondness for the players he had on his basketball team. "They are the kind of kids you want to date your daughter," he said. "But on the court, I want them to be jerks. I want them to be cocky, arrogant, confident, tough suckers who are going to battle on the court. Off the court, we can wear our shirts and ties and be nice kids and go to church."

I'd use the metaphor "warrior," rather than "jerk," but the desired attitude seems to be the same.

■ ■ ■

I am impressed by Bill Romanowski, reputed to be the wildest, most aggressive, nastiest linebacker in the NFL. He is also known, off the football field, as the consummate and caring gentleman. He is well-spoken, active, and giving in his community. He seems to adjust his behavior to what the environment calls for. He has not compromised his persona. Rather, he has established it. Whoever he is, he is effective—wherever he is.

Athletic competition is confrontation. Athletes must realize that and reconcile any differences they have between their understanding and their approach. If efficacy comes from aggressiveness, and caution or timidity assures ineffectiveness, their choice should be clear to them. Their goal should be established and vigorously pursued. That is the need of every nice guy. Otherwise, he will not be much better off than the nice guy in a Bryce Courtenay novel, who became "powerless as those around me plundered my spirit with the gift of themselves."

■ ■ ■

The coach addresses the mental game by helping the athlete:

- To understand that some of the finest, "nicest" people away from the competitive environment have been the fiercest, most confrontational competitors.
- To understand why so many people have as an agenda the need to please others.
- To identify himself and his tendencies, in this regard, as a person and as an athlete.
- To understand that the ability to adapt to the appropriate conduct required in any given environment, without compromising his own values, is one characteristic of a self-actualized person.
- To know and remember that aggressive behavior is a major attribute of every successful athlete.
- To set specific goals related to behavior during competition that address being aggressive and confrontational, rather than being timid and a nice person.
- To live and perform from the "inside out," rather than from the "outside in," meaning, act upon what he knows is right and appropriate, rather than what he feels would satisfy and please others.
- To develop "a warrior's heart" and a sportsman's ethic during competition.

O

Outcome

(Review APPROACH, section 3)

A bad beginning makes a bad ending.
Euripides,
Greek dramatist

The word used more often than outcome is *results*. Whether one chooses to say outcome, results, score, or statistics, he is still talking about ends. Athletes spend too much time thinking about ends. Outcomes. (So do many coaches.) Their time would be better spent addressing the means—how to have it happen.

"Everything we do has a result. But that which is right and prudent does not always lead to good, nor the contrary to bad." These words, written by the German writer Goethe, are as applicable to sport as they are to life in general. Perhaps more so to sport.

The athlete executes his task well. His approach is excellent; the result is not. The athlete executes his task poorly. His opponent slips and falls. The approach is not acceptable; the result is just what was desired. Thank you, Mr. Goethe.

■ ■ ■

Sports history is rich and fully recorded. Books of statistics abound. Averages of all sorts are broken down, analyzed, discussed, and debated. The baseball box score was invented in the 1870s. Young boys read and memorized players' statistics. Races are run in record time. Tournaments won the most number of times. Golf scores recorded as new lows. Numbers of victories recorded as new highs. Everything an athlete does is documented statistically, for better or for worse.

Well, not everything. Statistics do not tell a true story about *behaviors*. They only tell about the results of the behaviors. And even that depends on how one interprets the term result. For example, if a pitcher executes a pitch well, he might consider the good execution a result. He might, but it's not likely.

■ ■ ■

Mark Davis won the Cy Young Award when pitching in relief for San Diego. "Numbers" became his nemesis. "I hate numbers," Davis said in May 1990, after having signed a big contract with Kansas City during the previous winter. "I don't look at them this year. I didn't look at them last year or the year before that. Numbers are in the past, and they don't help me get anyone out. I just know what they can do when they get into your mind and make you think things you don't need to think," he said.

"When your numbers are good, then a pitcher puts pressure on himself, and says, 'I've got to keep it up.' When a pitcher's numbers are not good, he puts pressure on himself, by saying, 'I've got to get it down.'"

Davis delivered a sermon I have given many, many times—to athletes who told me, "I have to put up numbers." And to those who were desperately trying "to keep their numbers from slipping away" from them. Davis knew too well the danger of numbers and pressure. After having signed a big contract with the Royals, he struggled mightily and never came close to the level of performance he had reached with the Padres in 1989.

■ ■ ■

Statistics are the results that fans, media, and some administrators scrutinize. (Coaches should know better.) An athlete is a *performer*. If he accepts what happens—outcome, instead of his approach and execution, he'd better learn a thing or two that goes beyond his inappropriate interpretation.

He should reconcile himself to the fact that he has no control over results that take place once he has executed his task. If he executes well but gets a bad result, he must *respond* by understanding that he did what he wanted to do (and what he could control) and that he should do it again. And again. Regardless of the result, which he knows he *cannot* control.

■ ■ ■

Years ago, a young left-handed pitcher, originally with the Toronto Blue Jays, came to the Oakland organization. A Harvard graduate, Jeff Musselman had talent and intelligence. But he lacked an essential understanding in regard to the cycle of approach—result—response. While discussing the topic, he revealed this lack. "When I execute a great pitch but get a bad result," Musselman said, "I think, 'Now what do I do? I just threw this guy a great pitch and he hit it hard.'"

"Throw another good pitch," I said. Instead, Musselman tried to throw a "better pitch," which invariably was overthrown and ineffective. Common and unacceptable. My answer, he said with a laugh, was "too simple." He had been seeking something more profound.

■ ■ ■

Athletes who aren't getting the outcomes they want often lose confidence in their execution. Some try harder—attempting to force outcome. Their muscle tighten, they lose their technique, and distort their focus. Others try to change their approach, because they begin to believe that the way they're going about their task is not the right way. They make unnecessary and counterproductive adjustments. Or destructive changes based on this lack of confidence.

The coach who sees technique break down should suspect that the athlete is preoccupied with outcome. He should intervene.

■ ■ ■

Disappointing consequences may seem limitless to an athlete. He may think them to be too frequent, too imposing, too often ill fated. But in the short term—clock time, that is—they can be reduced, weakened, made irrelevant by the immediate focus on behavior. On the execution of the next task.

Though he can't control an outcome, an athlete can certainly influence it, as Euripides suggested in the epigraph. A bad approach will likely lead to a bad result. A good approach, one that does not regard result, will greatly enhance an athlete's performance—and, more often than not, provide him with a satisfying result.

■ ■ ■

The coach addresses the mental game by teaching the athlete to:

- Understand that he has no control over results, if by results he means outcome after the task has been executed.
- Recognize that good results are most likely to come from good approaches and responses.
- Recognize that statistics and standings become part of an historical record, but they are results, which are not part of his focus during competition.
- Be aware that it is inappropriate to set result goals, because he has no ability to control them, as he does behavioral goals.
- Know that when he effectively executes a task, he is doing his job, regardless of the result.
- Understand that mental discipline is required to consistently

execute specific and repetitive tasks, especially when results may not reinforce his motivation to do so.

- Take responsibility for his approach and response, and disregard results during competition.

P

Perspective

If it all ended tomorrow, it'd be sad, but I could cope. I'll be a
success in life, no matter what. I've gained a healthy perspective.
Swimmer Natalie Coughlin,
holder of two world records, 22 U.S. records,
anticipating the 2004 Olympics in Athens

Olympic skating champion Scott Hamilton said his coach had a term he
liked to use: *Refined indifference*. Said Hamilton, "Refined indifference is a
sports psychology precept: Train like there's no tomorrow and then accept whatever happens. Once you step on the ice realize that whatever
is meant to be is meant to be. This can be applied to facets of our everyday lives as well." Natalie Coughlin certainly has done just that.

■ ■ ■

A coach can help his athletes develop a healthy outlook. I'm still
amused by one of my well-intended but lame attempts to go above and
beyond my players' "everyday life"—and the high school state basketball championship they'd just won.

The team was on the bus after their triumph, still very much excited.
Players thumping the inside roof of the bus with their palms, in time
with blaring music from a radio. Singing, cheering, general chaotic joy.

And this was my thought: "Coaches try to give their kids a good perspective after a heartbreaking loss. They tell them the sun will come up
tomorrow and stuff like that. It becomes a rationalization for losing—to
try to soften the blow. Well, here's my chance to give them some perspective after *winning* a championship. This should mean something
now."

With that profundity in mind, I turned in my front row bus seat and
looked at my two co-captains, sitting directly behind me. (One, now a
pediatrician, the other a genetic counselor.) A seemingly perpetual

famine existed in Africa, and that was what I thought of as I said to them: "I just want you to understand that there are more important things going on in this world than this."

One of the co-captains responded immediately and emphatically: "Not tonight there isn't!"

My wife, sitting next to me, gave me a smug look, which clearly conveyed her thought: "Very bad timing."

■ ■ ■

The athlete's perspective toward himself, his needs, and his performance will dictate his body's behavior. Every time he's unhappy with any aspect of his being or performance he should examine his perspective. Examine whether he's performing out of his emotional system or his rational system. Is he acting out what he thinks—or what he feels?

His brain should be in control, telling him what to do (positive functional commands), rather than allowing his emotions to distract him by imposing how he feels onto his behavior. His emotions may very often be based on concern with results and an anxiety related to negative anticipation.

■ ■ ■

The athlete should hold thoughts that are "big"—about himself, his life or his sport—at a distance. A large object held too close to one's face will block out the world beyond it. A large thought must be seen from a distance. That's why it's so easy to help a friend solve a problem, though the very same issue can confound us. "Step out of the frame, and it's easier to see the picture," I tell athletes.

Item: A writer for the *New York Times* wrote that NBA guard Stephon Marbury "resorted to looking at the big picture." Resorted?

Marbury himself explained how he coped with the difficulties his team was facing. "My mind is mentally worn down, but I won't break," he said, refusing to complain after a third consecutive routing of his team. "I know I'm able to get up every day and walk and talk. That's the best thing. There are people that are paraplegics that will never, ever walk. There are some people that would love to be in my situation. . . . That's how I keep my mind in perspective."

After hearing some of my complaints when I was a sick child, my father said to me, "If everyone in this world got in a circle and threw their troubles in the middle, you'd be glad to get your own back." Perspective.

■ ■ ■

The fuller view, as illustrated above, directs the athlete to life beyond himself and his performance. It also helps him to recognize his life and performance as it is, rather than as he wishes or needs it to be. It allows him the health of knowing reality and facing it with common sense and courage. It allows him to be rational, rather than emotional about his mistakes and shortcomings. His goals and his results.

The smaller view is essential during performance. An athlete's perspective must be narrowed so that, in the context of his specific activity, he must have a limited focus. Entirely different from the perspective of his life issues. Attention to the task at hand is all that should matter. Mental discipline, of course, is the major requirement when distractions intrude on the athlete's ability to attend to execution. His ineffective performance is creating by ineffective thought patterns.

■ ■ ■

Many athletes ask me to provide them with relaxation techniques. "Sure," I'll say, "but first tell me why you're having trouble relaxing." The answers are varied, but most are related to a poor perspective, to imaginings and fears that distort their realities. It's hard to relax when you're anxious (scared?) and anticipate failure because of your point of view.

An anxious athlete feels tension in his muscles and well as in his mind. He doesn't concentrate on the task well, of course. A poor outlook can do this. *Has* done it to many athletes, many times. The athlete with an unhealthy perspective says, "This is a threat." A healthier point of view is "This is a challenge." The former of the two says, "I can't." The latter says, "I can."

The strongest statement is "I will." But what if an athlete *does not*? Well, he'll just make an adjustment next time. He'll ask himself the questions suggested elsewhere in this book: "What was I trying to do? What went wrong? What am I going to do next time?" This, instead of making excuses or cursing his fate—or himself.

■ ■ ■

We're all products of everything that's ever happened to us. So, from our early years, our perspective has been shaped, in part, by positive people or negative people who influenced us. Energetic people or lazy people. People who were mentally strong or mentally weak. And so on.

But our experience doesn't have to be our fate. It may help explain why we are as we are, but if we happen to be unhappy with our perspective, we can choose to change it. Or choose not to change, in which case we become a victim of our past. We would be better served if we learn to distinguish between what is inevitable—beyond our control—and what we can choose. We can choose to think and act.

■ ■ ■

The coach addresses the mental game by teaching the athlete:

- That a healthy perspective allows the athlete to see his world objectively and rationally, rather than with vision clouded by emotional needs.
- That a perspective on life should be *wide*, taking in all aspects of the athlete's daily life and performance.
- To identify the nature of his perspective. By asking the athlete, "How do you tend to view the issues or tasks you face?" (Optimistically or pessimistically? With confidence or uncertainty? With hope or despair? Etc.).
- To begin to develop a healthier perspective through his awareness.
- To trust in his ability to cope with difficulties and to approach them aggressively, rather than submissively or fearfully.
- That a healthy perspective encourages self-confidence and helps the muscles to be relaxed. The opposite is true of a distorted perspective, which provokes self-doubt and a sense of urgency.
- That the brain is an athlete's valuable tool for building a proper perspective. And by encouraging the athlete to think clearly, to step back and "get out of the frame."
- That a performer's perspective should be *narrow*—limited to function and focus.
- That he has a choice to see and be what he wishes. "See" with a healthy outlook; "be" with a healthy attitude.
- How to evaluate his performances by having him ask himself "Did I execute what I wanted to do?" If not—by then reminding him to make adjustments based on understanding, rather than negative reaction. And to then know what he wants to do during the next competitive moment.

Playing with Pain

Nothing is got without pain but dirt and long nails.
English Proverb

In 1976, gymnast Shun Fujimoto competed in the Olympic Games with a broken leg. He was awarded a gold medal. Afterward, Fujimoto said, "Yes, the pain shot through me like a knife. It brought tears to my eyes. But now I have a gold medal, and the pain is gone."

Runner Grete Waitz suffered from cramping in her thigh during a long distance race. She focused on running to win. "It has to do with your will, and how much pain you put in your running. At 23 miles, I saw the time and I knew I had a chance to break the record." She did.

Item: From *The Ultimate Athlete* by George Leonard: "We know very little about pain. It seems mechanical in that it's somehow connected to reflex action, and yet it's highly subjective and can't be easily quantified. . . . The perception of pain is increased by anticipation or dread or tenseness. If you fight or shrink away from it, that only makes it worse. In some sense, pain is a judgment. It is not a fixed quantity."

■ ■ ■

The mind has the capacity to exert control over the body's nervous system. Norman Cousins referred to the various functions of that system as "something of a miracle in itself." He said, "The very absence of an awareness of the life process gives rise to the notion that we are totally deprived of any control over them. Yet some measure of control is well within our capacity."

An athlete's capacity to bear pain must be accompanied by his determination to put his focus elsewhere. Given what we know about biochemistry and individual differences—as they relate to pain—we can say that one athlete doesn't feel the same level of pain as another. Getting beyond the pain will therefore require more mental discipline from one athlete than it will from those with a "higher pain tolerance."

When tennis player Jennifer Capriati was sixteen years old, she learned about increasing that tolerance. Playing in the 1993 Australian Open, she took her pain and sick feelings onto the court. When the match began, she disciplined her mind and focused on her task, "and everything seemed to take care of itself," she explained. Actually, *she* took care of it, with appropriate attentiveness to task.

Baseball Hall of Fame great Joe DiMaggio had his own cure: "You ought to run the hardest when you feel the worst."

■ ■ ■

Vince Lombardi believed pain brought him closer to perfection. That is, the ability to bear the pain.

Item: Included as one of the epigraphs for this book are words written by L. Pearce Williams, a history professor at Cornell when those words appeared in the program for the 1971 Cornell-Rutgers football game. The following, also part of that article, spoke of a sandlot football game Williams had participated in at the age of twelve, an experience that "focused (his) attention on the importance of pain and the reaction to it."

> One boy, determined to break his opponents regardless of personal agony, demoralized eleven other boys, all as big as (or bigger than) he, and as good as (or better) football players. Their undoing was their inability to understand how the human will can drive the body to do things that defy reason.

I have never forgotten that day and the lesson I learned. Like my teammates, I had a healthy fear of pain, but I realized that this fear could be overcome and that the man who could overcome it had a distinct advantage over those who lived in its thrall. . . .

In the years since, I have used that lesson well. Pain, in one sort or another, is everywhere. It is painful to confront a problem in mathematics that you cannot solve. It is excruciating to roll blank paper into a typewriter and have no words come for hours. . . .

These are mental agonies, but they are no less real than the physical, and I am convinced that learning to live with and transcend physical pain can give one the inner strength to conquer the mental variety.

■ ■ ■

As a minor leaguer, Mark McGwire came to me before a game and asked for some advice. His shoulder was hurting him badly, and he wondered if he should play. I told him to go see the trainer and find out of playing would damage the shoulder—cause an injury beyond the pain that existed. He came back within the hour and said the trainer told him he wouldn't damage it. "Then there's no question: you play." He did, and had a game-winning double. More important, he learned something about the difference between being controlled by pain and being *in* control of it.

■ ■ ■

The coach addresses the mental game by teaching the athlete:

- That pain is increased when he anticipates it.
- That pain is reduced when he puts his focus elsewhere.
- That pain will not inhibit performance when his intense focus is on the task at hand.
- That to conquer pain is to conquer fear.
- That playing with pain enhances mental toughness and self-confidence.
- That being in pain is not the same as being injured; that he should not damage his body further by participating.
- That playing in pain is appropriate only if the pain does not inhibit his ability to perform at an acceptable level.

Poise

If you can keep your head when all about you are losing
theirs . . . you'll be a Man, my son!
Rudyard Kipling,
"If"

Hemingway called it "grace under pressure." Writer Paul Theroux used a term that is a favorite of mine: *Un-get-at-able*. As in the dugout expression, "You can't get to this guy." Poise is their subject.

An athlete who has poise is able to maintain his composure during "times that will try his soul." That is not to say he will not entertain some distracting internal responses. But he will not externalize them. He will "keep his powder dry." Cy Young Award winner Tom Glavine comes immediately to mind. His demeanor is impeccable. No observer knows what he is thinking or feeling, and that is the way it should be. He is methodical and consistent in his behavior on the mound. He will not let anyone "see him sweat." Peter Gammons described Glavine's mound behavior to me, with pride in his eye and tone, as "good old New England stoicism."

But poise is more than outward appearance, though that is important enough. (See BODY LANGUAGE, section 3.) The Viking warriors believed that no good purpose could be found for showing fear. Such display, they felt would signify to observers that they had lost their independence—freedom. An athlete's emotional display reveals his loss of self-control. A performer who has "total" poise has the ability to control his emotions, his thinking, and his *behavior*. His is a serenity of mind over chaos.

The psyche is an amazing piece of the human "works." Mysteriously it seeks to restore balance when we lose our way. Sometimes athletes make it too hard for it to be successful. When this happens, the psyche is in chaos; the athlete is in trouble. He has lost his poise.

■ ■ ■

Many athletes have "partial" poise. When speaking of Tom Glavine, I refer to what observers may see. He is not a "stalker" when competing. His serenity is total, insofar as the observer can tell. Yet other athletes may stomp around when matters seem to become unglued. As long as the *performer* doesn't come unglued, the *situation* can be dealt with effectively. The proverbial bottom line is how the athlete behaves as he executes his next task.

Glavine exemplifies total poise. His performance seems to be effortless. When Glavine was with the Braves, his pitching teammate, John Smoltz, was an example of "partial" poise. Smoltz can be seen making facial expressions or body suggestions, but he seems to regain his composure—his poise—quickly, before delivering the next pitch. That's what truly matters.

■ ■ ■

A perfectionist can never be fed by his achievements. They always fall short. By adjusting his self-assessment, major league pitcher Kevin Brown has allowed himself to approach performance with a clearer vision of his purpose and a greater expression of poise.

Item: Record-setting swimmer Natalie Coughlin (*USA Today*, August 12, 2002): "I don't mind the mistakes. They're just easy ways to make me go faster. If I were perfect, it would be depressing."

NHL goalie Ed Balfour has had struggles similar to Brown's. After a blowup with his coach Ken Hitchcock, both then with the Dallas Stars, Hitchcock said he needed to improve the way he dealt with Belfour's fragile psyche. He blamed himself for allowing matters to continue without intervention for a number of months and for not seeing warning signals. He recognized that the goalie is a volatile perfectionist, one who chooses between "fight or flight" when faced with an unpleasant circumstances.

When that happens, all poise slides out of the rink.

■ ■ ■

The danger for young athletes is to believe that regaining poise during competition is easy to do. It is not likely that a performer who habitually expresses his emotions during competition will get it back. For some, it is easier to maintain poise than regain it. Often, an athlete who "loses it" does not get it back until he's on the bus or back in the locker room. Having lost his poise, he lost his self-control—to the extent that he could not have "his wits about him" and gather himself. "I just flat-out forgot everything I had to do to fix myself," I've been told, by an athlete who lost control of his thoughts and his poise. Others simply say, "I lost it."

■ ■ ■

Such statements illustrate how an important mental tool that can be lost in the heat of the moment. Panic, anger, or frustration can result in loss of "memory." Those emotions can also produce vague or distorted messages in the brain. The athlete's judgment suffers as well. Doubt and indecisiveness result. Irrelevant and distracting thoughts gain control.

Physical effects also result from loss of control. Breathing is adversely affected. (I have seen many athletes hyperventilate during competition.) Muscular tightness inhibits proper blood flow. Range of motion is reduced and the body becomes less "free." The ability to focus on the task is reduced or eliminated.

■ ■ ■

The loss of poise has a ripple effect. An athlete should always strive to have an internal peace, in spite of adverse or chaotic conditions outside him. (See ADVERSITY*, section 3.) Poise, as Kipling's words in the epigraph suggest, helps make the man. The woman, as well.

■ ■ ■

The coach addresses the mental game when he:

- Helps the athlete to understand that poise is an indicator of self-control.
- Helps the athlete to understand that body language indicates attitude, and attitude, at such times, will dictate behavior.
- Consistently reminds the athlete of the mental and physical effects of loss of poise.
- Reminds the athlete to gather himself and his thoughts when conditions begin to affect him adversely.
- Encourages the athlete to work diligently at harnessing emotional responses to external events.
- Watches for warning signs that an athlete may be "losing it" and intervenes.

Preparation

As soon as I see a couple of mental mistakes, that's telling me you're not ready to play.
Byron Scott,
NBA coach

The instinct of elite athletes runs parallel to the view held by Boy Scouts: be prepared. Confidence and self-belief are greatly enhanced when plans for consistency are developed and employed.

In 1983, future Hall of Fame pitcher Tom Seaver told me, "My confidence is not in my talent; it's in my preparation."

The value of routine has already been established in this book. Routine—set behavior—plan. Habitual acts. Call it what you will, effective preparation is grounded in such behavior.

Diet, sleeping habits, and workout schedules are part of an athlete's preparation. The self-discipline required to prepare himself *away from* the competitive arena can be as formidable as what it takes *on* the field. In some cases, more formidable.

Self-proclaimed "gamers" rationalize that they're *ready* when they "get between the lines." It's the excuse of those who cannot hold up under what they consider to be too much painful discipline: the discipline of conscientious preparation. They're obviously not disciples of Euripides, who wrote, "Do not consider painful what is good for you." And their "game" is far beneath the level of those who are committed to total preparation. And, for that matter, far below their own potential, whether they care to admit it or not.

■ ■ ■

I've already mentioned that the two words I hear most from athletes are "I know." Athletes are, for the most part, aware of what is required in order for them to be effective. They also know that a gap often exists between their knowledge and their behavior. There are those who *usually* do what is necessary; others *often* do what is necessary; some *rarely* do. . . . Those who *never* do what is necessary are not around long enough to be otherwise convinced.

Excellent athletes *always* do what is necessary, meaning they behave in ways that will enhance their performance, rather than detract from it. Their consistency is the lock on their performance. Preparation is the key to that lock.

■ ■ ■

Athletes who wish to be consistent must make a commitment. First, they should formulate goals, which will help them determine what aspects of their game—physical and mental—they need to work at. Then they should develop a program of routine, which will allow them to habituate behaviors, so that these behaviors will become "second nature" to them. They then must have the mental discipline and stamina to follow these routines, regardless of how they may be feeling at a given moment or on a given day.

An athlete's preparation should become a compilation of all the good and appropriate habits he has on and off the field. (See HABITS, section 3.) His eating, sleeping, and conditioning habits should come as a result of a plan put into action. If they are habits of neglect, they will be habits of failure. Sloppy thinking is not the characteristic of successful athletes. Preparedness developed through positive and determined thinking succeeds and endures.

■ ■ ■

Part of an athlete's preparation may be affected by the social demands of others—including teammates. Examples: an athlete knows it is time for him to work out, but a friend puts pressure on him to go to the movies. Or a cousin wants to extend a visit deep into the night, when the athlete knows he should be getting rest in preparation for the next day's competitive event.

The athlete should be confident that *he* knows what's best for him—better than others do. He should act upon what he knows. In addition to commitment and self-discipline, courage is required. Not everyone can easily say, "No." The athlete must decide what is most beneficial to him and make choices based on that understanding.

■ ■ ■

Conditioning is part of preparation. An athlete should, in accord with the coach—and/or the weight trainer and medical trainer—establish a regimen that works for him and the needs he has, according to the sport he participates in.

■ ■ ■

Preparation is the athlete's getting ready for battle. The military purpose is to have an advantage over a warring opposition. The athletic purpose is to have the competitor perform at his best. Still, to compete is to battle, so I succumb to the temptation of employing a military metaphor. "The more you sweat in peace, the less you bleed in war."

Preparation related to performance is required during the performance itself—with each task—before the performance and between performances. (The "after" and "until.") Positive, task-oriented thinking; narrow and sustained focus; aggressive, controlled actions; poise; the ability to "regroup" through self-coaching—all prepare a performer for his next task in competition.

He should always be ready to do battle.

■ ■ ■

The coach addresses the mental game by teaching the athlete to:

- Understand that appropriate preparation will help him be a more confident and effective performer.
- Understand that a major ingredient of his preparation is consistency.
- Establish off-field and on-field routines, making behavior compatible with circumstance.

- Prepare mentally by establishing individual keys, cues, and triggers that keep him properly attentive to task.
- Reiterate, according to need and time, all the mental cues he previously developed before competition.

Pressure

Pressure creates tension, and when you're tense, you want to get your task over and done with as fast as possible. The more you hurry . . . the worse you probably will play.
Jack Nicklaus,
professional golfer extraordinaire

Pressure comes when you're not doing well or you're not prepared. When you're fully prepared, there should be no pressure.
Bob Gibson,
Hall of Fame pitcher

[Manager Davey Johnson] takes the pressure off and allows you the freedom to produce.
Wally Backman,
major league infielder

Coaches' messages can produce tightness in athletes—and in themselves. Anxiety about outcome is the single most intrusive inhibitor to effective performance. Coaches can help players by allaying their own fears or by hiding them from the athletes. (See BIG GAME/EVENT and URGENCY*, section 2.)

The pressure to perform in a manner that ensures good results will create behaviors in many athletes that work at cross purposes with their goal. And the goal of the coach. The healthier the point of view, the more likely inhibiting pressure will be preempted. (See PERSPECTIVE*, sections 2 and 3.)

■ ■ ■

Cliché: you either feel pressure or apply it. Well, there is a long line on the continuum between these two extremes. The trick is to get the athlete as far over toward the application point—thereby getting him as far away from the "feeling" point.

Language takes the athlete in one direction or the other. The language of function—"how to"—takes him toward relentless execution of task, which enables him to apply pressure.

But the more common human tendency is to express oneself in

terms that focus on worries, fears, and imperatives. "I have to" and "or else" are just two the athletes typically employ. Coaches have favorite imperatives they hurl at the athletes: "very important," "critical," "must game," "must win," "we'd better," and so on. (These terms have been noted under other topic headings.) They are words of pressure, words of weight. What Shakespeare called "the be all and the end all."

■　■　■

In a psychology class I was teaching, the subject of pressure (and stress)—because of problems real and imagined—was to be discussed. I brought a big, tin, empty linseed oil can into class the day the topic was to be treated. And an air pump. At the beginning of the class, I gave a demonstration. First, I took the cap off the opening of the can and put a rubber stopper into it. Then, the thin hose from the air pump was inserted into a hole in the stopper. The pump was to be used to extract air from the can.

Slowly I pumped the air out of the can. A crackling noise began to sound as the can's shape gradually changed. The sides were collapsing. I pumped faster; the noise became more pronounced and the can collapsed and shriveled. When I stopped the can's shape was completely distorted.

"What happened?" I asked.

"It collapsed because of the air pressure outside," came an answer.

"It folded because there was nothing left inside," I responded.

Prior to the demonstration, we had noted that air applies fifteen pounds of pressure per square inch on every surface. The pressure put on the can's external surface was fifteen pounds per square inch. The pressure inside the can had been the same—until I sucked the air out of the can. Because there was no longer any air inside, to combat the pressure from the air outside, the can "folded."

"The same physical principle applies to us," I said to the students. "We have air inside us that keeps our bodies intact. Our psyches follow the same principle. The pressing problems or issues we have all can create pressure. But these issues won't dent us or buckle us if we have what it takes to stay whole. It takes coping mechanisms. The can's internal force is air; our internal psychological force is whatever coping mechanisms we have," I said. Though oversimplified, the point seemed clear to them.

An athlete's healthy perspective, conscientious preparation—mental and physical—his focus on and execution of task, and his rational responses all qualify as "coping mechanisms."

■　■　■

Part of the oversimplification mentioned above is that pressure is a perception. What Athlete A perceives as a threatening situation, Athlete B sees as an exciting challenge. Different athletes interpret the same environment and circumstance differently. For example, I know players who buckled playing professionally in New York. (I refuse to say New York buckled them.) And I know players who have thrived there. A person's reality is what he believes it to be. (Karl Wallenda once said, "Being on a tightrope is living; everything else is waiting.")

Still, if the environment truly presents difficult situations that must be dealt with, the coach should do everything possible to help the athlete. An athlete who has "the right stuff" will survive, at least, and thrive, at best, in spite of whatever external problems exist. He'll cope. He will manage himself and, to that extent, "manage" his environment. He won't control the externals, but he will control the internals—thereby applying equal pressure from within. He will not cave in. Coaches can help by putting the air into the athlete, rather than taking it out. By saying the right stuff, the right way.

A better cliché? Skirt it and exert it. That is, the athlete avoids pressure through an intelligent and healthy competitive perspective and puts it on the opposition—if they are susceptible—through a relentlessly aggressive approach to competition.

■ ■ ■

I'm certainly not cavalier about the various issues athletes must face—many presented by particular factors of environment or circumstance. But I've heard too many people pay too much attention to too many problems, rather than paying attention to possible solutions. The "problem" of pressure is just one more misdirected focus. "How can we deal with it?" That is the question I ask players on a regular basis (after we determine that the issue is real, rather than imagined).

What an athlete is forced to deal with is an internalization that inhibits his ability to relax, to enjoy what he does and to do it well. Crucial games, important performances, "must" plays to be made—all the descriptive terms noted earlier can give the athlete a feeling of being tight in his own skin. Again, the coach should wish to loosen it for him, rather than pinching it tighter.

■ ■ ■

The coach addresses the mental game by:

- Teaching the athlete that perceptions and language can encourage the creation of pressure and help to prolong the feeling.

- Understanding that he, the coach, *may* be responsible for having created whatever pressure exists, and he *is definitely* responsible for helping the athlete cope with it effectively.
- Encouraging the athlete to develop coping mechanisms away from the field, such as alternative thinking processes and alternative activities.
- Encouraging the athlete, during competition, to gather himself when he's feeling the pressure of a situation—to breathe deeply, relax his muscles by moving shoulders and arms, concentrate his focus on the task he is to perform—and then employ self-talk, using a positive, functional, task-oriented key (what it is he's going to do).

Quitting

When defeat first creeps into the mind it is not at all unwelcome.
There is a strange pleasure in giving up.
Sebastian Faulks,
The Girl at the Lion D'OR

I liken the feeling alluded to by Faulks' words in the epigraph to a snow death. The easy "letting go" poet Emily Dickinson wrote about. Giving up.

An athlete who "quits" during competition expresses any of a number of internal weaknesses. The complex emotions that take over his *perspective* and *behavior* indicate that he has submitted to powers that are stronger than his understanding of what appropriate behavior is. The quitting, in his situational *perspective*, becomes appropriate to his screaming *needs* to protect his psyche. It actually exposes it, making him more vulnerable in the long term.

But long term is not what instant gratification is about, and, hard as it is to believe, he *is* gratified when he shucks the responsibility to persist in an activity in which he feels the results to be inevitably unrewarding, the further expenditure of mental energy futile and exhausting, and/or humiliation a very possible consequence of further effort.

A number of terms have been italicized above. At this point in the book, it might be useful to note again—with emphasis—how many topics in sections 2 and 3 are reiterative and overlapping. The emphasis of interrelatedness should, once again, point out how addressing the mental game covers a wide scope of human needs, feelings, and tendencies.

As illustrations, listed below are topics that have been unhitched from the quitter's wagon:

- Positivism
- Mental Toughness
- Mental Discipline
- Relentlessness
- Courage
- Motivation
- Aggressiveness

- Goals
- Poise
- Responsibility
- Pressure

The athlete's attitude toward adversity directs him toward giving up, letting go.

■ ■ ■

"Giving in" and "giving up" are distinctly different behaviors as has already been expressed. Giving in is deferring, I believe. Giving up is surrender. Quitting.

While neither behavior is acceptable for a competitive athlete, quitting, in my view, marks and scars an athlete, who most visibly enacts behavior on the stage in the middle of the competitive arena.

A performer accurately identified as a "quitter" might just as well wear a scarlet Q on his uniform. His will be a lonely athletic existence. Coaches should do whatever they can to help vulnerable athletes avoid the experience. It *can* be avoided—with the coach's involvement based on some forewarning (signs) and the athlete's desire to be a competitor, rather than a "caver."

■ ■ ■

Thomas Tutko, an early and important influence in the field of sport psychology, felt that "it is in the very nature of a player not to participate when all is lost, not to put out totally." If this view is accepted, the question remains, "When does an athlete concede that 'all is lost'?" Answer: Not until the competition is over.

The athlete's ego, if he quits, is readying itself for the pain of perceived failure. Science tells us that this is done to reduce that pain of that failure. In other words, the ego protects itself by saying, "This isn't really important to me." The message allows the athlete's body to shut off intensity, to stop caring—to shut down output.

To battle, to fight the fight, would be to fight the relief the ego now seeks. It would be to say that the event still matters. Such a self-statement would result in the ego feeling the pain and anguish that comes with what is, after all, a failure. Basic psychology. An athlete's ego encourages him to quit in order to protect itself in the short term.

This is a very normal—ordinary—athlete. But what his ego gains in the short term becomes a loss in the long term. Excellent athletes understand both the focus of the moment (short term) and the perspective of time (long term). Extraordinary competitors behave accordingly. They prepare their egos to take the hurt.

I am pleased to have the acquaintance of many athletes who would sooner "eat their egos for lunch" than allow those egos to be gratified by quitting.

■ ■ ■

Many players have told me what is now commonly expressed in the world of sport. "The agony of losing is greater than the ecstasy of winning." This is exactly because of what psychology confirms. Players who don't quit hurt more, because they *invest* more. They're proud of their investment—and it pays off in a significant way. It reinforces behavior, regardless of outcome. It is the mental toughness every competitor is proud to call his own. He trains his ego, whether he knows psychology or not, to be pained by *poor effort*. That is the competitor's pride. Never giving in—never giving up.

■ ■ ■

Every athlete must know what can happen to a person when expectation meets disappointment. At that line, he will fight many battles. He should fortify himself. First, with perspective. It isn't a quality, as courage is, but it allows an athlete to prepare himself in a philosophical way, at least, for occasional failure in the game—and more frequent frustration.

■ ■ ■

The coach addresses the mental game by helping the less warrior-like athlete to:

- Understand that, during competition, athletes can sometimes believe—incorrectly—that "all is lost."
- Adopt a philosophy that "*all* is never lost" while competing in an athletic competition.
- Be aware of his tendencies in this regard.
- Understand that quitting reinforces a sense of incompetence or inadequacy in the long term, whereas relentless competing produces the opposite.
- Train his ego to be rewarded by effort and persistence, rather than results.
- Be prepared for the times when performance expectation meets disappointment.
- Value impeccable behavior through mental discipline at such times.
- Evaluate his responses to adversity and disappointment on a regular basis, making appropriate adjustments as required.

Relentlessness
(Review QUITTING, section 3)

Victory belongs to the most persevering.
Napoleon I (Bonaparte)

The falling drop at last will wear the stone.
Lucretius,
Roman philosopher and poet

For an athlete, relentless behavior is an expression of his will to win. An expression of mental toughness. The primary reward is, once again, in the behavior, not in the result. But invariably, a "way to winning" is in being persistent. To persist in doing the right thing. In executing tasks well and responding to adversity with courage and determination.

When I worked with the first of two major league expansion teams, I began the habit of having T-shirts made up for the players each spring training. The theme was always related to relentless behavior, to subjecting themselves to what John Cheever called the discipline of continuousness. To the relentless pursuit of what is challenging or difficult.

The T-shirts had symbols or words such as unyielding, staying power, running through the finish line, never conceding anything—and just plain (expletive deleted) relentlessness. And I spoke to the teams about the value in it for them—as athletes and as people.

Coaches should concede that this kind of toughness can be learned by so-called soft athletes if the subject is addressed and reiterated regularly—as instruction, rather than ridicule of an athlete's softness.

■ ■ ■

"It does not matter how slow you go as long as you do not stop." Well, perhaps speed is more important to Coach than it was to Confucius, but the persistence can be appreciated by both.

Vince Lombardi expressed an appreciation of it through his relentless teaching of fundamentals: sweep right, sweep left. Over and over in the pursuit of perfect execution—leading to the relentless expression of his players' collective will during competition.

■ ■ ■

Tennyson, in his poem "Ulysses," wrote:

> One equal temper of heroic hearts
> Made weak by time and fate, but strong in will
> To strive, to seek, to find, and not to yield.

Relentlessness is the reciprocal of quitting—yielding—giving up. It is an aggressive, persistent, attack-mode attitude. It defines a warrior. The relentless performer gives himself intensely, entirely, and constantly to competition.

"Paralyze resistance with persistence," Ohio State football coach Woody Hayes used to say. The relentless athlete works consistently to do just that, offering an internal persistence to his opponent. He has "left nothing out there" after his performance. He is fully extended. Spent. He may be beaten, but he will never surrender. His sense of self is rewarded by this unyielding behavior.

A relentless attitude combats distractions, such as minor pain, fatigue, weather conditions—or the score. Athletes with severe flu symptoms, for example, have performed effectively and been in a state of virtual collapse—*after* the performance. Their sympathetic nervous system gave them as much as they demanded of it. Those who make no demands get little in return. Bob Gibson made demands. He was able to pitch with a broken leg. Gymnasts and hockey players have done likewise.

"You just pitch," Greg Maddux explained to a reporter who noted that his team had "supported" him with only two hits in the game. "You don't worry if you're up ten runs or down ten runs. You just make pitches. Regardless of the situation, you just have to get guys out. So who cares what the situation is?"

On one occasion before a game a couple of years ago, Maddux, in thinking about the relentless execution of pitch by pitch, said to me, "It's scary. Nothing else matters. I've learned that if I let down, it can all turn around in a heartbeat." He does not let down.

■ ■ ■

Steffi Graf had a reputation of being a relentless competitor on the tennis court. Monica Seles described Graf's approach with admiration. "Steffi will never give you a free point, even when it's 5-0, 40-love." Irrespective of score, of circumstance—of feelings. Keep executing the task at hand. Keep competing. Keep bearing down. Stay focused. Relentlessly. All athletes have the capacity; not all have the determination. (See WILL, section 3.)

■ ■ ■

I've seen athletes who battled through adversity, working to find a way to get it done. They appeared to be hanging on with suction cups. Japanese athletes describe such a quality as *gambate*—working hard, never giving up.

Sometimes the suction cups don't hold. But, as Lombardi was fond of saying, it's not about how many times a person falls; it's about how many times he gets up. Dorothy Fields wrote the lyrics for a 1936 Jerome Kern tune that I first heard on the radio when I was a very young boy. The song begins:

Now nothing's impossible, I have found,
For when my chin is on the ground,
I pick myself up, dust myself off,
And start all over again.

I read these words as an adult: *Percussus resurgo*—"Struck down, I rise again!" And again.

■ ■ ■

The coach addresses the mental game by:

- Teaching the athlete to value the behavior of competing fully until the performance is completed.
- Helping the athlete to develop a philosophy that recognizes relentless behavior as its own reward.
- Teaching the athlete to understand that execution should have nothing to do with score or circumstance.
- Teaching the athlete to evaluate his *behavior* after each performance, setting as a goal the relentless execution of tasks, irrespective of any internal or external factors.
- Reminding the athlete that the development of any attitude is a process—one he must continue to work on with diligence and consistency if he is to develop a relentless attitude.

Response*

People ask me what makes a great skier. It takes the gift; but besides the gift it takes that availability of mind which permits total control of all the elements that lead to victory—total composure.
Jean-Claude Killy,
three-time Olympic Gold Medal winner

"Approach, outcome (result), response." That is the sequence of the three events that take place during competition. It is actually a cycle, these events being repeated throughout performance.

APPROACH and OUTCOME have been treated earlier in this section. A performer's approach, as noted, is entirely within his control. Outcome is not within the performer's control.

The athlete's response is pivotal. How he acts after the previous event—the result of an executed task, an official's call, a teammates blunder—will often dictate the quality of his next approach. Meaning that if an athlete's response is a poor one—loss of poise, loss of purpose, loss of focus—he is likely to take that distraction into his next approach. The next task, therefore, will not be executed with maximum effectiveness, to say the least. *The athlete has complete control of his response.* But he often will *lose* control of his thoughts and behavior. If he forfeits them, he forfeits whatever edge he hopes to establish as a competitor.

Every athlete faces ongoing challenges to his makeup and attitude. For example, when all is going well, he can respond with continued focus—or with a complacent loss of focus. When he faces difficulty, he can respond with frustration, anger, submission. Any response that addresses the problem, rather than the solution will perpetrate that problem.

Relentless devotion to task is the attitude and the behavior that must be developed. It is the response an athlete should demand of himself if he wishes to be exceptional. The intellectual response to adversity, once again, is simple enough. Three questions, asked of himself: "What was I trying to do?" "What went wrong?" "What do I want to do next time?"

In looking at those questions, the reader will see this: if a task is well executed, *nothing went wrong. That* is the proper response. Of course, the outcome might not have satisfied the performer. Stuff happens. He must recognize that there's nothing he can do about it—and deal with it by relentlessly executing the next task. *That is the only acceptable response.*

Courage, intelligence, and mental discipline are required if an athlete is to have consistently appropriate responses during his performance. It's that simple—to *say.*

It's not necessarily harmful, though not ideal, for a performer to react to a result with an emotional response. However, he must quickly purge himself of that emotion, and regain his composure and focus before readying himself for the next task. No negative response should be brought to it. Ever.

■ ■ ■

"So, if you have a good approach, and there's a bad outcome, and you *respond* badly to that, what's your next approach going to be?" I'll ask an athlete rhetorically.

"A bad one," I answer. "What will have happened is: a good approach, a bad result, a bad response. Which will then lead to a bad next approach and, most likely, another bad outcome. And down the drain the performance swirls.

"On the other hand, consider this sequence," I say. "Good approach, bad outcome, good response. What's the next approach likely to be?

"A good one. So, then have an ongoing sequence in which the two things an athlete can control will *always* be good. That's all he can do to give himself a chance to succeed. And those who are disciplined enough to do that are very likely to be successful. That's the understanding and trust every performer should have: that good outcomes will come, if his approaches and responses are good."

■ ■ ■

Every sensible person knows he'll face situations he will either take for granted or be troubled by. He understands that intellectually. But in order to handle these situations well, he must have his emotional responses under control. He must get his answers from his rational system. "What do I want to do here?" That is his operative question—his appropriate response.

■ ■ ■

Many, many years ago, the Greek philosopher Diogenes was asked why he begged money from a statue. He replied, "I am practicing disappointment." He was working on his response, albeit with cynicism. No harm; he was a philosopher, not a competitor.

■ ■ ■

The coach addresses the mental game by helping the athlete to:

- Understand that his response to any event, situation, or circumstance is entirely within his control.
- Understand that a negative response during competition— whether it is frustration, anger, or any other distracting reaction—will adversely affect his approach to the next task.

- Understand that disappointment is inevitable and that the manner in which he handles it will determine his level of maturity, mental "toughness," and efficacy as a competitor.
- Respond to adversity by making adjustments that are within his control through self-coaching, rather than self-pity.
- Disregard what he cannot control, that is, outcome/results.
- Trust that a good approach and a good response are means that are most likely to bring about good ends.

S

Self-Coaching

Self-reflection is the school of wisdom.
Baltasar Gracian,
The Art of Worldly Wisdom

And self-coaching is the school of achievement. The wisest athletes know how to assess their needs. The best achievers know how to integrate that understanding into their performance.

Infantrymen in the midst of battle can't ask their drill sergeant what he thinks is best to do. Sailors on a firing line cannot refer to their *Blue Jackets Manual*. Whatever is required at that moment, in that circumstance, is their exclusive responsibility.

Self-coaching is the athlete's technique of reminding himself how to respond to the circumstance—to the moment—during the heat of battle. It is the ability to employ positive, functional self-talk that will "coach" his mind to direct itself appropriately to the task at hand.

■ ■ ■

My message to athletes—amateur and professional—has been that each of them is the most important coach he'll ever have. By this I do not mean to imply that an athlete won't gain abundant and valuable insights from others. But only the player himself can integrate this information into behavior. Or *not* be able to apply what he's learned.

■ ■ ■

Conventional wisdom tells us that most athletes make midcompetition adjustments. Some are necessary; some are not necessary; some do more harm than good. It's the athlete's responsibility to know which to make, when to make them and how to make them. It all starts with self-study, which is a major part of the curriculum in the school of wisdom.

Seattle pitcher Jamie Moyer, not known for imposing "stuff," nevertheless has been a very effective pitcher over the years. He studies opposing hitters. Scrutinizes them. He has put together a notebook with information on just about every hitter he has faced. He certainly knows more about some of them than they know about themselves.

The study includes hitters' patterns, strengths, and weaknesses. Moyer's greatest discovery is not about these tendencies, however. The greatest revelation to him is that many opponents never adjust. They will continue to behave in the same way, despite apparent inability to get the job done. And Moyer will continue to take advantage of such opponents.

The point here is that the performer is only doing to the opponent what the opponent allows him to do.

■ ■ ■

Here are a few "essentials" for the athlete:

1. A performer must examine quickly what's happening during competition. His difficulty may be psychological (e.g., having distracting thoughts or trying to do too much); philosophical (e.g., taking the wrong shot at the wrong time); mechanical (e.g., forgetting his keys for establishing getting out of the starting blocks).

   No one knows what an athlete is thinking except the athlete himself. No one else can coach him immediately before and during his execution.

2. A performer must have the presence of mind to take the time to gather and control his thoughts. When things are going wrong for an athlete, his instinct is to get out the "wrongness" quickly. So he accelerates his thinking process and accesses his body movements. He rushes himself and very often spins out of control.

   Unfortunately, the tendency is counterproductive. The athlete must learn to slow himself down, gather his thoughts and composure, make a mental and/or physical adjustment and with an aggressive mind but relaxed muscles approach the next task.

3. A performer must coach himself in positive terms, telling himself what he wants to do, rather than what not to do.

   Self-coaching that is emotionally reactive and negative will be ineffective. An initial response may be emotional, but the performer must quickly "get to his brain." Sustained unhappiness about an execution is distracting and immature. The athlete should tell himself what to do (vs. what not to do)—and how to do it. This all takes place within a very limited time frame.

■ ■ ■

Atlanta outfielder Andruw Jones was asked about his success under his hitting coach's watchful eye. His response: "My coach is myself. 'You're the one who has to go out and do it.' That's what he tells me all the time."

■　■　■

The athlete who doesn't coach himself effectively most often understands what should be done. But he allows the wrong thoughts to preempt that understanding. As I've often said and written, the two words I hear most from athletes are "I know." Though those words may excite me in a classroom, they aren't enough in athletic competition.

Australia's Olympic superstar Cathy Freeman, before the 400-meter race in the 2000 Olympic Games, on what she has called one of the biggest nights of her life, remembered to coach herself effectively. She repeated, over and over, "Do what you know. Do what you know." That coaching reassured her; it relaxed her—it reminded her.

■　■　■

The coach addresses the mental game by teaching the athlete:

- To take the responsibility of learning how to coach himself during competition.
- That, when he's unhappy about what's going on during competition, he must take the first opportunity to pause and make himself aware of the problem.
- To remember his individual mental and mechanical keys, in order to make the necessary adjustment.
- To coach himself by saying what he wants to do, rather than what he doesn't want to do.
- Talk from his brain, rather than his emotions of the moment.
- Exhale deeply, to relieve possible tension.
- Examine and monitor his internal "conversations" related to circumstance, competition, and himself.
- Understand that self-coaching indicates what he thinks and feels about his "world" and himself—and should be grounded in objective reality.
- Recognize that positive self-talk will enhance his ability to perform, whereas negative self-talk will focus on and encourage failure.
- Understand that positive self-coaching should be accompanied by involved attentiveness to what is being said.
- Talk about himself in self-affirming, nonjudgmental language.

- During competition, talk about the task and how to approach it.
- Understand that he is human and therefore fallible—less than perfect—and must learn to coach himself accordingly, with appropriate self-talk, rather than with inappropriate self-condemnation.

Self-Esteem

I had no confidence in myself whatsoever.
Sally Ride,
astronaut

Dr. Sally Ride suffered from very low self-esteem in high school. Her father, during what she called "a casual conversation," said to her, "You know, you've got to reach for the stars."

That casual and seemingly platitudinous remark figuratively and literally "launched" her, motivating her to propel herself beyond her self-image.

When people stretch themselves, they reach beyond what they *believe* their grasp to be. Beyond their perceived abilities and capacities.

■ ■ ■

While coaching women's basketball in Vermont, I implored one of our starting players—a skillful defender and rebounder—to shoot the ball when she had the opportunity. When she was open for a good shot. She had a good touch, but lacked the esteem, thinking herself only as a player who would guard the other team's best scorer. She passed up too many good opportunities that the offense had worked hard to get. Naturally, opponents began to leave her open and guard our scorers more effectively.

"I want you shoot the ball, Sue!" That was her mandate and my mantra at practice every day. "I don't care if you miss your shot; we'll get the rebound," I said, with an air of certainty that was not verifiable. She reluctantly took more shots, without exceptional results, negatively or positively.

But she did shoot more. And just the act of expressing some courage made her self-esteem soar. She saw no terrible consequences of missed shots.

Later in that season, her senior year, Susan played in her final game. It was for the state championship. Incredibly, she took the first three shots of the game for our team. More incredibly, to the spectators and, apparently, to the opposing coach, she made all three. We were ahead 6-0. It was a wonderful start for our team and for Susan Andrews.

After the game, the reporters asked me about her offensive performance. She had scored 10 points. I remember telling the newspaper writers: "Well, after she made her third shot, I looked over at the other bench, and the coach had a look on his face that said something like, 'What the hell is going on here?'"

What had gone on was that someone had learned that she could grasp if she would reach. She did just that, and self-esteem and self-trust grabbed the desired results.

But self-esteem should *not* be based on results of performance, which is how athletes often define themselves. Behavior, approach, courage, intelligence: these are some of the traits with which an individual builds an esteemed self.

■　■　■

Initially, my instinct was to consider SELF-ESTEEM to be a section 3 redundancy. After all, CONFIDENCE and PERSPECTIVE have already been discussed. But there is an extensional meaning of self-esteem that I wished to clarify, based on experiences with precocious athletes over the years, and this attempt seemed important.

"It is difficult to make a man miserable while he feels worthy of himself," Abe Lincoln said in one of the many speeches he delivered as president of the United States. "Worthy of himself." That's the operative phrase. When talking with athletes, my subject is usually "performance" or the athlete as a performer. They wear uniforms, but I must often remind them that there is a "self" under that uniform.

A youngster, who is precocious, whether it is as a musician, a mathematician, or an athlete, has his precocity in front of others—and himself—always. He is identified for his great and exceptional talent, rather than for whatever self is behind it. Behind it—hidden from public view, and, very often from the person "himself." What seems to matter is what he does, rather than who he is. And this is how his early years train him.

A coach has a hand in that training. He may help the athlete gain great confidence in his talent and skill. He may teach the youngster to have great belief in his ability to achieve. But this self-esteem will be based on his singular achievement and the exaggerated approval of others.

On this, the athlete's identity will be built. It is a shaky foundation. He'll feel "worthy of himself" when he performs to the level of expectations. For most athletes, the level is indicated by statistics and victories. That will be part of the youngster's learning curve. He'll an avid and eager learner, in this regard. But will he learn much about self-worth as a whole person? The more precocious he is, the less likely he will be considered a whole self.

When a person considers his entire self to be a performer, failure becomes very personal and very dramatic. Self-esteem plummets. Players say, "I'm a failure." I try to correct them. "You've failed at a task, but *you* aren't a failure." It's a hard sell, and often requires the building of a foundation of self that had not previously existed.

■　■　■

Many examples come to mind. One particular player, a glaring example of a person who had low self-esteem, had a very fine major league career and was recognized as being an outstanding ballplayer. As a man, he is intelligent, kind, considerate, trusting, handsome, and articulate. At the end of his playing career, he was very troubled. He had always had social insecurities, based on the fact that he did not see all his personal attributes; he only recognized his efforts on the baseball field—his statistics. Those around him during his youth focused on his baseball prowess. So when his "numbers" began to identify him as significantly less than the player he had been in the past, his self-worth became significantly less as well. He had little (nothing?) to fall back on. It was an emotionally exhausting ordeal he went through, in order to gain a new—and healthier—perspective of himself. An esteem that had not previously existed.

This is not an isolated or exaggerated example. It is "out there." Let the coach beware. If he does not help an athlete develop and identify an early self, that individual will become a symbol of his performance, rather than the substance of who he really is. And he will fail to recognize his substantial self, giving himself approval only when his numbers allow and confirm that approval.

■　■　■

Unrealistic expectations, subtle but constant criticism, one-dimensional treatment (as an athlete, rather than a person), the burden of others' needs being satisfied through the young athlete—all will inhibit the development of a healthy and self-actualized self. It can distort the individual's view of himself and influence the view of the adult he or she becomes.

"Public influence is a weak tyrant compared with our own private opinion," Thoreau wrote. "What a man thinks of himself, that is which determines or rather indicates his fate."

A few words about public opinion. First, in general, people out there are more considerate and less interested in us than we think. In addition, their judgments of athletes are fickle and fleeting. People have more to do than spend their time judging and condemning. Their immediate expression of opinion is neither objective nor sustained. Nor should it be an influence on the individual player.

The self-consciousness that a young athlete might have is a false pride, a form of egotism that persuades him that what others think and say about him has more meaning than what he says about himself. Naturally, the athlete with high self-esteem, then, is fortified. The athlete with little self-esteem is under siege and vulnerable. He must recognize that he, not spectators, parents, or the media, is the problem and the solution. The coach should be a part of that solution.

■ ■ ■

An athlete who continually refers to his inadequate performance is, to use Lawrence Durrell's metaphor, "tied to the wheel in the sinking vessel of [his] self-esteem." His belief and confidence have eroded. He comes to discount his successes and magnify his failures, thus always confirming a negative self-image. He will be cautious, rather than aggressive. He will be distracted, rather than focused. He will expect to do poorly, rather than expect to do well. And he will tiptoe through life, intimidated by car salesmen and plumbers, never realizing his own self-worth, despite being a good son, a good friend, a good teammate, a good husband and father. A good young man.

■ ■ ■

Maxwell Maltz, in his marvelous book *Psychocybernetics*, wrote, "Of all the traps and pitfalls in life, self-esteem is the deadliest, and the hardest to overcome, for it is a pit designed and dug by our own hands." Under the influence of others, a young athlete may accept a design created by them—but he, most certainly, will "dig his own pit." A coach should not provide the shovel.

■ ■ ■

The coach addresses the mental game by teaching the athlete to:

- Understand that he has many dimensions as a person, beyond being just an athlete.
- Recognize that self-esteem should be based on all the traits and behaviors of an individual, rather than on a singular, albeit highly developed, ability and skill.
- Understand that his identity is related to his substance (who he is), rather than the symbolic representation of him (what and how he does).

- Work at being more well-rounded, valuing more in life than just athletic performance.
- Learn to participate for himself, rather than for others.
- Learn to diffuse the effect of public opinion by understanding its nature: exaggerated, self-gratifying, subjective, and temporary. And less interested in him than he thinks.
- Perform regular reality checks on himself, assessing daily behaviors—on and off the field—in order to evaluate himself fully.
- Set his own standards and goals, based on his values, and hold himself accountable through the daily evaluation noted above.
- Use affirmative language when talking about himself, rather than the language of self-disparagement.
- Be an advocate, rather than an apologist, for what he values and believes.
- Look people in the eye during conversation (regardless of his stats).
- Take responsibility, rather than blame.
- Look at life and himself objectively.
- Express his sense of humor.
- Learn to tolerate uncertainty.
- Take risks.
- Be honest, rather than being deceptive or a game player.
- Identify his defense mechanisms and have the strength to work at breaking them down, recognizing that he does not need to continually justify himself to others.
- Like himself—and deserve it.

T

Task at Hand

Everything should be made as simple as possible, but not simpler.
Albert Einstein,
scientist

Keep it simple, stupid. That's a widely held philosophy. Matters become complicated, not because of information, but, rather, because of interpretation. Matters are further complicated when significance is given to irrelevancies.

Keeping it simple means knowing what matters and what does not matter. That is what Einstein meant. Quite often, however, athletes tend to complicate their world with their needs, their fears, their desire to succeed. My expressed view to them is that sport is simple; people are complicated. Many of them tend to think that there must be more to the game than executing a task successfully. In terms of behavior, there is not. Each singular execution of task has a "perfect simplicity [that] is audacious" (George Meredith).

The greatest truths are the simplest, and so are the greatest athletes. Not simple-minded, but simple in their approach. They think small; they are focused on task. They do not allow extraneous issues and circumstance to take them out of their game plan—which is *simply* to attack and execute.

All big thoughts are unmanageable, out of a performer's control. *Carpe momentum.* The moment, the now must be seized.

Living in and for the moment makes it easier for the athlete to adapt to situations as they change. His focus is narrow; the requirements are limited to that time and space. All attention is concentrated on executing the next task: a shot, a block, a stroke. He can understand that; he can control that. It is small and elemental. That task at hand is his exclusive concern, and always should be.

■ ■ ■

The only life a person can lose is the one he's living at the moment. To forfeit the moment, for an athlete, is to relinquish his control and ability to effectively accomplish his task. If great wisdom is in knowing what to do next, an athlete who is attending to anything other than the moment—the next task—forfeits his wisdom as well.

Many topics in this book have also addressed the need for this concentrated attention to task. That concentration, as has been noted, will be prepotent. It will power the athlete's mental energy—his mind, his muscles, his eyes—toward the execution of task. Nothing else will matter. Nothing else will intrude on the performer's now.

The greater his ability to establish such focus, the more often he will—naturally and without effort—"be in the zone." Some athletes will achieve it more naturally than others. But it can become an acquired instinct. The acquisition is through the process of disciplined preparation. And then, in dealing exclusively with the task at hand. Focusing on it—and executing it.

That's as simple as *I* can keep it.

■ ■ ■

The coach addresses the mental game by encouraging the athlete to:

- Adopt the mantra of one task at a time, which is always his immediate and essential concern during competition.
- Understand that any other thoughts in his head during competition will diminish his ability to concentrate appropriately on his task.
- Remember that his behavior is within his control; results are not.
- Recognize that he should function in the present—the now—rather than fretting about the past or fantasizing about the future.
- Reiterate the philosophy of dealing exclusively with the task at hand, especially when media, parents, and friends wish him to conjecture on matters beyond his control.

U

Urgency*

Bode Miller blew away the competition in his "all-or-nothing" second slalom run, giving him a silver medal in the combined. It was the first medal by a U.S. Alpine skier in eight years. Miller had fallen in the downhill and slipped on the first slalom run. He was 15th after the downhill portion. The second run was different in result. Gold medal winner Kjetil Andre Aamodt of Norway said, after watching Miller's second run, "I've never seen anybody ski so fast."

What he saw was a result of Miller's adjusted mental approach. A sense of "urgency" based on his desire to win was replaced by an understanding of how he skis when he's at his best. "Need" ("I gotta do well") was replaced in his internal system by "want" ("I know what I should do").

■ ■ ■

Conventional wisdom and scientific studies speak to the point that athletes perform better when they are in a relaxed state. A sense of urgency is the antithesis of relaxation. At best, an athlete's urgency inhibits his ability to function well. At worst, it makes him dysfunctional.

A feeling of urgency can have as many causes as there are athletes. Each individual brings his perspective and needs to each event in which he competes. If one athlete feels the need to do well to prove himself, he can manifest this need by trying too hard. If another is competing in a "must game" for his team, his urgent response will work at cross-purposes with his intention—to win the big one. He is very likely to try too hard, becoming overly aggressive and less controlled.

Excessive concern, worry, or fear produces the same symptoms: a loss of a controlled mental and mechanical pattern. When desperation sets in, thoughts become disjointed and scattered. Muscles tighten, the execution quickens.

A relaxed state speaks to the athlete by saying, "Be easy, trust it, stay on task, let it flow." Urgency speaks another language: "Hurry up, force it, I'd better . . ." Urgency is "I have to" and "I must." It induces tension and fear. Urgency is "or else." Urgency is do or die.

■　■　■

Some language patterns are conducive to adjustment and an effective approach to performance, others to maladjustment and an ineffective approach. Words and phrases that result from the athlete's sense of urgency rush his thoughts toward judgments related to consequences. His concentration and muscles follow those thoughts—all going in the wrong direction.

Urgency induces loss of control, loss of purpose, loss of balance, loss of focus, loss of tempo, loss of trust—to name a few losses. Illustrative behavior can be seen just about every day, in just about every game. It happens, to varying degrees, to just about every athlete. The greater the sense of urgency, the greater the loss of all the elements of an effective approach to task.

■　■　■

Real crises test mental discipline. Perceived crises test the athlete's view of the world and of himself. Whichever tests him, a controlled behavior helps him to pass. Urgent behavior induces failure.

The coach should recognize which of his athletes have tendencies to behave in such a way—to try harder at key moments in competition or when they lose trust in their ability to perform well. Trying harder is trying to force something to happen. The athlete believes his greater effort is going to produce a desired result. It isn't. A calming intervention by the coach can help the athlete regain—or gain—perspective and self-control.

The greatest help will come from a reaffirmation of a healthy point of view and a renewed understanding of what works and what does not work in competition. First, an athlete who performs with a heightened sense of urgency has made everything matter too much. The "or-else syndrome" takes over. Dire consequences are always close to his surface thinking. A better perspective is required.

Second, the athlete, having gone through the experience of performing at this high level of urgency, understands its power over him. He must further understand what measures he should take to transfer that power. In my experience with athletes, this has been done with constant and frequent reiteration of a desired approach. "Brainwashing."

Daily work on mental discipline and preparation helps train the athlete to (a) establish a more effective approach, and (b) recognize when it breaks down during competition and make an adjustment. This, rather than allowing the urgency to cut off his head and have him perform like the proverbial chicken.

Finally, regular relaxation exercises are appropriate for an athlete who regularly performs with a feeling of urgency. Philosophy deals with the issue; techniques deal with the symptoms. An urgent athlete should deal with both.

■ ■ ■

The coach addresses the mental game by helping the athlete to:

- Understand that a sense of urgency will take him out of the relaxed state that helps him to maximize his ability.
- Recognize the causes of urgent behavior and work at developing a more realistic perspective.
- Reiterate and/or review his philosophy of effective performance on a daily basis.
- During competition, be aware of any tendency to accelerate his tempo and rush his execution of task.
- Make the necessary adjustments at such times, gathering himself, slowing his thought process, using calming self-talk, and refocusing on task.
- According to need, develop a routine for using breathing exercises and relaxation techniques.

V

Visualization

If you can learn to think about something in a systematic and detailed fashion, it becomes a part of you. Your body knows it has been there before.
Harris & Harris,
Sports Psychology: Mental Skills for Physical People

Visualization is the technique of recalling information in images and physical forms, rather than in language. Some people learn more effectively with their eyes than with their ears. With others, the opposite is true. My approach is to present the concept and process to athletes, allow them to see how simple the procedure is and encourage them to give it a try. The rest is up to them.

■ ■ ■

The first and most obvious value of visualization is in the fact that it can be utilized away from the field: on a living room chair, reclining in bed, sitting in front of a locker. All provide an environment for using the technique.

Having recognized the ability to "rehearse" away from the field, the athlete can be further encouraged to use the practice by knowing that research has found that mental practice is often more useful than physical practice. Stories abound to verify these studies, including the one about a prisoner of war who had never played actual golf in his life, but who spent years playing visualized golf—thirty-six holes a day—to make his days in captivity more tolerable. When he became a free man, he also became a very respectable golfer. Immediately. His mental rehearsal had prepared him well.

■ ■ ■

Athletes who conscientiously prepare for performance may wish to include some form of visualization in their program. Prerequisite for its successful use is that the athlete understand what makes visualization work and that he then believes in its value for him. Some athletes are initially skeptical about their ability to visualize. I simply ask them to recall what they were wearing at their sister's wedding or their senior prom. "What was your date wearing?" I then ask. And I ask for other details. That data, stored in the subconscious, is easily recalled by an athlete.

His conscious mind determined that this information was significant to him, and he filed it for future reference, should it be needed. Sensory experience was thereby registered at the conscious level and stored at the unconscious level. "Memory in pictures," I tell athletes to simplify the idea—sparing them an explanation of Karl Albrecht's definition. Visualization, Albrecht wrote (*Brain Power*) is "all non-verbal thought forms that (the) brain organizes into a spatial pattern, *not just a mental picture.*" (Emphasis mine.)

∎ ∎ ∎

The POW who played "mental golf" had pictures of people swinging golf clubs in his memory bank. He had observed; therefore he had the images. His eyes had seen golf being played, his conscious mind stored the images for future reference, and he recalled them when he needed them. He was able to "recreate" doglegs to the right, doglegs to the left, water hazards, sand traps, and a good golf swing. He had these pictures, though he had not had the physical experience.

Athletes have had the physical experience, and therefore have kinetic memory as well as visual memory. That's an experiential advantage. Visualization will help the athlete to program his nervous system and his muscles. And, as noted, he has an experiential reference point to assist him in "getting it right," especially in regard to mechanics.

∎ ∎ ∎

Joyous or traumatic memories are so vivid that the emotions from those moments are often reproduced. It's an example of memory controlling the muscles and the nervous system. This power can be utilized before the fact. The athlete sees himself participating in the event—the game or the singular task. He can mentally simulate crowd noise, tension level, and circumstance. Called subjective visualization, this technique allows the athlete to include and adjust his emotions within the experience. (Being a spectator is objective visualization.) He then directs his intentions with self-talk. "Quick to the puck; stick down." And he sees the execution of those commands.

Jack Nicklaus claimed he visualized every golf shot he took before he took it. But the movement and time between golf shots allows for that. The pace of some sporting events does not—on a regular basis. My recommendation to athletes is that they rehearse either the night before they perform or in the locker room before each competition. "When your head hits the pillow, use the next ten minutes for putting a tape in your head of your best performances," I tell athletes. "See yourself performing at the top of your game, executing every task effortlessly and effectively. You'll usually fall asleep with the tape still playing."

■ ■ ■

Visualization requires concentration. An athlete who begins the process and soon loses interest will not benefit from an activity he cannot sustain. Just as every concentration exercise requires mental discipline, so too does every visualization exercise. Visualization serves more than one master.

Many exercises can be used to develop and practice the technique, through observation, imagination, invention, and recall. A keen observer sees much. When entering a hotel/motel room in which he has never been, the athlete should notice the spatial relationship of the furniture, the window and door locations, anything unusual about the room. He should be attentive to detail, observing all, rather than just being another "piece of furniture" in the room. He should see colors (bed spread, picture on wall), feel texture (curtains), smell fragrances (wood, room freshener). He should "get the picture."

A different setting can be invented. The athlete can sit and visualize himself water skiing, riding a horse, playing golf, or eating a favorite meal at a restaurant. The accompanying sights and sounds should be included. And smells. And tastes.

The athlete can imagine finding a gemstone in his travel bag, for example. He senses its color, observes its size, and feels its texture.

He can recall past events and recreate the setting and images he has retained at a lower level of consciousness. A gathering of friends, a skiing experience. A wedding or prom, as mentioned above. Some special visit during childhood. Any vivid recollection will serve.

■ ■ ■

The above are examples of exercises that can be helpful in developing an athlete's ability to create and sustain visual images. Their ultimate value is in the developing and enhancing of the athlete's ability to "see" himself perform—to visualize effective execution.

■ ■ ■

The coach addresses the mental game by encouraging the athlete to:

• Understand the concept and purpose of visualization.
• Understand the technique used to visualize.

- Understand the value of visualization.
- Work on practice exercises in order to enhance his ability to visualize effective performance.
- Utilize and further develop his sensory abilities through keen observation, imagination, invention, and recall.
- Visualize peak performance from his past, seeing himself in "flow" experiences of execution (possibly "feeling" the muscles and emotion during that performance).
- Incorporate mental rehearsal into a regular preparation program.

Will

(See RELENTLESSNESS, section 3)

[A] thousand wishes but no will.
Will Durant,
The Reconstruction of Character

Will is power. Will is determination and resolve. Will is self-discipline. It is the imposing of desire into behavior. Many value it; not that many exert it.

One of my first remarks when speaking to athletes addresses a very basic human tendency. "Everyone wants to succeed," I say. "But not everyone has the will to do what it takes to succeed." Most enthusiastically acknowledge the importance of asserting their mental energy and say they intend to.

"Men are distinguished by the power of their wanting," wrote novelist Barry Unsworth. But their wanting, without willing, achieves little or nothing. The undistinguished behavior of broken resolutions is "normal." But it is a normalcy other than what elite athletes should seek for themselves.

■ ■ ■

A "warrior" is the person—the athlete; a powerful will is his psychological weapon. The designation of an individual as a tough competitor is a reference not to his physical capacity, but, rather, to an indomitable will. Most of the misfortunes an athlete faces during competition are a result, I believe, of weakness of will. He has gone into battle with a blunt weapon—or with no weapon at all. The strong determination an athlete has for getting it right connects him to his appropriate concentration. As it does to positivism, aggressiveness, and all the other traits and behaviors he values. The expression "He wills himself to win" speaks to that point.

Even when an athlete's internal system is invaded by self-doubt or fear, his determination enables him to disregard these intruders. He

341

redirects thoughts and immediately regains control of his approach and performance. Self-control requires a strong expression of will.

■ ■ ■

A story of Native American origin tells of the ordeals an adolescent boy is required to face and conquer before his tribe considers him to be a man. A long, solitary walk was one of the requirements. Five miles. Before he departed, an elder would tell him, "If you can walk five, walk six." After a will becomes strong—it becomes insistent.

"When will is as taut as a bowstring, the ant can overcome the lion." That's what an African tribe's "lesson" is to their boys with "manly" aspirations.

Cancer patients have offered many examples of the assertion of will extending life, as opposed to resignation—giving up—ensuring death. More often than a "normal" person thinks, he is able to take himself beyond that norm. With will power.

■ ■ ■

The coach addresses the mental game by helping the athlete to:

- Be aware of the power of a strong will as it imposes itself on behavior.
- Understand that ordinary people most often express intentions without expressing the resolve required for those intentions to become reality.
- Reestablish his broad goal of being extraordinary, rather than ordinary.
- Be certain his specific goals are expressed in behavioral terms, allowing for their achievement through his determination and daily attention.
- Recognize that the expression of a strong will affect all aspects of his performance in a positive way.
- Remember that self-improvement as a person and as an athlete is a process, an arduous one for those who are determined and persistent.

X-Factor

x: any unknown . . . factor (or) thing.
The American Heritage Dictionary

*She was afraid of the dark as she was afraid of the unknown, and
what was the unknown but the force of evil?*
John Cheever,
The Wapshot Scandal

The twenty-fourth letter in the alphabet: students learn to use it in algebra class. Athletes often use the term *x-factor* when they refer to the unknown—which can be a troubling concern, if not a "force of evil."

The *future* is the unknown athletes are factoring. But in their equation, the x-factor will always remains an unknown, until it's revealed as the immediate *present*—the "now."

The now is what an athlete *can* know, *can* manage, and *should* address. His musings on the future are surely distracting and potentially anxiety producing. The unknown, wrote H. L. Mencken, "sits . . . calmly licking its chops," ready to devour the performer who has lost his way—who has strayed from the path of the next task he is to execute.

The now is all that athletes truly have. (All *any* of us have, for that matter.) What they do with it will determine the extent of their effectiveness. Past and future must not intrude. The task about to be performed is the most significant task the athlete will ever have. That's the viewpoint he should bring to it. Having done that, he then focuses on the next task—the new now. When executed, that task becomes the past and focus is then given to the one that follows. And so on.

Through such a progression, the irrelevant unknown becomes the relevant known. The "x" is no longer x. It has been transformed by *action*, not by time.

So the athlete will always have an identifiable now to deal with. He need not and should not deal with the x-factor. Because he cannot—except in his distracted mind.

■　■　■

One young minor league pitcher I had been talking with in 1984, strayed just two pitches into the future. The unknown was lurking there as well, "licking its chops."

The day after his relief appearance, he approached me and revealed what "had happened" to him during the previous night's game. He explained that, after having taken the sign for the next pitch, he brought a thought and picture into his mind and his "mind's eye." They were related to the pitch that would follow the one he was about to execute.

"I was about to throw a fastball inside—move the guy off the plate," the pitcher said. "Then I saw myself throwing a slider away after that—while I'm on the rubber! I was thinking about that slider when I threw the fastball. It was away, where I wanted the slider to be. He [the right-handed hitter] smoked it against the wall in right."

He continued, "But I'll tell you something. At that very moment, it kicked in. I mean I really understood the idea of one-pitch-at-a time. I understood right out there what had happened to me. I was thinking way ahead of myself."

Way ahead is a relative term. But one pitch ahead—one execution of whatever the task may be—is still enough ahead to qualify as an x factor—the distracting unknown and irrelevant future.

■ ■ ■

Aeschylus wrote 2,400 years ago, "The future / you shall know when it has come; before then, forget it." Better yet, the performer should ignore it, before it needs "forgetting."

Sooner or later, there will not be a future for each of us. But there will *always* be a present. An athlete should devote himself to that now during competition. It is what he has, what he knows, and what he is responsible to be attentive to. *Que sera, sera,* the song says. What will be, will be. The athlete's focus should be on what he's capable of influencing—of "making be," rather than what might or might not be—somewhere in the land of x.

■ ■ ■

The coach addresses the mental game by teaching the athlete:

- That the future is beyond his recognition and control.
- That the ability to effectively perform is reduced by a focus on the unknown future, rather than the manageable now.
- To understand that take care of the task at hand is a mantra specifically used to direct attention to his most important approach.
- To realize that the regular tempo and flow of his game is

enhanced or diminished by his ability or inability to maintain a disciplined focus on the now.

- To monitor and evaluate this ability during and after each performance.
- To make necessary mental adjustments to his focus during competition through awareness and the use of self-coaching techniques.
- To understand that the future will become the present through his actions, which always take place in the present.
- To determine, therefore, to have his mind and actions always functioning in the same time zone.

Yes-But Athletes

I see you nodding your head that you know what to do, but I hear
you blaming the music because you haven't done it.
Spoken to me by one of my older sisters, who was trying to
prepare her little brother for his first dance

I call a particular type of athlete, "Mr. or Ms. Yes-but." When being
given instruction or criticism, the individual invariably responds by saying, "Yes, but, I . . ." Or "Yes, but, it . . ." Or "Yes, but, this or that . . ."

Whether it should be categorized as an explanation, an alternative
point of view, a reason, an excuse, it is a failure to properly listen to
whatever words are being offered. The yes-but response is an indication
that the person will not "get the message." The athlete is focused on
what he wants to say, in order to preempt what he doesn't want to hear.

It is a defensive behavior (review EXCUSES, section 3), and it can be
seen in a variety of shades. "I know, but . . ." is one. Or—a long dis-
course that most often indicates a rational understanding of what's
right, followed by "But, . . ." and an explanation of why what he knows
is right is really wrong. Or the "reason" why the right idea wasn't integrated into behavior.

Athletes who employ these devices cannot learn easily, first of all because they're already thinking of defenses while they are being coached.
They aren't good listeners. Their insecurities (e.g., the need to please or
never appear to be wrong) and bad habits get in the way. They avoid
their responsibility to learn because they avoid responsibility for the
many things that lead to learning.

I tell the athletes who behave this way that whatever comes before
the "but" I don't believe. That is, I don't believe that *he* can believe it—
truly. Until he takes responsibility for avowing its truth or accuracy
without qualification or rational rebuttal, the words before the "but" are
just "lip service" offered to the other participant in the conversation.

An athlete who is a "warrior" doesn't hide behind the flimsy fortress
of "Yes, but . . ."

■ ■ ■

The coach addresses the mental game by making it clear to the athlete:

- That the tendency to offer initial agreement followed by explanation or disagreement is most often a defense mechanism.
- That such defensive expressions are used to avoid unpleasant truths (or criticism), to avoid trying to learn something that is difficult, to be resistant to an idea for whatever particular reason he may have.
- That one of the greatest failings of such an athlete is that when he dismisses what he has said "yes" to, he fails to seek a strategy for a mistake he has made or a remedy for a situational failing. He inhibits learning, performance, and adulthood.

Z

Zeal

What a great place for me to complete the body of this book: in the soul of the athlete who loves to compete, who is joyous in his participation, fervent in his desire to be a winner.

Zeal: "enthusiastic devotion to a cause, ideal, or goal and tireless diligence in its furtherance" (*The American Heritage Dictionary*). Terms and phrases I've used to describe some of the true competitors I've been lucky enough to coach or counsel have been: enthusiasm, vitality, energy, joyousness, spirit, passion—fire in the belly.

These athletes bring enthusiasm to practice and performance; vitality to their learning and the growth of their teammates; energy to every activity, cerebral or physical; joy that crowds a gymnasium or a locker room; spirit that soars.

Perhaps Hazlitt's zeal for zeal in the epigraph overstates the case a bit. I tend to side with William Fuller, who said, "Zeal without knowledge is fire without light." Many factors contribute to success and zeal makes a significant contribution. But zeal has to be informed by intelligence, controlled by self-discipline.

I've often told athletes who were too zealous that if we looked out at a field filled with spirited, swift thoroughbred horses, they would make a beautiful picture as they ran wild—"But they won't win a race without a bit and bridle." Their spirit shouldn't be broken, but it must be controlled. Unbridled spirit is not enough for a competitor.

Without proper control of his thought patterns and his body, the athlete's zeal can become exuberant dysfunction. The Greeks said it 2,500 years ago: "Nothing in excess." They advocated a proper balance. Maintained with consistency, I'd add.

■ ■ ■

There are also those athletes whose inner joy and enthusiasm for competition is not made evident by their body movements. Some who I've been around have even been accused of being "lazy" or called "dead ass." The evaluators, in the cases that come to mind, were wrong. Henry Aaron is a notable example of someone who played with ease and grace. So, early in his career, many thought he "didn't care."

Coaches should not base their view of an individual's attitude on external signals exclusively. Aaron's performance, by the way—an external—indicated the kind of athlete he truly was.

An individual does not have to jump up and down in order to qualify as an enthusiastic and spirited athlete.

However, I have come across athletes who have told me, in essence, "I'm saving my energy for when I need it (in a crucial competitive situation)." My response is consistent: I inform the individual that energy can't be stored; it doesn't get built up when it isn't used. "Put it in gear now and keep it in gear."

■ ■ ■

Writer F. Scott Fitzgerald, who should have known, said, "Vitality shows not only in the ability to persist but the ability to start over." Zeal fuels a relentlessness spirit that never gives in. It is a form of mental toughness. Optimism wins over pessimism. Strength over weakness. Determination over despondency. All this comes from vitality (*vita* = life), the zeal that directs the best in us toward the goals we've set for ourselves.

■ ■ ■

The coach addresses the mental game by:

- Conveying to the athlete his own positive enthusiasm for the sport, for competition, and for teaching and learning.
- Monitoring the athlete's behaviors during competition, in order to be aware of circumstances when excessive enthusiasm may inhibit, rather than enhance, his performance.
- Helping the high-energy athlete learn how to control and channel that energy using techniques such as regulated breathing and calm, function-directed self-talk.

Appendix A—Leader List

The following list was used in workshops on "Leadership and Communication" with the staff of the Oakland Athletics and the Florida Marlins, when I worked for those organizations.

The Coach as an Effective Leader or Nonleader?

The LEADER helps clean up; the other presides over the mess.

The LEADER appeals to the best in each athlete; keeps his door open; is a problem solver, an advice giver, a cheerleader. The other is invisible—gives orders to his staff and athletes and expects them to be carried out perfectly.

The LEADER thinks of ways to make people more productive, more focused on team goals. The other thinks of personal status and how he looks to others.

The LEADER is comfortable with people around him. The other is uncomfortable.

The LEADER arrives early and stays late. The other is in late and leaves on time.

The LEADER has the common touch. The other is strained with minorities or people different from himself.

The LEADER is a good listener. The other is a good talker.

The LEADER is fair. The other is fair to those above him and uses those below him.

The LEADER is decisive. The other is tentative.

The LEADER is humble. The other is arrogant.

The LEADER is tough—and confronts tough problems. The other is elusive—and avoids as many problems as possible.

The LEADER is persistent. The other hangs in only when he has something personal at stake.

The LEADER simplifies. The other complicates (making things look difficult).

The LEADER is tolerant of open disagreement. The other is intolerant.

The LEADER has strong convictions. The other looks to others for a philosophy, rather than for suggestions.

The LEADER does dog-work when necessary. The other is above that.

The LEADER starts with a trust of people. The other trusts only words and statistics.

The LEADER delegates responsibility. The other will do everything and decide everything. — OR

The LEADER takes his rightful responsibility. The other is glad to let to others do everything.

The LEADER wants anonymity for himself, publicity for his team and athletes. The other wants the reverse.

The LEADER often takes blame. The other looks for a scapegoat.

The LEADER gives credit to others. The other takes it for himself—and complains about his lack of good players.

The LEADER gives honest, frequent feedback to his athletes. The other has information flow one way—into his office.

The LEADER knows when and how to discipline people. The other ducks unpleasant tasks and/or has poor timing and touch when addressing them.

The LEADER goes where the trouble is to help. The other resents the trouble and wants it to disappear.

The LEADER has respect for all people. The other has respect for those who make him look good or those he needs to please.

The LEADER is consistent and steady under pressure. The other improvises, equivocates, passes the buck.

The LEADER prefers eyeball-to-eyeball communication. The other prefers messengers and meetings.

The LEADER is straightforward. The other is tricky and manipulative.

The LEADER is consistent and credible to the team. The other is unpredictable, often saying what he thinks they want to hear.

The LEADER admits his own mistakes and assists the athletes when they admit theirs. The other never makes mistakes and blames those who do.

The LEADER is open. The other is secretive.

The LEADER avoids making promises he can't keep. The other indiscriminately promises much and delivers little.

The LEADER is focused with great intensity on the team's values and objectives. The other is focused on himself.

The LEADER tells the athletes the team comes FIRST. The other may deliver the same message but sees himself as Number One, and acts accordingly.

The LEADER sees mistakes as an opportunity and responsibility to teach. The other sees mistakes as punishable offenses.

The LEADER maintains a high standard for execution of task in practice and competition, while understanding that humans are imperfect. The other maintains unrealistic expectations and holds everyone accountable for perfection—except himself.

The LEADER has energy and enthusiasm. The other calls coaching "a job" and acts as if it's an ordeal.

The LEADER is loyal to his athletes and staff. The other is loyal to himself.

The LEADER is positive and optimistic. The other is negative and pessimistic.

The LEADER COMBINES and BALANCES COMPASSION and STRENGTH. The other has only one of those traits—or neither.

And still, the LEADER recognizes and trusts his own individual way of doing all the things he has learned from experience are required to be effective and exceptional. The other has been used by experience, rather than being one who has used *it*—by learning from it.

Appendix B

"THE GUY IN THE GLASS"
by Dale Wimbrow, *The American* magazine, 1934

When you get what you want in your struggle for self
And the world makes you king for a day,
Just go the mirror and look at yourself
And see what that man has to say.

For it isn't your father or mother or wife
Whose judgment upon must pass.
The fellow whose verdict counts most in your life
Is the one staring back from the glass.

You may be like Jack Horner and chisel a plum
And think you're a wonderful guy.
But the man in the glass says you're only a bum
If you can't look him straight in the eye.

He's the fellow to please—never mind all the rest,
For he's with you clear to the end.
And you've passed your most dangerous, difficult test
If the man in the glass is your friend.

You may fool the whole world down the pathway of years
And get pats on the back as you pass.
But your final reward will be heartbreak and tears
If you've cheated the man in the glass.

Appendix C

Below are words from one of the many posted sheets that caught my eye in one of the many locker rooms I've passed through. The source was not noted on the sheet then nor is it known to me now.

What I do know is that the "we" refers to those who have coached—and those who have learned from coaches.

WE LEARN WHAT WE'VE LIVED

If we lived with criticism, we learn to condemn.
If we lived with hostility, we learned to fight.
If we lived with ridicule, we learned to withdraw.
If we lived with shame, we learned to be guilty.
If we lived with tolerance, we learned to be patient.
If we lived with encouragement, we learned confidence.
If we lived with praise, we learned to appreciate.
If we lived with fairness, we learned justice.
If we lived with security, we learned to have faith.
If we lived with approval, we learned to like ourselves.
If we lived with acceptance and friendship, we learned to find
    love in the world.

Appendix D—A Winning Way

A winning way is to choose and discipline one's mind:

- To get something out of every situation, rather than complaining.
- To be prepared, rather than just show up and call himself "a gamer."
- To be consistent, rather than occasional.
- To be early, rather than just on time—or late.
- To do more, rather than just enough—or less.
- To want to learn, rather than want to explain or excuse.
- To be mentally tough, rather than mentally lazy or intimidated.
- To think about solutions, rather than worry about problems.
- To concentrate on what to do, rather than on what may happen.
- To be aggressive, rather than passive—or submissive.
- To know his or her limitations, rather than trying to do more than capability allows.
- To confront adversity, rather than running from it—or denying it.
- To recognize that adversity is part of sport—and life—rather than magnify the adverse situation and seek sympathy.
- To share with and help others, rather than be selfish.
- To think and act positively, rather than negatively.
- To be energetic, rather than complacent—or lethargic.
- To know, rather than assume.
- To seek responsibility, rather than seek refuge in excuses.
- To think and act in winning ways, rather than just want to win.

■ ■ ■

While living in Prescott, Arizona, I was asked to speak at Yavapai College. On a bulletin board in the locker room was a sheet of paper that caught my eye. The heading read "Scoreboard for a Winner." I liked it, and it was included in *The Mental Game of Baseball*. I wish to share it here, as well. No author's name was in evidence.

■ ■ ■

SCOREBOARD FOR A WINNER

- A Winner takes big risks when he has much to gain. A Loser takes big risks when he has little to gain and much to lose.
- A Winner focuses. A Loser sprays.
- A Winner says, "Let's find out!" A Loser says, "Nobody knows!"
- When a Winner makes a mistake, he says, "I was wrong." When a Loser makes a mistake, he says, "It wasn't my fault."
- A Winner isn't nearly as afraid of losing as the Loser is secretly afraid of winning.
- The Winner works harder than the Loser and has more time. A Loser is always too busy to do what is necessary.
- A Winner takes a big problem and separates it into smaller parts, so that it can be more easily manipulated. A Loser takes a lot of little problems and rolls them together until they are unsolvable.
- A Winner goes through a problem. A Loser goes around it and never gets past it.
- A Winner makes commitments. A Loser makes promises.
- A Winner shows he's sorry by making up for it. A Loser says, "I'm sorry," but he does the same thing the next time.
- A Winner knows what to fight for and what to compromise on. A Loser compromises on what he shouldn't and fights for what isn't worth fighting about.
- A Winner learns from his mistakes. A Loser learns only not to make mistakes by not trying anything different.
- A Winner says, "I'm good, but I'm not as good as I ought to be." A Loser says, "I'm not as bad as a lot of other people."
- A Winner tries never to hurt people, and does so rarely. A Loser never wants to hurt people intentionally, but he does so all the time without even knowing it.
- A Winner listens. A Loser just waits until it's his turn to talk.
- A Winner would rather be respected than liked, although he would prefer both. A Loser would rather be liked than respected, and is even willing to pay the price of mild contempt for it.
- A Winner is sensitive to the atmosphere around him. A Loser is sensitive only to his own feelings.
- A Winner feels strong enough to be gentle. A Loser is never gentle. He's either weak or a petty tyrant by turns.
- A Winner respects those who are superior to him and tries to learn something from them. A Loser resents those who are superior and tries to find kinks in their armor.

- A Winner explains, and a Loser explains away.
- The Winner feels responsible for more than his job. A Loser says, "I only work here!"
- The Winner says, "There ought to be a better way to do it!" A Loser says, "That's the way it's always been done."
- A Winner paces himself. A Loser has only two speeds, hysterical and sluggish.
- A Winner knows that the verb "to be" must precede the verb "to have." A Loser thinks that enough of the verb "to have" is what makes a verb "to be."

(That is) a fatal mistake in the grammar of existence.

■ ■ ■

There are a few "mistakes," if you will, in the list itself: generalizations, exaggerations, and so on. The labels—"Winners" and "Losers"—are, themselves, generalizations. Nevertheless the ideas presented in the list should provoke thought about all that goes into doing things in a "winning way."

Appendix E—The Final Word on the Mental Game

Below is the major part of a column written by Greg Boeck. It appeared in *USA Today*, July 3, 2002. As one who was taken to race tracks at an early age by my father, and as one who continues to go with anyone who will accompany me—or alone, if no one is available—I am happy to use this timely information, so indicative of the importance of addressing the athletes' mental game.

■　■　■

"Horse trainer Leon Bard . . . successfully diagnosed quarter horse Zip First as claustrophobic, thus giving the 2-year-old a chance to win the All-American Triple Crown at New Mexico's Ruidoso Downs.

Bard turned horse shrink when Zip First reacted negatively to his three-walled stall at Ruidoso Downs before the time trials for the Ruidoso Futurity, first leg of the series. 'He freaked out. He wouldn't eat or sleep,' Bard says.

The colt had his first loss in five races, although he ran fast enough to qualify for the Futurity. Bard hauled Zip First back to his stable in Bryan, Texas, determined to learn what upset his colt. He installed an infrared camera in the stall and monitored Zip First's behavior on a 19-inch TV in his bedroom.

He saw a happy, content horse who reveled in looking out all four sides of his open stall. 'When he would get up, he wanted to look around,' Bard says. 'I knew what it was: He couldn't stand to be closed up.'

So Bard bought a 12-by-13-foot portable stall for $1,200, hauled it to Ruidoso Downs and put it under the shed at the stables. 'It was like home away from home for him,' Bard says. Zip First won the Futurity and $233,443, more than justifying the stall's cost.

Said Bard, 'He's as happy as can be.'"

■ ■ ■

Every athlete is happy to have an enlightened and caring coach.

About the Author

Harvey Dorfman's background has been in education and psychology . . . as a teacher, counselor, coach, and consultant. Harvey was a goalie on his college's national championship soccer team and the coach of a high school state championship basketball team.

In 1984, he developed and implemented a sport psychology program for the Oakland Athletics baseball team, working full time as an instructor/counselor. He left Oakland in 1994 to work for the Florida Marlins and was with them through their '97 championship season. The following year, he worked for the expansion Tampa Bay Devil Rays.

Harvey has worked with two professional hockey teams: the Vancouver Canucks and the New York Islanders. He has also done consulting work for the Calgary Flames and the Washington Capitals of the NHL.

His freelance work in sport psychology includes work with a professional female bowler, amateur and professional golfers, an Eclipse Award–winning jockey, a professional tennis player, a skier on the U.S. Olympic Disabled Team, a weight lifter, and a current NFL quarterback. He also worked with a singer of the San Francisco Opera Company.

In 1999, Harvey became a full-time consultant in sport psychology and staff development for the Scott Boras Corporation, an agency that represents professional baseball players.

He wrote, with Karl Kuehl, *The Mental Game of Baseball*. He has also written *The Mental ABC's of Pitching* and *The Mental Keys to Hitting*.

Harvey has also been a freelance journalist, his work having appeared in the *New York Times, Boston Globe, Miami Herald,* and *Los Angeles Times,* among others. For eight years, while teaching in Vermont, he wrote a weekly column entitled "Miscellany" for the *Rutland Herald.* His "Mind Game" column appeared in *Pro,* a quarterly magazine for professional athletes. He lectures at major universities and for corporations on psychology, self-enhancement, management strategies, and leadership training.